B-29 Superfortress

B-29 Superfortress

The Plane that Won the War

By Gene Gurney

The War Vault
2019

B-29 Superfortress: The Plane that Won the War by Gene Gurney. First published in 1963. Revised edition published 2019 by The War Vault.

Copyright 2019 by The War Vault.

This book or any portion thereof may not be reproduced, scanned, digitized or used in any manner whatsoever without the express written permission of the publisher except for the use of brief quotations in a book review or scholarly journal. All rights reserved.

First printing 2019.

ISBN: 9781688233850.

Contents

The Birth of the Giant 7
How Will It Fly? 15
The War Drums Roll 27
The Journey Begins 32
Journey to War 37
"A Damned Trucking Outfit!" 47
Rodeo Over Bangkok 52
Ding Hao! 61
Betty Over Target 68
Summer Operations 76
The Hard Way Back 94
To The Marianas 115
A New Year, An Old Story 124
Rescue at Sea 136
Iwo or Ditch 147
The Giant Pays Its Way 151
Now We're in Business 172
The Journey's End 184
Epilogue 203

The Birth of the Giant

THE B-29 WAS THE LOGICAL EVOLUTION of the Boeing Airplane Company's pioneering work with four-engine aircraft. Boeing officials were convinced that in a field developing as rapidly as the airplane, the company that hesitated would soon be left far behind. While they were busy improving the twin-engine plane, Boeing designers were looking ahead to a plane so much bigger and faster that it would require four engines. There were many questions to be answered: How heavy could a plane be made and still remain structurally sound? At what point would it be impossible for a pilot to control the plane? Would there be an engine capable of supplying all the power that would be needed?

In 1934, when the Air Corps asked for preliminary designs for a long-range bomber, Boeing sent its president, Claire Egtvedt,[1] to the Air Corps Matériel Division[2] at Dayton. There he learned what was wanted: an airplane weighing 30 tons, capable of carrying 2,000 pounds of bombs a distance of 5,000 miles. Was he interested in the project? He most certainly was!

With only a month to develop preliminary data, Boeing prepared a design for a giant four-engine plane with a wingspan of 150 feet, a totally new kind of plane. Boeing's entire staff of design engineers and aerodynamicists worked day and night on it. Because old engineering data were of no use on a plane this big, they had to start from the beginning, building and testing the critical parts as they went along.

Boeing was awarded the contract. This was the plane that became the XB-15. Next came the request for another bomber: Bomb load, 2,000 pounds; required top speed, 200 miles per hour; required range, 1,020 miles; desired top speed, 250-miles per hour; desired range, 2,200 miles; a crew of four to six; multi-engined.

---

[1] Clairmont L. "Claire" Egtvedt (1892–1975) was born in Stoughton, WI, the son of first-generation Norwegian-Americans. A talented draftsman, he was recruited out of college in 1917 by Boeing and put to work designing aircraft. He rose quickly, becoming chief engineer by the early 1920s.
[2] Air Materiel Command (AMC), based at the Wright-Patterson Air Force Base. Today, it houses the National Museum of the United States Air Force, alongside Wilbur Wright Field.

Claire Egtvedt went back to Dayton. Boeing designers were working on a four-engine transport, and they were thinking about a bomber of the same size. But the specifications said "multi-engined," a term the Air Corps used for planes in the twin-engine category.

"Would a four-engine plane qualify?" Major Jan Howard, the engineering chief at Dayton, checked the circular that had been sent to the aircraft companies. "The word is 'multi-engined,' isn't it?" he answered with a smile.

Egtvedt hurried back to Seattle.[3] A flying airplane would have to be ready in one year. It would take all of Boeing's manpower and most of its capital. They would have to risk everything on that one big bomber!

Egtvedt took his problem to Bill Allen, the company lawyer.

"Bill," said Egtvedt, "I don't want to jeopardize the future of this company. You know what little we have left here. If we undertake this four-engined bomber there'll be lots of unknowns. The design studies for the XB-15 made that clear enough."

"Do you think you can build a successful four-engined airplane in a year?"

Egtvedt looked out of the window at the buildings of the plant.

"Yes, I know we can."

Before the year was up, shortly before sunrise on the morning of July 28, 1935, Egtvedt's bomber was off with a roar on its first flight. Noting its five machine-gun turrets, newspaper reports called it, "an aerial battle cruiser, a veritable flying fortress," and Flying Fortress became its name. Major General Oscar Westover, the chief of the Air Corps, called the Flying Fortress "the most successful type of plane, everything considered, ever developed for the Air Corps."

But airmen knew they were going to need more range and more armament. They talked to Boeing about the problem of

---

[3] A successful 28-year old lumber entrepreneur from Detroit, Michigan, William E. Boeing was at a flight exposition in Seattle in 1906 when he fell in love with aviation. Ten years later, he founded The Boeing Company. Today, the company thrives, probably even beyond the young William Boeing's wildest dreams. Boeing International remains one of the world's largest aircraft manufacturers and amongst the top five global defense contractors.

combining high speed with long range. There was no immediate prospect of another contract. The War Department, still not convinced that a four-engine bomber had a place in the country's defense plans, had asked the Air Corps to put no four-engine bombers in its estimates for fiscal 1940 and 1941.

Nevertheless, the B-17 was scarcely off the drafting tables before Boeing engineers were at work on ways to get a plane farther, faster, and higher than the Flying Fortress. Once again, they were moving into the unknown. But they knew what the Air Corps wanted: a superbomber.

In June of 1939, the Kilner Board issued its report calling for the development of a long-range bomber. In September Hitler invaded Poland. Boeing was told, "Keep working on that big bomber. We're going to have a new requirement soon."

The official notice reached Boeing on February 5, 1940. It requested detailed data and drawings for a 5,333-mile, high-altitude, high-speed bombardment plane. It was marked "Urgent."

Preliminary designs for the new big bomber were submitted early in April 1940, by Boeing, Lockheed, Douglas, and Consolidated and were rated in that order by an Air Corps evaluation board. Lockheed and Douglas later withdrew from the competition leaving Boeing and Consolidated to go ahead with the construction of experimental models. Consolidated's model, called the XB-32, underwent so many design changes that only a few of them had gone into combat when the war ended. Boeing's work on a superbomber, its "Design 341," had given it a head start on the project. Its model, called the XB-29, became the plane that was to play such a vital role in World War II.

Boeing designers and engineers had encountered many problems in designing and building a plane to surpass the Flying Fort. They had to develop a flap of monstrous size and effectiveness that could be fastened to a highly loaded wing to facilitate the giant plane's take-off and reduce the distance otherwise required for landing. After four years of building models and testing them in the company's wind tunnels, they felt that they had the answer.

The war in Europe had shown that the best defensive armament for a bomber was multiple guns mounted in power turrets. Power-operated gun turrets had been developed for the B-17, but they wouldn't work on the B-29, which was to have a pressurized body. From a design viewpoint, Boeing engineers wanted to keep the big plane streamlined and free of exterior turrets. The Army Air Force, interested above all else in getting a fighting airplane, was inclined to favor turrets in spite of the drag they would produce.

The solution to this dilemma was provided by General Electric, which had been developing an electronic remote-control system. Its engineers, working with Boeing and the Air Technical Service Command, adapted the system to the guns of the B-29. The result was the radically new Central Fire Control System, which allowed guns mounted outside the airplane to be fired by a gunner who had no manual contact with his weapon. In addition, maximum use of the five-gun sites was insured by allowing the gunners, with the exception of the tail gunner, to control more than one set of guns at a time. Each gunner had primary control of certain guns and secondary control of others, so that the man with the best view of the approaching enemy could command extra firepower. If a gunner were injured, someone else could fire his guns. A signal system among the gunners made possible this exchange of control.

The center of the system was a small black box housing a computer, which automatically made allowances for such factors as wind and plane velocity. A signal was transmitted to the guns, which the gunner fired with thumb triggers. In case of damage to the computer system, the gunner could take over and direct his guns himself.

Split-second opening of the bomb-bay doors was another refinement worked out for the B-29. When the B-17 started on its bombing run, the opening of the bomb-bay doors served as a signal that it would maintain a constant speed and a steady course in order to give the bombardier a chance to track his target accurately. This allowed enemy fighters to lurk out of range until the bomb-bay doors started to open; then they could attack knowing that the pilot of the bomber could take no evasive action on the "run." Several methods of speeding up the action of the B-29 doors were considered. Eventually a pneumatic bomb door actuating device was developed which, when perfected, snapped the doors open in seven-tenths of a second and closed them in three seconds.

For many years, aeronautical engineers had been experimenting with pressurized cabins as the solution to the problems of anoxia and bends encountered at high altitudes. Anoxia, or lack of oxygen, is one of the greatest hazards of high flying.

As the airplane climbs, air pressure decreases, and at 10,000 feet and above it is not sufficient to force into the lungs enough air to give the body adequate oxygen; lack of oxygen results in lassitude, extreme fatigue and, finally, unconsciousness and death. Aeroembolism, or aviator's bends, is another hazard of high flying.

At sea-level pressure, oxygen and nitrogen both dissolve in the blood. As pressure decreases at high altitudes, oxygen still is absorbed, but the nitrogen is released in bubbles that may jam in a vein, blocking the blood vessel. This causes severe pain and may result in permanent injury. Once bends has set in the only recourse is to return to a lower altitude where pressure forces the nitrogen back into solution.

Until the development of the pressurized cabin, high-altitude flying was possible only with the use of oxygen masks. They were used satisfactorily by the crews of the B-17 on short missions, but on extended ones the cumbersome equipment and breathing oxygen for long periods of time impaired the efficiency of the men. In 1938 the Army had asked Boeing to work on the pressurization of the B-17, but Boeing's engineers found that it would not be practical. Boeing had succeeded in pressurizing its 307 Stratoliner, the first pressurized transport plane ever built, and incorporated many of its features into the B-29, a plane built to fly and drop its bombs at high altitudes.

In the B-29 there were three sections that would be occupied by crew members: the nose, the waist, and the tail. Two others, the bomb bays and the after section, did not need pressurization. The problem of transferring crew members from the pressurized nose section through the unpressurized bomb bays to the pressurized waist section was solved by installing a tunnel large enough for a man to crawl through between the nose and the waist. The tail gunner was to be isolated in his pressurized tail section during pressure flight.

Compressed air was piped into each pressurized section from a supercharger on the inboard engines. This air was heated or cooled as needed, making an automatic air-conditioning system.

Although small bullet holes might be patched while the bomber was pressurized, it was planned that when the B-29 approached its target, where antiaircraft fire and enemy fighter opposition would be greatest, the crew would don oxygen masks and plug in their heated flying suits, and the plane would be depressurized. Thus, the crew need not be distracted by battle damage at a vital moment. The system worked out for the B-29 increased cabin pressure as the plane rose from sea level to 8,000 feet. Above this point pressure was maintained by introducing air into the cabin while the flow out of the cabin was gradually decreased.

The XB-29 (experimental, twenty-ninth bomber design purchased by the Army), for which Boeing was given a contract in late June 1940, had been Boeing's Model 345, the culmination of the series of models its engineers had turned out in their effort to improve on the performance of the B-17. The XB-29 had a wingspan of 141 feet 2 inches; its length was 93 feet 2 inches. Loaded with 2,000 pounds of bombs the plane had a range of 5,333 miles. At 25,000 feet its speed was 282 miles per hour. It was to be powered by four Wright air-cooled engines, and its design gross weight was 100,000 pounds.

Boeing began the construction of a full-scale wooden mock-up of its Model 345. The long-range bomber was at last a project.

The summer and early fall of 1940 found the American people watching the struggle in Europe with increasing interest. The German army was moving with rapier precision. And on July 23, 1940, General Arnold wrote to General George C. Marshall, Chief of Staff, stressing the fact that the Germans, if they succeeded in establishing advanced bases in the Americas, could reach the United States with existing types of aircraft. To offset this possibility, the General stated the United States would need planes equal to the Nazis' in range and far greater in numbers; and even if we were successful in this venture, to deal the enemy a knock-out blow, it would be necessary to hit his homeland.

Less than a month after his memo to General Marshall, General Arnold received a report from the Mock-Up Committee at Wright Field which had approved in detail the wind-tunnel model of the XB-29. He immediately ordered Boeing to build two experimental models; this was later increased to three.

Structural testing of the component parts of the XB-29 was undertaken by Boeing simultaneously with the actual construction of the experimental models; something completely new in the annals of the aircraft industry. Many portions of the plane's control system actually were flight tested before any of the completed experimental bombers had been airborne. In the last quarter of 1940, various surfaces, scaled down to the size of the smaller B-17, were flight-tested on a Flying Fortress assigned to that specific mission.

By the spring of 1941, B-29 ailerons were ready to be tested, and once again the B-17 was called upon for the test. A radically new landing gear was finished shortly afterward. The first set of wings was completed and attached to a fuselage section; then 300,000 pounds of pressure was applied.

TENS OF THOUSANDS OF DESIGNS WERE MADE, discarded, and replaced, as thousands of designers on the shores of Puget Sound worked around the clock to keep the program moving. At last came a major test of the completed airframe. Army specifications stipulated that the plane had to withstand a free drop of 27 inches. To meet this, the big bomber was fitted out with enough weight inside to simulate full equipment: fuel, crew, bomb and ammunition load; it was raised 27 inches from the floor, then dropped. The Superfort successfully went through a series of these drops, some in a horizontal position, others in an inclined position.

In another test, different sections of the plane were riddled by 20-mm. cannon shells and .50-cal. machine-gun bullets to determine just how much gunfire the bomber could take. Still another test found the Boeing engineers deliberately blowing up, by measured air pressure, a completed fuselage of the B-29. This showed them exactly how much the pressurized sections of the Superfortress could withstand before they broke at the seams. It was a tribute to Boeing engineers that no major section had to be redesigned.

By this time the Preliminary Design Unit of Boeing's Seattle Engineering Division had finished its over-all plans and turned them over to the Project Unit for detailed designing; but the detailed designs had not been completed. There was still much wind-tunnel testing to be done on such parts as engine nacelles. Then, too, materials were hard to get, and tools and jigs had to be designed and built. Because of these obstacles, the first work on the experimental models of the XB-29 had to be done piece by piece and section by section as parts became available, regardless of logical sequence.

As various parts and subassemblies were finished, production men sat down with men from the Project Unit to work on the designs that would be needed next; then work would be speeded up on the completion of those parts so that the next designs could be made. In spite of the complexity of the job, Boeing was expending every effort to meet the Army's demand for speed and more speed in the production of the experimental models.

Through the summer and autumn of 1941, work on the XB-29 models progressed, and in November, as the Japanese situation became tense, even greater efforts were made. Then, on December 7, the Japanese made their attack on Pearl Harbor, and the American people awoke to the fact that they were at war.

Despite the Japanese attack, the War Department adhered to its earlier decision to use the very long-range bombers exclusively, or at least predominantly, in Europe until the collapse of Germany; it was an accepted fact that eventually they would have to be used in an offensive against Japan. Although the experimental models had not yet been completed, revised plans called for greater numbers of the new bomber. It was recommended that bases in Alaska be readied against the time when the B-29 could be deployed against Japan.

For the next eight months, the War Department had its hands full as the Japanese continued their offensive and the training of millions of Americans went into full-scale operation. Air activities in the Pacific were limited to strategic defense, strikes at enemy shipping, and support whenever possible in the battle for bases nearer to Japan. At this time, the defeat of Germany was predicted for late 1944; by then the B-29 would be in quantity production and ready to play an important part in the war of tremendous distances in the Pacific. However, no detailed target studies of Japan were made. By and large, Pacific planning marked time until the situation in Europe clarified itself.

How Will It Fly?

ON THE HOT, CLEAR AFTERNOON of September 21, 1942, Edmund T. Allen, the slight, balding chief test pilot for the Boeing Aircraft Company, climbed into the first completed XB-29 and prepared to take off. The XB-29 had hopped fifteen feet off the runway three different times in preliminary taxiing exercises a few days before, but this was to be a real test flight. At 3:40 the plane was airborne. Anxious designers, engineers and mechanics waited for the answers that only the test flight could give them.

Seventy-five minutes later, the XB-29 flashed over the field, flared out, and touched its wheels to the runway. Eddie Allen[4] stepped from the plane to be surrounded by the waiting crowd. Breaking into a smile, he said, "She flew." Coming from Allen, that was the highest compliment the plane could have received.

The first B-29 had been airborne, but the AAF and Boeing had not waited for the outcome of that test flight; the green light had already flashed on production of the very long-range bomber. This was a radical departure from normal procedure, which required a new plane to pass rigorous tests before any purchases were made. At the time of the first B-29 flight, orders for 1,664 Superfortresses were on the books.

Because of this speed-up, changes in design had to be made as production proceeded and problem areas began to show up. Everyone, including the Army, expected reverses.

Said Colonel Leonard Harmon, a B-29 flight test officer at Wright Field:

"We started building the planes knowing there would be errors, but realizing that we could eliminate bugs as they developed, not waiting for a perfect airplane as we should have had to do if we continued to nickel and dime ourselves by buying a few at a time and then building a new experimental model while some Board exclaimed, 'It's a good thing we didn't buy more of

---

[4] A much-admired pioneering figure, Edmund Turney Allen (1896-1943) or Eddie Allen, was a freelance test pilot who worked for Boeing and the other major aeronautical firms of the era.

these planes.' It was a bold effort when we went out to build planes from a set of drawings; some 8,000 drawings."

From Seattle, where the Boeing B-29 was designed and developed, to Wichita, Kansas, where the first production model was built, to the Bell plant at Marietta, Georgia, the wheels of the aircraft industry began to grind on a scale unprecedented in the history of aviation. Chrysler, General Motors, Goodyear, Hudson, Briggs, Cessna, Murray, A. O. Smith, and many other firms all over America played a big part in the B-29 production program. The complex task of directing this widespread manufacturing pool was shared by Boeing and AAF officials.

The final assembly plants were located at four widely separated places. A part coming from Grand Rapids, Michigan, would have to be built so that it would fit on a B-29 being put together at Renton, Washington; Wichita; Omaha, or Marietta. Boeing furnished all manufacturers and subcontractors with master gauges so that all planes and their parts would be built exactly alike. In order to supply these gauges, Boeing first had to make the control master gauges from which the masters could be produced. This was a most exacting tooling job, requiring tolerances to the ten thousandth of an inch.

Boeing supplied blueprints, templates, tooling and manufacturing procedure, and engineering to the firms in the program to give them the advantage of its experience. A bookkeeping organization was needed to coordinate this work and to keep each firm advised about the activities of the others. Thus, the Boeing-Douglas-Vega Committee was formed. It proved so successful that a similar organization, the B-29 Liaison Committee, was set up for the nationwide B-29 production pool. An AAF representative was chairman of the group; other members consisted of representatives from Boeing, Bell, Martin and Fisher Body. The committee was the medium through which all problems concerning B-29 production were discussed and clarified.

When the widespread B-29 production program was inaugurated in early 1942, North American Aviation Corporation was included, but Boeing-Renton and Martin had not yet been named participants.

Under the initial arrangement, Boeing was to continue its established plans, whereby completed bombers would be assembled at Wichita, and the Seattle plant would build B-29 subassemblies. Bell, North American and the Fisher Body Division of General Motors were to build completed airplanes, and Fisher Body also was to supply North American and Bell with outer wing panels, tail surfaces, ailerons, flaps, control columns, wing trips and completed engine nacelles.

Two circumstances changed this arrangement. First, increased demands were made on the Seattle-Boeing plant for Flying Fortresses; and it was decided to devote this plant exclusively to B-17 production, and shift Seattle's B-29 work to Wichita. Second, in August 1942, the Navy suddenly switched emphasis to land-based bombers, and asked the AAF for delivery of Flying Forts. The AAF was unable to fulfill the Navy's request but offered to trade North American's twin-engine bomber facilities, already slated for B-29 production, for the Navy's Boeing-Renton factory, which had been built to manufacture the Boeing Sea Ranger, a twin-engine flying boat. The Navy agreed, leaving the Sea Ranger an orphan.

Following the AAF-Navy swap, plans were made to convert the Boeing-Renton plant into B-29 production, and Renton was designated to take over North American's commitment. Later the AAF brought the Martin plant at Omaha into the pool and assigned to it the quota of completed airplanes originally allocated to Fisher Body. Fisher Body retained a major role in building sub-assemblies at eight of its war plants.

Tooling for B-29 quantity production posed one of the most difficult problems. While experimental models of the Superfort were under construction, engineering was still far from completed. In fact, engineering was not finished until almost a year after the tool program was inaugurated. This meant that tooling had to be anticipated in many cases, and the anticipation had to be correct.

The first step in the manufacturing procedure was to picture the B-29 as a production article and to determine how it could be broken down into component parts and finally assembled. In this, Boeing was guided by one major factor: it was necessary to reduce fabrication and assembly to the simplest of operations, so that hastily recruited, speedily trained personnel, many of them women, could build the plane in the shortest time possible. Critical labor shortages were imminent, and the bulk of B-29 workers would have to come from the ranks of semiskilled and unskilled labor.

All major jigs and fixtures were designed in Seattle and produced at Boeing's expanded Wichita plant. Fabrication tooling was predominantly of Wichita design and manufacture. After the Wichita plant started work on the B-29 and additional orders were received from the AAF calling for increased production, it was necessary to subcontract to the Briggs Manufacturing Company the B-17 work which Wichita was doing. As Superfort production requirements increased, Boeing converted its Seattle plant to B-29 production. The Seattle conversion was spectacular in that it was accomplished without shutting down the factory or losing a single hour of work.

After receiving the authority to build large quantities of the B-29, Boeing, in cooperation with the United States Employment Service, canvassed major cities west of the Mississippi River, interviewing everyone it could find who had had engineering training or experience. Engineering personnel were needed in the early days of B-29 production more than production workers. During this initial recruiting drive, some of those hired had been away from their profession for five or six years; others had engineering degrees with no practical experience. They were found working in drugstores, banks, bars, and on farms. Some were working as cowpunchers. Several hundred were hired during the fall of 1941, but there was still a need for many more trained and expert personnel.

In the spring of 1942, the Boeing Engineering personnel supervisor toured American colleges and universities to recruit graduating student engineers. Of course, the draft boards were counting on these students for future draft calls and conflicts resulted. All during the early forties the tug of war between aircraft manufacturers and Selective Service continued, but the college and university tour produced 400 employees. At the same time, hundreds of women were being hired to trace over engineering drawings. The women were trained by the Engineering and Science Management War Training Program of the War Manpower Commission.

With engineers of all types being hired for airplane work, Boeing saw the definite need of a training program for these new employees, and a Boeing Engineering school was established by the company. More than 90 percent of the people hired to do engineering work took a 4-6-week course before they began their job.

Engineering was only a part of the personnel problem. As the plants at Wichita and Renton expanded, the local labor supply was drained completely. Renton was in the position of having to draw on nearby Seattle for its labor personnel, and at Seattle, Boeing's Number 2 plant was drawing the bulk of its manpower from the city of Seattle. Boeing again conducted a recruiting campaign in cooperation with the United States Employment Service, this time in the Midwestern and Southern states where Boeing had a top priority employment rating. Recruiting teams went through cities, villages and rural areas. Individual workers and in some instances whole families were signed up. All this was done in conjunction with an intensive advertising campaign.

Women proved to be a major factor in solving the labor problem. At the Boeing Wichita plant, they constituted 39 percent of the employees. In all aircraft plants, the number of female employees increased as the war went on.

There were relatively few jobs that women could not handle in an aircraft factory; exceptions were tasks requiring great physical strength: foundry work, sandblasting, and operating cranes and derricks.

Women were employed as die-makers, and in fabrication of sheet metal, which involved riveting with guns weighing three to fifteen pounds. Other jobs included machine-shop operations, toolmaking, benchwork, spot welding, electrical repair work, tool design, engineering, drafting, electrical form work and assembly, radio tower dispatch duties, estimate and production illustration. Apart from the actual factory work, they took over administrative jobs, personnel direction, time-motion study, timekeeping, material inspection, and recreational work.

Few of the women employed in aircraft factories had any previous mechanical experience. A large number of the workers were married. Before they were hired, those with children had to produce certificates proving they had provided for independent childcare in a home with relatives or at a day nursery. At Boeing's Wichita plant 2,293 mothers were hired between August 1943 and June 1944. These women, collectively, had 3,671 children.

Women had a problem in adjusting to their "defense work." It was no easy task to turn out the family wash after ten hours with vibrating, clattering rivet guns. The turnover in personnel in some factories was as high as 80 percent a year. In order of importance, health, dissatisfaction with working conditions, conflicts between problems at home and working hours, family ties, and childcare were the reasons given for leaving a job.

But the women of America proved they could temporarily forsake a peacetime existence when emergency methods were required. Their help was a determining factor in the success of the B-29 production program. The Bell Aircraft Corporation was an example of the expansion produced in the aircraft industry by the B-29 program. On December 22, 1941, General Arnold advised Larry Bell, the corporation's president, that his company had been selected to build B-29 heavy bombers in a plant to be constructed near Atlanta, Georgia.

On March 30, 1942, ground was broken for the new plant and construction started. Less than a year later over 1,000 employees moved into the completed plant and offices. On December 20, 1943, Bell's first "All Georgia" production ship was completed.

Bell was faced with a serious labor problem from the beginning. Although attempts were made to employ workers from the Atlanta area, the draft and shipbuilding operations along the Atlantic coast had depleted the supply of skilled labor. In the spring of 1942, a number of Georgians were hired and sent to Bell's Buffalo plant to be trained and taught Bell's production methods. Simultaneously, a substantial number of Buffalo employees were sent to Georgia to form a nucleus for the new facility. In Marietta, a downtown factory building was rented, and for nearly two years it served as an upgrading center to train new workers. There were also numerous training rooms at the plant.

"The Marietta plant is probably the best illustration available of the difficulties we have had in production," said Brigadier General B. E Meyers, a troubleshooter from Washington assigned to help ready the B-29s for overseas flight and combat. "The people there were untrained, plant facilities were practically nonexistent, and there were none of the conditions that would normally seem necessary for a successful industrial venture. Believe it or not, people who were employed to make aluminum planes had to be shown what a sheet of aluminum looked like."

From the beginning, the Bell training program was highly successful in converting schoolteachers, salesmen, clerks, hairdressers, granite cutters, ministers, automobile mechanics, blacksmiths, bank tellers, farmers and housewives into expert aircraft workers.

The Bell plant differed from other B-29 plants in that it delivered to the AAF a combat-ready plane. The other B-29 plants delivered their finished product to modification centers (Bell and Bechtol, McCone & Parsons of Birmingham, Alabama, were the two major ones), where changes were made until they could be incorporated at the start rather than in the middle of the original factory's production line. At Marietta all modification was done under direct Army supervision.

The development of the complex operation involving thousands of contractors and subcontractors continued to run into obstacle after obstacle. Typical was the experience of the Murray Corporation of America, which was asked to expand the production of B-29 parts in its Detroit plant. The War Manpower Commission objected to any expansion because of the critical labor shortage in Detroit; the War Production Board also objected to an expansion of the company's activities in Detroit.

Shortly thereafter, the War Labor Board, in conjunction with the Plant Site Board, made a survey of Scranton, Pennsylvania, and concluded that sufficiently trained and semiskilled labor was available in that area. Scranton, as the center of the anthracite[5] mining industry, had been endeavoring for some time to bring in new industries to counteract the unstable economic conditions of the once great industrial city.

A site was selected in Scranton, but not without opposition. The president of the CIO local at the Murray Corporation, in Detroit, argued that the company was using the Scranton project to browbeat the union, that both labor and facilities were available in Detroit without the need of transferring to Scranton. The Defense Plant Corporation itself objected to the site, protesting the exorbitant cost of strengthening the Glen Alden Coal properties

---

[5] Coal, or 'Hard coal.'

under the site, as well as the price demanded by the company to surrender the right to mine coal under the site.

Several buildings on the site, including the Quackenbush Warehouse containing about 50 carloads of lend-lease material, and the Brookside Distilleries would have to be removed. The demolition costs, the cost of moving the lend-lease material and the distillery, as well as the cost of new facilities for storage and distilling, were also thought to be excessive and were not included in the estimated costs of the expansion. And there was the possibility that damages would arise if the fermentation of thousands of gallons of wine was interrupted during a transfer.

To add to the difficulties, the Defense Plant Corporation stopped the work already authorized, but without benefit of a lease, because clear title to the land could not be obtained. One railroad claimed title to part of the land; another railroad bucked the project so as to have the site moved to its line. Initial cost estimates were finally revised upward by more than $3 million.

Subsequent events held up construction so that production originally scheduled for August 15, 1943, was delayed five months. Subsoil conditions, which called for footing excavations to an unusual depth, were so bad that adequate bearing was not found until the 25-foot mark. Sheeting lumber for retaining scaffolding was unavailable; seepage from the Lackawanna River caved in the banks. As an alternative to excavating individual shafts, a single mass excavation of the site was made by power-shovel.

Three levels of old concrete foundations and huge blocks of fused metal and slag, dumped from the foundry formerly occupying the site, had to be dynamited. So much unusable slag and cinder fill had been removed that backfill had to be hauled in at great cost over some of the highest hills in the region. As the depth of excavation increased the size of the pyramid-shaped footings, more concrete was needed.

Since the War Production Board insisted that steel bearing columns be eliminated, 27 extra piers were installed along the south side of the building so that a bearing wall could be substituted. Concrete had to be poured at single dumpings because the shortages of reinforcing steel for doweling made layer pouring impossible. To negate the hydrostatic uplift of the freshly poured cement, the pyramidal wooden forms had to be anchored. So as not to increase the mill demand for new steel, warehouse stock of greater tonnage was used; but greater tonnage meant uneconomical design.

There was a further development on the Glen Alden claim to the coal remaining on its properties under the plant. The laws of the state of Pennsylvania limited mining to two-thirds of the available supply so that the remaining one-third could be left in place to support surface land. The Glen Alden Company claimed to have left in place as a pillar support more than the one-third required, as well as more than the required barrier of coal. It was decided that Glen Alden could mine the area except for that portion directly under the plant; periodical inspection of the mine and timber supports would disclose any weakening of the pillar supports. This resulted in a large saving on the original estimate of $170,000 to be paid to Glen Alden.

Because boilers for the new plant could not be obtained at first, production started on power from a steam railway locomotive on the plant siding. Eventually, boilers from a colliery in Dunmore, Pa., abandoned because of a cave-in, were transferred to the Murray plant. And finally, the plant was in full operation.

That was the way it went, not in one, but in hundreds of places, as B-29 production fell far behind the goals set by the Combined Chiefs of Staff. So, in October 1943, General Arnold called on W. S. Knudsen of General Motors to help speed up the B-29 program. Of this assignment, Lieutenant General Knudsen later said: "It was hell for the first three months at Wichita. At first the B-29 program was an engineering and production problem. In particular, we were greatly troubled by plane engine shortages, but by rushing Chrysler-Chicago plant completion and enlisting their best engineering technicians, we finally overcame initial difficulties, eliminated motor bugs, and met a high schedule demand. The B-29 was the problem of a million little things."

One of the greatest of these problems was the 3350 Wright engine with which the B-29 was powered. The four engines with turbo-superchargers could each develop 2,200 horsepower at sea level. The largest engine ever installed on an airplane; it was first tested early in 1937. Less than a hundred of them had been built when the Army Air Forces Matériel Command adopted the engine for the Superfortress. By November 1943, some 2,000 engineering changes had been made in the engine; 500 of these required changes in tooling. During the testing of the experimental planes, test crews were plagued with engine failures and engine fires. Some of the fires were minor, but some of them were serious, and on February 18, 1943, an engine fire caused Aircraft Number 2, XB-29, to crash, killing Eddie Allen and ten vitally important members of the test flight section of Boeing Airplane Company.

The flight had been planned as a test of power-plant performance and cooling, propeller governing, and two-engine performance. It was to have taken three hours; it lasted seventeen minutes. The weather was good—ceiling 8,500 feet, visibility five miles. At 12:16 Eddie reported his position at Lake Tapps, twenty miles south of Boeing Field at an altitude of 5,000 feet, southbound. At 12:21 he reported his position south of Renton at 2,400 feet, descending, and requested landing clearance: "Number One engine is on fire, propeller feathered, trouble not serious."

At 12:24 Eddie reported his position over Lake Washington Bridge at approximately 1,500 feet. No mention was made of fire. One minute later the controller of the Seattle tower overheard a member of the XB-29's crew call to Eddie on the plane's interphone, "Allen, better get this thing down in a hurry. The wing spar's burning badly."

Eddie's unhurried request to the control tower to have fire equipment ready, "I'm coming in with a wing on fire," was the last heard from the giant aircraft.

Even as Eddie spoke, the fire was burning away the wing and eating into the cabin. Forty-five seconds later the electric power at Boeing Field failed; the B-29 had struck a high-tension wire, knocking out the system. Fifteen seconds later the burning plane crashed into the fifth floor of the Frye Packing Plant with its devastating weight of more than 100,000 pounds. The aircraft was destroyed; its eleven crew members were killed. Many employees of the packing house and several firemen died in the awful conflagration that followed.

At the moment of the crash, Army Corporal Kenneth J. Cristner and a detail of seven men were on their way to the Seattle Civic Auditorium to weigh in for boxing matches to be held that evening. Traveling north on Airport Way in an Army truck, they saw the burning plane and watched anxiously as it struggled to reach Boeing Field. Suddenly there was a blinding flash of light and then a loud explosion; the plane had hit the packing plant.

Corporal Cristner and his men jumped from their truck and raced into the burning building. While the others ran to the top floor to help employees who had been trapped there, Cristner, using two phones simultaneously, called the fire and police departments. This fast action on the part of the eight soldiers helped keep the casualty figures low. One of them, Private Sam Davis, carried four Frye employees out of the holocaust in heat that singed his eyebrows and burned his clothes. They never reached the Auditorium for their boxing engagement, but they did receive the Soldier's Medal for their heroic efforts at the Frye plant.

The tragic loss of the Number 2, XB-29, and its crew was a severe technological blow to the men who had labored so long to design, develop, and build the giant bomber, and it was a severe setback to the men of the Army Air Force. The death of Eddie Allen alone was a catastrophe, for he was Boeing's best test pilot and he knew more about the infinite mechanical complexities of the giant airplane than any other man. He had joined Boeing in 1939 as head of its Research Division and had directed the planning and testing that led to the B-29. The famed Boeing 117 airfoil, the wing that eventually carried the heavy bomb loads over record distances in the Pacific, was developed by the man he brought in to head the company's aerodynamics section, George Schairer.

When Major General Benjamin T. Chidlaw presented Eddie's Air Medal to his young daughter, Turney Allen, he said, "It is impossible to measure accurately his contributions to air supremacy or to do it justice. It is written in the accomplishments of heavy bombardment in every theater of operations in which the Air Forces operated."

At the time of the fatal crash the B-29 was still a highly classified project; the plane had never been photographed and was covered with canvas when not in flight. In news releases the crashed plane was called "a four-engined bomber," and so stories describing it as a B-I7 were carried by the Seattle newspapers and papers all over the country.

One paper almost destroyed the veil of secrecy. It was the Seattle City Transit Weekly, a paper published for the employees of the transit company. One of its bus drivers was near enough to the scene of the crash to get some very good pictures of the plane before it burned entirely. He gave them to the editor of the City Transit Weekly, who used them to illustrate a story of the fire. Publication day brought the FBI swooping down on the offices of the City Transit Weekly. All but a few of the 500 copies that had been printed were recovered, and the B-29 remained a secret.

The accident that killed Eddie Allen held up the B-29 program for several months; every possible step was taken to eliminate fire hazards. In June, Aircraft Number 3, XB-29, made eight successful flights, after which it and Number 1 were turned over to the AAF for armament and further testing.

The War Drums Roll

DESPITE THE DISCOURAGING PRODUCTION picture and the delays caused by the many modifications that had to be made before the B-29 was ready for battle, the potential power of the plane was so great that combat commanders were busily working out valid reasons why they should get some of them as soon as they were available.

The bulk of the bombers had been scheduled for the Eighth Air Force, so General Ira C. Eaker[6] was more intimately aware than other theater commanders of the delays in production back in the United States. In March of 1943, he asked Washington to give him a date for the arrival of the B-29s in England; because it would take at least nine months to strengthen airstrips and enlarge airdrome facilities, he had to know as soon as possible.

General Arnold advised Eaker that the first B-29s were expected to leave in January 1944. He sent along the airfield requirements, but he could not tell Eaker exactly when delivery would be made or what the eventual B-29 strength would be in that theater. General Eaker, who was in the process of planning his Combined Bomber Offensive to crush Germany, decided to leave the B-29 out of his plans and give the job to the B-17s and the B-24s already in the theater.

As 1943 wore on, the use of the B-29 in Europe became less likely and important. The Combined Bomber Offensive was approaching its climax, and the tremendous force of B-17s and B-24s on hand seemed adequate for the assigned task. Too, the addition of four B-29 groups, all that would be available before the anticipated fall of Germany in the autumn of 1944, would not revolutionize our striking power in Europe.

General Lewis H. Brereton, shortly after his arrival in India in February 1942, had requested B-29 airfield specifications from General Arnold. In June of that year General Delos Emmons, commenting on the tactical phases of the Battle of Midway, stated that the B-17 was deficient in range for Central Pacific

---

[6] General Ira Clarence Eaker (1896-1987).

operations and suggested that every effort be made to send the B-29 to that theater.

A few months later, General Millard Harmon wired General Arnold from the South Pacific requesting B-29s for bases to be established at Bora Bora. And another request came from Lieutenant General George C. Kenney,[7] commander of the Fifth Air Force. Later, when the decision not to send B-29s to the Fifth Air Force was made, both General Kenney and General MacArthur protested, but to no avail.

When the first production models of the B-29 began to roll off the line in July of 1943, the future of the big bomber was still not entirely clear. Some industry leaders were urging that the B-29 project be discontinued because of the serious defects that were showing up. "Write off the deal; we'll play along on another plane," they told General Arnold and the Air Forces. But the General and his aides believed in the B-29, and there wasn't time to design and build another plane. No more time could be wasted.

Where could the new long-range bomber be used to the best advantage? The war against Japan was still defensive in nature. The Japanese had been checked at Midway in the west, the Solomons in the south, and were being thrown out of the western Aleutians in the north. The British campaigns in northern Burma and the Akyab region had failed, and in war-weary China, the Japanese were consolidating and extending their holdings. Except for allocations to the Navy, our military effort in the Pacific had been strictly subordinate to our effort in Europe.

In May of 1943, however, the war in the Pacific came up for discussion at the trident conference in Washington. With both United States and British commanders from Asia in attendance, the acceleration of the war against Japan was studied. It was still thought that Germany would be defeated late in 1944, allowing redeployment of forces to the Pacific. Meanwhile, the situation in China had been deteriorating rapidly. It seemed imperative that we adopt a more vigorous policy in that area if China were to be kept in the war.

---

[7] General George Churchill Kenney (1889–1977) published his memoirs *Air War in the Pacific: The Journal of General George Kenney, Commander of the Fifth U.S. Air Force* in 1949.

By this time a fairly reliable estimate of a target date for the deployment of the first B-29 units could be made. While this date was too late in 1944 for the plane to play any considerable role in the anticipated victory in Europe, it easily fitted into a schedule of operations for the Far East. So, the B-29 became a prominent factor in both long-range strategy against Japan and in proposals for early aid and encouragement to the Chinese. There was little opposition within the Combined Chiefs of Staff to the diversion of the heavy bomber, long intended for Europe, to the Far East.

A plan called setting sun was drawn up, which called for the construction of a number of airbases along a 400-mile axis north and south of Changsha, China. Within 1,500 miles of these bases lay most of the industrial areas of Japan, and it was assumed that the B-29 could fly effectively in that radius with a ten-ton bomb load. Ten groups of 28 B-29s each would be deployed to the Changsha area by October 1944, and 20 groups by May 1945. Logistic support for the B-29 groups would come by air from India. It was not expected that there would be any Pacific island bases available in 1943 and 1944, making China the only base for aircraft attacking Japan.

General "Vinegar Joe" Stilwell, fighting the Japanese in the China-Burma-India theater, was asked for an opinion of setting sun. Immediately he wired Washington: "Plan as a whole is logistically impracticable within the time limits set." He pointed out, among other things, the inadequacy of the port at Calcutta.

But Vinegar Joe had an alternative plan, coded twilight, whereby Changsha bases would be used only as advance bases while the main B-29 force would be kept at airfields in the Calcutta area which was relatively free from air attack. His idea of permanent bases in the rear with planes operating from an advanced staging area eventually was used, but twilight as a whole was rejected.

Meanwhile, another possibility for B-29 bases was introduced in September 1943, when a new plan for the capture of the Marianas was proposed. It had always been assumed that the area would be used for advanced naval bases, but now the Marianas were suggested as a site for B-29 operations. It was recommended that Truk and Yap be bypassed as earlier targets in order to move the target date for the Marianas from early 1946 to mid-1944.

So, a detailed study was prepared which called for interim basing of the B-29s in China, with eventual movement of operations to the Marianas as the most promising base area. It was suggested that China could be used as a training ground for the B-29s where bugs could be worked out of the untested airplane.

It was clear that the B-29s would have to appear in China; the urgent need of measures to encourage the Chungking government was reiterated at each successive conference of Allied leaders. General Arnold asked General Wolfe to develop a plan for operating the B-29s in China. The "Wolfe Plan" was a modification of General Stilwell's TWILIGHT and set up a self-supporting project by basing 150 B-29s in the Calcutta area to serve as transports for a striking force of 100 B-29s based in an advance area around Kweilin.

Wolfe himself thought his plan had certain weaknesses. It was logistically inefficient, and the advanced airfields and their supply lines were vulnerable to enemy attack, but he thought the calculated risk was worth taking. He continued to work on his plan. After General Stilwell pointed out that it would take at least 50 infantry divisions to protect the advanced bases if they were located in Kweilin, it was decided to locate the bases in Chengtu.

After further refinements, the plan, entitled "Early Sustained Bombing of Japan" was turned over to the Joint Planning Staff. Its code name became Matterhorn.

Among the several nations, services, agencies, and individuals concerned, there were divergent opinions, strongly maintained, as to where and how the B-29 could best contribute to the defeat of Japan; and Matterhorn was by no means universally accepted as a good plan. Objections to it delayed its final acceptance until April 10, 1944, when an official commitment of the initial B-29 units was made. By that time their advance echelon had been in the CBI (China-Burma-India) theater for months, and the flight echelons had begun to arrive at the operational bases prepared on the assumption that the B-29 would have to appear in China.

The choice of Chengtu rather than Kweilin as the base area for heavy bombers was dictated by its greater security against both ground and air attack. It was always recognized, however, that the establishment of B-29 bases at Chengtu might bring sharp retaliatory air action from the Japanese, and that fighter defense must be provided.

The natural decision was to vest responsibility for that defense in General Claire Chennault even though his inadequate forces would have to be strengthened in order to perform the additional duty. In March, the Fourteenth Air Force activated the 312th Fighter Wing under the command of Brigadier General A. H. Gilkeson and gave it the job of providing air defense for the B-29s in China. Selected to make up the new wing were the 33rd and 81st Fighter Groups, P-40 veterans of the North African, Sicilian and Italian campaigns. The units could not be released from Italy until after the Anzio operation; they were flown to India in mid-February and reequipped with P-47s.

In order to expedite the delivery of the P-47s, the Navy was asked to transport them, assembled, to Karachi on escort carriers rather than disassembled in cargo ships. The Navy agreed to ferry out 100 of the P-47s, leaving 50 to go by regular transport. The 100 planes arrived at Karachi on March 30 and two weeks later transitional training began.

General Stilwell, in typical temper, exploded when he learned that fighter protection for the B-29s in China would not be operational before May or June. He asked that B-29 strikes be postponed for at least a month. His request was refused because General Arnold was under considerable pressure to end the long delay in initiating B-29 operations.

The result was that the 59th Squadron of the 33rd Fighter Group retained its P-40s and left India for China immediately. The other two squadrons of the 33rd and the 81st Group followed as they were equipped with P-47s.

As it turned out, Japanese attacks on Chengtu, which was very close to the enemy lines, did not prove to be as violent as was feared; the B-29 program was never greatly hampered by the lack of fighter protection of its advanced bases.

The Journey Begins

THE B-29 WAS STILL A FAR CRY from a combat plane when on May 15, 1943, General Wolfe met with Major General Davenport Johnson, the commander of the Second Air Force, to establish training policies for the crews who were to be gathered from all over the world to fly the new long-range bomber.

On June 1, came word that the 58th Bomb Wing had been activated with General Wolfe commanding. Originally based at Marietta, Georgia, the new wing was soon moved to training fields on the plains of Kansas, where its headquarters were set up at Smoky Hill Airfield near Salina—the first operating organization of the 20th Bomber Command.

There in the summer of 1943, just a few short months away from combat, crewmen were being assembled. The B-29 training program was beginning, and the group stationed at Smoky Hill had all of one B-29! Slowly, a few more planes arrived as the summer wore on, and as fast as they did, double crews were trained for each one. Each man was taught two jobs. Gunners were gunners one day, the next day specialists in armament, central fire-control repair, electricians, or engine repairmen. The bombardiers spent long hours learning how to operate the radio, while the navigators forgot their slide rules long enough to learn how to drop bombs. The flight engineer went to school for the better part of a year learning his trade; then he learned how to operate a gun.

While training progressed, the chief topic of conversation among the men was where they would be sent. Everyone figured the B-29s were going into action soon, but there had been no official word as to where. A hint of what was to come was contained in a request from General Lawrence S. Kuter of the Air Staff's Plans Section for a special test flight. The test was to simulate an attack on Tokyo by 100 B-29s from a base in the Changsha area exactly 1,500 miles distant. The plane was to carry ten tons of bombs and travel at a speed determined by a formation leader. The attack could be planned for any daylight hour, with allowances made for crossing enemy-held territory en route. It was hoped that the information obtained would aid the Air Staff in making plans for the B-29.

The supply section of the 58th Bomb Wing was especially concerned about the ultimate destination of the B-29 because spare parts had to be shipped ahead. If they were to go to India, initial shipments of parts would have to start at least four months before the planes left in order to reach Calcutta in time. With no definitive answer available, the first shipments were loaded on boats for India on the basis of educated guesses.

As the end of 1943 approached, there was no more need for speculation; they were going to the CBI. By the end of January, it appeared that the first 150 B-29s might be ready by early March. That became the target date for their dispatch to India. Production problems were still a source of constant worry to the men planning the battle commitments of the plane. Years of testing and modification were being compressed into months. Men who were trying to learn in weeks what ordinarily should have taken many months noticed, as the new planes came in, that more and more changes had been made. One day a weary sergeant, examining a newly received plane, suddenly yelled: "Where the hell did they put the toilet?" An engineer explained the lavatory had been shifted to a different section of the plane in an attempt to achieve better balance.

Modification centers in Georgia, Alabama, Texas and Oklahoma were working around the clock, and still there weren't enough planes. A new center was opened in Omaha, where the Glenn L. Martin plant was making B-29s and Continental Air Lines took over part of the Denver airport to operate still another center.

In spite of the work of these modification centers, Superforts unfit for battle were arriving in Kansas. In November of 1943, Colonel Harman sent a report to the AAF Matériel Command's Production Division listing defects that were showing up in the B-29s. The report was based on more than 2,800 hours of flying and listed as sources of trouble ignition, exhaust valves, engines, exhaust cylinder-head temperatures, electric-power regulation, carburetor airduct baffles, exhaust turbo oil leakage, exhaust turbo hood mounting, exhaust turbo shrouds, fuel-cell leakage, and a dozen other items.

The situation got no better with the new year. Airplanes with highly nonstandard equipment were emerging from the modification centers. Modifications were being made hurriedly, and in some cases without complete inspection. Matériel shortages, accessory shortages, lack of skilled workers, and a general organizational confusion were causing the trouble.

Officers and enlisted men at Pratt, Great Bend, Walker, and Salina did their best with the planes that were arriving from the modification centers in various stages of completion. They worked day and night until exhaustion drove them to their bunks.

In February, unable to stand the situation any longer, Colonel Pearl H. Robey went to Washington to tell Headquarters the planes could not possibly leave for India on March 10 as they were supposed to; and to prove why. He was immediately shown fancy production charts, the lines shooting off into the heavens as factories reported increased output.

"The only chart I've got shows zero B-29s; none," said Robey. "We haven't got one that can fight. You can push a B-29 through a factory door and maybe even fly it away, but that doesn't prove it's ready for war."

According to Robey, in order to get each of the B-29s in shape for actual warfare, 54 major modifications had to be made on each plane as it rolled off the assembly line. Improvements were vital in the electrical system, the central fire control, the radar, the propeller-feathering system and the engines. And it was important that the planes be equipped with tires that wouldn't flatten after a few landings.

A list of modifications and of every piece of equipment a plane would need was drawn up; and the list ran into a booklet. The Air Technical Service Command ordered modification centers to deploy experts to the Kansas bases immediately to get those planes already delivered into shape for overseas shipment. And on March 9, one day before the scheduled departure date, General Arnold himself flew to Salina and asked how many B-29s would leave the next day for India. His answer was a flat "None."

The General was known for his fast and positive action. He immediately let fly a list of orders that were considered absolutely impossible. Phones began to ring all over the country. "What's the dope? Arnold wants every part required to complete modification.

No, not next month—tomorrow, tomorrow morning." And so began the famed "Battle of Kansas."

Troubleshooter Major General B. E. Meyers was placed in charge of the representatives of the contracting firms and AAF agencies and the GI and civilian mechanics whose job it was to get the B-29s ready for overseas flight and combat. He asked for no paperwork except simple notes about work completed, and hours were to be as long as a man could stand on his feet. The last plane was to be ready to leave no later than April 15, armored and fully equipped.

The work had to be done under the most rigorous conditions outdoors because hangars were scarce. Men were issued high-altitude flying clothes to withstand wind and sleet. General Meyers was constantly on the phone, calling Chicago, Oklahoma City, New York. Air Transport Command planes were arriving in a steady stream delivering parts for the B-29s.

As each plane was finished, it was carefully loaded. When the Superfortresses left Kansas, they would be fully armed except for bombs, and they would contain all their equipment. Gross weights at take-offs would be high, and the weight of each plane had to be measured exactly.

The flight schedule for the 58th Bomb Wing called for a single B-29, with a spare engine aboard, to fly to England before the others left for India. This mission would give the Superfort a shakedown test in a long overwater flight and provide a camouflage for the mass migration to India. The value of such a cover plan was obvious. The existence of the B-29 had long since ceased to be a secret: knowledge of the abnormally long runways being built at Calcutta and Chengtu could not be kept from Japanese Intelligence, and it was easy to figure out that the runways were not being prepared for B-24s or C-46s. When the B-29s arrived in India, their physical presence could not be hidden for long and their target would be known to all.

The cover plan called for the dispatch of the Superfort to England by way of northwest Africa. In England the plane was to be shifted about from field to field until its presence was widely known and an impression would be given that the bomber was about to appear in Europe to lend its weight to the Combined Bomber Offensive. Along with this controlled lack of security there was to be a publicity campaign to create the belief that the

B-29, though designed for very long-range bombing operations, had not lived up to expectations and was being modified to serve as an armed "super-transport." Because of the pressing need for aerial transport over the Hump, several of the modified planes were being sent to India on an experimental basis; the new fields were being prepared for them. General Stilwell gave "news" releases to that effect in his theater.

So, in mid-March, Colonel Frank Cook, flying under secret orders, took off from Salina in Superfort 963. His flight plan took him nonstop to Miami. Taking off from there at night, Colonel Cook flew south for one hour over the Atlantic, then he changed course and flew north to Newfoundland. The last leg of his flight took him to England where a German reconnaissance plane took pictures of the B-29 only forty-five minutes after it had landed. For the next two weeks, "963" was open for inspection by the brass of the ETO while the preplanned publicity campaign was put into operation.

Back in Kansas, shadowy figures flitted through the chill early morning of March 26. There was haste, but no confusion as the silhouettes appeared briefly, their backs hunched by barracks bags, then noiselessly faded back into the dark. A flash of brilliant light cut through the darkness as the door leading from the operations shack quickly opened to allow Colonel Leonard Harman out, then the light was abruptly cut off as the door slammed shut.

Soon the whine of the engines of the world's biggest bombers broke the silence, growing louder and louder as engine after engine was started, until the air was filled with a thunder that seemed to shake the very ground.

With Colonel Harman at the controls, the first big bomber rumbled down the runway, then strained upward into the overcast. It was quickly followed by another—and another—and another. At last, the journey of the giants had begun.

Journey to War

Following Colonel Harman that morning, and in the next few weeks, would be aerial armadas of the 40th, 444th, 462nd and 468th Bomb Groups. Each plane was manned by a hand-picked crew gathered from every theater of war and rushed back to the United States for a few brief months of training. They were facing a momentous undertaking. The long hop to far-off India would be a real test for the big bomber. And everyone had questions. How would the ship perform on long hops? How would she handle the gales over the Atlantic? The dust storms in India? How far would she fly on 10,000 gallons of gas? Would the engines hold up?

There was every reason to question those engines. For of all the bugs that had turned up in the sky giant, the most troublesome had been the engines. But now no time remained for experimenting; the first planes were taking off to be followed by daily groups of nine or ten planes. The initial complement would total ISO Superforts.

The first leg of the journey was a 2,500-mile nonstop flight to Gander Bay, Newfoundland, over northern New England and New Brunswick. With Colonel Harman in the lead all the Superforts in the first group, except one forced down at Presque Isle, Maine, completed the trip. At Gander the airmen were jubilant over the performance of their new plane; the average time for the 2,500-mile flight was 11 hours. Few realized that in the one uncompleted mission they were receiving a subtle preview of things to come.

Colonel Harman was able to slip out of Gander after a short servicing stop, but most of the planes following him encountered blustery gales and lay snowbound for 48 hours. When the storm finally ended, canvas covers were rapidly stripped from aluminum wings and eager crews piled into the planes. Once again, the engines turned and crescendoed into roars. Soon the first plane moved down the cleared runway, rose majestically into the skies, and climbed in fast turns up to 17,000 feet. Then its long nose was pointed toward Marrakech, 3,000 long miles across the icy, storm-swept Atlantic.

One by one the other planes followed: "Liberty Bell," "American Beauty," "Georgia Peach," "Last Resort," "Princess Eileen," "Deacon's Disciples," "Black Magic," "Andy's Dandy," "Miss Minetta," "Totin' To Tokyo."

As the Superforts droned over the endless gray waves, the crews began to realize that there was a lot of water between them and Marrakech, and there was a lot they didn't know about their new airplane. When it came right down to basic facts, what did they know about cruise control, this newfangled engine maintenance, emergency procedures, the thousands and thousands of intricate gadgets which were a part of this aerial Big Bertha?[8]

The dazzling speed with which the plane had been rushed into production and the speed with which these first crews had been trained precluded top performance in both machines and men.

Just eight months had elapsed since the Kansas training bases had been established; since then ground, administration, and air crews had been pulled together and trained for combat service overseas. Because of the shortage of planes some crews had flown only 18 hours in the B-29 before leaving Kansas; only one long-range training mission within the continental United States and safely spaced between storms had been flown. The urgency of international commitments allowed neither the time nor the equipment for the careful training that would have been desirable. The B-29 had been rushed into combat. The flight testing of the experimental planes, the setting up of production lines, the modifications and the equipment changes had all been done in a hurry. Inevitably, command of its full potentialities and thorough knowledge of its complex operation had not been achieved.

The Superforts all crossed the Atlantic without mishap. Ranging between 17,000 and 19,000 feet and traveling at an average speed of 300 miles an hour, they made the hop in 10 hours or less. There was excitement when the advance echelon sighted the low black coastline of northwest French Morocco. Crewmen peered intently down at the 300 miles of fertile farmland bordering the Grand Atlas Mountains leading into Marrakech, the

---

[8] 'Big Bertha' was the nickname bestowed by soldiers upon Germany's advanced siege howitzer of World War I, the 42 cm *kurze Marinekanone* 14 L/12.

second stop on the flight to India. American boys from Memphis, Salt Lake, Dallas, Tacoma, Phoenix, Medicine Hat, Caribou, Butte, Boston and Kansas City were seeing for the first time the strange lowland beneath them.

From the bare brown wastes of the northern verge, crossed by random rivers and crude roads, the landscape to the south gradually softened, flared into ripening green and black fields and the white walled beauty of Casablanca. This highly cultivated country was their North African target, and circular brownstone Marrakech the bull's-eye guiding them into land.

To American eyes, the city, shining brown in the early morning light, looked like an ancient Arab citadel. Said Major Carl Coco, pilot of Liberty Bell, "Marrakech looked so beautiful from the air, but as we found out later, it sure did stink on the ground."

Metropolis of 20,000 French and 200,000 Arabs, continental France superimposed upon Moslem mystery, Marrakech remained Arab to the crewmen who explored it on foot. French bicycles and Parisian girls did offset the proud, dark-skinned natives wrapped in swaddling clothes, bending six times daily toward Mecca; the impressive tile-trimmed palaces surrounded by dark little huts; the roadside litter and the open sewers.

The length of their stay at Marrakech varied from a few hours in the case of Harman to several days. For at Marrakech the Superfort developed serious mechanical trouble—a mysterious loss of power. Flight engineers uneasily watched the heat indicator needles climb toward the danger mark as the B-29s took off, register overheating as the planes attempted to reach the 16,000 feet of altitude needed to cross the Atlas Mountains.

And at Marrakech a Superfort was lost. After a number of planes had managed to take off, the remaining airmen were idling along the runway watching another Superfort prepare to leave on the next leg of the journey—a 2,400-mile jump to Cairo. With engines roaring, the plane started to roll. As they followed its progress down the runway, the men noticed that the plane wasn't lifting. They opened their mouths to shout a warning, then helplessly snapped them shut. With a final surge, the Superfort ran off the smooth runway, piled up in the soft farmland beyond, and burst into flames. Speed on the part of the men nearest the accident saved the lives of the 11 crewmen, but $1,000,000 worth of bomber burned to ashes and twisted metal.

Was this the plane that was supposed to win the war?

Superfort commanders set their course across the deserts of Algeria and Libya, finally dropping out of the skies to the scorched runways of John Payne Field at Cairo. But the fabled charms of the city on the Nile did not prevail on the American airmen. They were not the same eager youths who had landed in Africa a few short days before. They were puzzled; they had a problem: What the hell had gone wrong with their plane?

The disappointing take-off from Marrakech and the poor performance of the ships on the third leg of the trip made it imperative that engines be changed, instruments be checked, and each plane be given a general overhauling. This meant a delay of three to six days while civilian aircraft specialists, who had just arrived in Cairo from the United States, and the crew chiefs and flight engineers went over each plane.

Jake Harman's plane led the others out of Cairo on the fourth leg of the trip, a 2,400-mile hop to Karachi over the grass-green Nile Delta, the brown Arabian Desert, and ancient Persia. Here the crewmen experienced weather such as few dreamed could exist anywhere on earth. Temperatures ranged to 110 or 120 degrees in the shade, and on the hardstands where the planes stood there was no shade. Thermometers inside the Superforts soared to 185 and 195 degrees. Engines came within 20 degrees of overheating while standing dead still; more than one engine, just started, became overheated and blew a cylinder before the crew chief had time to shut it off.

Two planes were completely lost at Karachi, one of them plunging into the sea, never to be seen again. Knots of anxious crewmen gloomily surveyed their planes. If the Superfort acted like this on a regular flight, what would happen when it came to actual combat? None of them could guess. Instead they serviced their planes and made ready for the final 1,500-mile flight to northeastern India and the new 20th Bomber Command bases. Still leading the armada was Jake Harman.

According to schedule, all the B-29s were to arrive between the first and the fifteenth of April. At noon, Sunday, April 2, at Chakulia, General Kenneth B. Wolfe, Commander of the 20th, and his staff assembled to await the arrival of Harman's plane.

Twice before false alarms had brought them rushing to base operations, but this time Colonel Harman himself had radioed his ETA (Estimated time of arrival).

Because this was a "historic" first, public relations officers staged an elaborate welcome with a fighter escort aloft and reporters and photographers on the ground. Suspense, mounting minute by minute, burst in a roar when the plane was spotted in the west. It flew steadily in, buzzed the field in a thunderous earth-shaking dive, swung around and settled smoothly on the long runway. Jake Harman and the crew of his Number 663 slid out of the silver belly to the enthusiastic greetings of the administrative, ground and maintenance men of Chakulia.

It had taken the lead plane just seven days to make the trip. Singly, in pairs, and in small groups other planes arrived in the days that followed. By April 15, thirty-two planes were at their stations, leaving dozens of their numbers behind to await major repairs along the route. All the planes in transit were grounded from April 21 to 29 after a fifth serious accident occurred. Investigation showed that most accidents had resulted from engine failures, some of which could be traced to mistakes made by inexperienced crews. When flight was resumed the planes arrived more rapidly; 130 Superforts had reached their home fields by May 8.

For General Wolfe the arrival of the Superforts was the culmination of a long struggle. Active in the B-29 program since its beginning, he had gone through the development, production, and training stages; and now the end was in sight: combat. Armed with a directive from the Commanding General to commit the B-29 to combat without delay, Wolfe had arrived at New Delhi on January 13, 1944. Two contingents of his staff officers had preceded him to survey airdrome sites, transportation and supply routes, climatic conditions, and troop facilities.

They found big problems. Under the supervision of the Combined Chiefs of Staff, six British airfields in east India had been tentatively selected as bases for the B-29s. Located in Bengal, in a 100-mile arc northwest of Calcutta, these fields at Kharagpur, Chakulia, Charra, Piardoba, Dudhkundi, and Kalaikunda were woefully inadequate for planes the size of the Superforts. However, they represented an engineering start, and all were accessible by road and rail from Calcutta, which was to serve as the chief port of entry for the 20th Bomber Command's equipment and supplies.

The British had already begun work on runways and buildings; they were to continue until American engineers could take over in January. Located as they were on the flat Bengal plains, the bases could be enlarged and rebuilt to accommodate both B-29s and ferry ships, and eventually would be adequate rear staging areas for the projected combat missions from China.

When General Wolfe arrived in mid-January, he found that a substantial start had been made by his hard driving advance staff. In addition to speeding the work on the Bengal bases, General Wolfe had to establish his forward area bases at Chengtu, move up the equipment and personnel that would be needed there, transport supplies for his people, and build a stockpile for his initial combat missions.

As the 20th's original "Project Officer," Wolfe swung into high gear. He flew over the entire China-Burma-India Theater, surveyed every projected B-29 base on both sides of the Hump, and interviewed all topside theater officers, including General Joe Stilwell and General Claire Chennault, on problems of strategic operation, airbase construction, defensive measures, and the logistics which would provide him with men, food, bombs, and gasoline.

His meeting with General Chennault took place at the Burma-India Sector headquarters of the Tenth Air Force. In this area the B-29 was still a deep, dark secret; therefore, it was with considerable surprise one morning that the intelligence officer learned he was to clear his office immediately for a meeting that would include Generals Wolfe, Chennault, Stratemeyer, and other Allied leaders. There was considerable speculation among headquarters personnel as the meeting progressed and no satisfaction when the generals finally emerged: they went directly to their planes and departed without a word. And the headquarters staff could obtain no information from the Tenth Air Force representatives at the meeting.

But in the office where the meeting had been held an intelligence officer found a series of maps. Penciled routings were traced on the maps—the routings leading directly to Japan. The officer, realizing something big was in the wind, but not quite sure what, quickly burned the maps.

A few days later, he and other members of Intelligence got their first solid clue to what had gone on behind the locked doors at the meeting. A Japanese airman, shot down and captured before he could lose himself in the hills, was brought to Headquarters. As he was taken into the interrogation room, he quickly asked, "Where is the new sky giant?"

"What sky giant?" queried the American.

"The B-29."

To most of the combat-worn men of the Tenth, the Jap's inquiry was the first knowledge they had of the new bomber. Meanwhile, General Wolfe conferred with New Delhi officials, British and American, who could provide him with useful information. Next he visited Panagarh, where the Command's temporary headquarters had been established, and Kharagpur, where the first contingent of his command had arrived. Completing a tour of the two bases and four satellite fields, he then recommended to Major General George Stratemeyer, ranking Air Force officer in India, that the Kharagpur, Chakulia, Piardoba, and Dudhkundi bases be swiftly enlarged as principal B-29 dromes,[9] with both service and tactical groups, and that the Kalaikunda base be developed as an auxiliary supply and staging field.

As his next move, General Wolfe flew the Hump to Kunming. There he conferred again with General Chennault and with his chief engineer, Colonel Henry Byroade, who was in charge of airbase construction in the Chengtu area. Rounding out these talks with flights to Chengtu and Chungking, Wolfe completed arrangements with the Chinese Minister of Communications, Dr. Tseng Yang-fu, for the immediate construction of four forward area fields, at Hsinching, Pengshan, Kwanghan, and Kiunglai, all within a 50-mile radius of the old university city of Chengtu. Fifty thousand coolies were to be drafted into service at each of the bases. The General left with the Generalissimo's[10] assurances that the forward staging areas would be ready for combat operations in three months.

---

[9] Location for test flights; an aerodrome.
[10] Chinese leader Chiang Kai-shek's full title was His Excellency Generalissimo Chiang Kai-shek.

During Wolfe's fortnight of Hump-hopping across the Asiatic world, the Bengal base-builders had been busy, but they had run into unexpected and unrelieved difficulties incident to India: the natives, the climate, the British, the dust, the insects, the contaminated water, the shortages, and the complete lack of modern facilities for transportation, communication, and construction. In terms of the President's commitment-to-combat date, progress was much too slow.

General Wolfe threw himself with characteristic energy and directness into the snafued Bengal base building project. He took off in his C-47 and headed straight for General Stilwell's advance headquarters in the North Burma jungle. Two days with scrappy, battle-bound "Vinegar Joe" and he had attained his objective: the loan of one of Stilwell's invaluable engineer battalions, then building the Ledo Road, and the diversion of another to rush completion of the 20th Bomber Command's east India bases.

The 382nd Engineer Construction Battalion, on loan from the Ledo Road, arrived by air late in January and began a round-the-clock extension of the red clay fighter strip which formed the airfield at Kharagpur. When the 853rd Engineer Aviation Battalion arrived in India on February 1, it was sent to Chakulia. The first trickle of men, machines, food, and fuel began to flow into Kharagpur and the adjacent bases despite the cramped railway situation, the crowded, narrow-gauge tracks, and the pint-sized freight cars.

Plopped down in the remote bush country of a remote land, a tiny knot of airmen faced as formidable a task as ever faced a GI. In strict secrecy and isolation, they had to create a functioning Little America deep in India. The handful of engineers, aided by Indians who did the jobs that could be accomplished by unskilled labor, literally sweated the bases into workable landing fields. They knew there would be no Air Medals handed out when the job was done. But with mounting energy they toiled, fighting against the rapidly nearing date when the first of the B-29s was scheduled to arrive.

As the month of February neared its end and the dry winter heat reached the 100-degree mark daily, every American, British, and native agency in India was enlisted to accelerate construction. At Kharagpur and the other fields, the runways, taxi ways, revetments and hardstands had been built by the British for fighters and medium bombers. A compromise was affected between the use of existing facilities and the construction of entirely new installations. The intricate internal situation required constant coordination between American and British engineers, between Anglo American and Indian agencies, and between the services of the U. S. Army itself.

The work was difficult, and the hours were long. During March, with the advent of the B-29 only a matter of days away, men worked on into the dusk and half the night to ready the fields. They were too tired to listen to reports of planes already on the wing; reports that were at once exciting and mysterious. Instead they had a fight of their own to win, and hours of work grew longer and longer.

On the morning of April 2, they forgot their aching backs and lined the runway at Chakulia to watch Jake Harman land the first of the B-29s. The impossible had been partly accomplished. Two of the five fields, Chakulia and Kharagpur, were operational.

By May 8th, 130 B-29s had landed in India. Newly arrived maintenance crews swarmed in and out of the planes, unloading spare engines and parts, getting the Superforts ready for combat. Their first problem was the burning wind: it was so thick with dust that breathing was a struggle; the dust clung, even after washing, and during the humid nights it seemed to soak into a man's guts. Their second problem was more serious: the planes were still acting sluggish, and there were still a hundred and one guesses as to cause.

"It's the engines," said the crew chiefs. "Change 'em and the planes will fly."

But there weren't enough spare engines to go around, not even enough to begin such a project. The only extras had been carried over by the B-29s themselves and had to be saved.

The order was to take off the engines and see what caused their failure. It soon became commonplace for one plane to undergo 30 major engine alterations a week, but the basic question went unanswered.

The ground crews complained of equipment shortages. How could they fix the planes without equipment? There was no answer for them. And there was no forgetting the heat; the scorching heat that caused overheated engines on take-off. During April and May airmen began to dread the training missions they were scheduled to fly. Finally, daytime flights were canceled, and training missions were started at five in the afternoon. Ten hours of precious engine time were devoted to a training program which included visual and radar bombing, air-to-air gunnery, and formation flying.

To the men who flew it, the B-29 was still a new airplane; a thorough knowledge of its complex operation had not yet been achieved. Every one of its 50,000 parts could cause trouble. The sky giant's performance left something to be desired. As they got closer and closer to combat, the men felt a growing hatred for the plane they were assigned to fly.

All was not going well on the ground either. Work was lagging at Charra, Piardoba, and Dudhkundi. These fields still could not accommodate the heavy bombers or the 19 C-87s which General Wolfe had brought to India in mid-January to serve as transports.

On April 24, the B-29s had been ordered to start the hazardous transportation of supplies over the Hump to stockpile the China bases for the first combat strikes against Japan. To many of the crews this was the crowning blow. Their planes were in debatable condition, and now they were to become supply jockeys. It was a great war!

"A Damned Trucking Outfit!"

BORN OF BATTLE NECESSITY, and with Allied leaders eagerly awaiting its debut, the B-29 suddenly became a flying boxcar, traversing the Hump to carry gas and vital equipment to China. The reason for this self-supply was simple. In order to forestall criticism from Generals Stilwell and Chennault that the strategic air attack would be pressed at the expense of land fighting in China, General Arnold had promised President Roosevelt that the B-29s would handle their own air supply, thereby relieving the already overworked Air Transport Command service across the hazardous Himalayas.

It was a tough promise to make. For the men of the 20th, it was a more difficult promise to keep. For over and above the fuel required to fly a B-29 from Calcutta to Chengtu and back, an additional 60,000 gallons of gas was required to reach Kyushu, the southernmost of the four main Japanese islands, and return to Chengtu. Seven hundred thousand gallons of gas would have to be ferried to Chengtu in order to supply one wing for one mission.

Twenty of the Superforts were ordered stripped for the supply operation, but the job proved so great that the 20th Bomber Command was forced to turn to the Air Transport Command for aid, and later combat planes between missions were used to augment the flying freighters. To keep the promise made by their general was one of the 20th's costliest assignments of the war. Each plane was required to make six round trips over the Hump with gasoline and bombs before it could go on to drop those bombs on Japan. And that was the reason for basing the Superforts so far back in India. There was no way to support them at Chengtu.

Among the crews assigned to fly the 1,200-mile run 30,000 feet over the rugged Himalayas, morale reached a new low. One night on pass a combat veteran of the Seventh Air Force, a crew chief who had been rushed back to the States from the Pacific, trained for this all-important assignment, and was now on a regular run over the Hump, expressed their disgust in a memorable toast: "Here's to the 20th Bomber Command—a goddamned trucking outfit!"

Flying the Hump was no picnic. The B-29s designed for a maximum load of 120,000 pounds were overloaded to 130,000 pounds, and they carried it over mountains that were not only the highest in the world but also the most treacherous. Hundreds of Americans had died in the Himalayan wastes before the B-29 was built, and hundreds more would die in its vast ranges. The weather was the world's worst, subject to sudden snowstorms, violent downdrafts, and 20-degree subzero temperatures.

The first flight of B-29s over the Hump took place on April 24, 1944, the same day that the first of four forward fields in China was declared operational for the big aircraft. Again, Jake Harman flew the first plane, while at the controls of the second were Brigadier General "Blondie" Saunders and Colonel William Blanchard. It was the start of nearly ten months of Hump operations, and a big day in the history of the 20th.

Captain William O'Malley, navigator for Saunders, described the trip:

"We took off at ten in the morning with General Saunders as command pilot, Colonel Blanchard as pilot, and Major Berton H. 'Tex' Burns as copilot. On the way up we flew directly over the Japanese lines in the vicinity of the Kohima Road and the Imphal Plain, without incident. The flight over the Hump was by-God amazing; perfect weather, incredible mountain valleys and gorges, tiny villages on the lesser mountains. We sighted three huge peaks about 200 miles distant. An ATC safety pilot told us nobody knew how high they were.

"After finally getting over the Hump, we flew above an overcast through which we let down into the Yangtze Valley. And there was China! A most amazing landscape of thousands of cultivated rice paddies. For the first time in my life I had the feeling of being in a different world; one that could not be described with a 'Well, this looks like Texas,' or 'This looks like Iowa.'

"The airfield at Kwanghan looked wonderful from the air. The landing was apparently quite an event. Thousands of coolies lined each side of the runway. After getting out of the plane, we lined up, and motion and still pictures were taken. General Chennault and his staff greeted us, as well as Chinese officials and American engineers. Everywhere the Chinese would smile and yell 'Ding Hao'—which means Very best."

Two days later, on April 26, a B-29 unexpectedly went into combat—the first of the Superforts to lock with the Japanese. On this day, two Superforts took off from India bound for China. One of these, aircraft number 42-6330 of the 676th Bombardment Squadron, 444th Group, left Chakulia at 12:45 A.M. Its cargo was 2,000 gallons of aviation gasoline for the Chengtu bases. The plane was piloted by Major Charles H. Hansen, with Colonel Alvin D. Clarke as command pilot and Lieutenant Harold H. Heinbaugh as copilot. Kurmitola was passed at 2 A.M. and Hailakanda in northeastern India at 2:55 A.M.

Scanning the thickening green-topped ridges near the Indo-Burmese frontier, Major Hansen suddenly sighted a dozen aircraft flying approximately five miles off at the 3 o'clock position and 2,000 feet below his 16,000-foot altitude. His warning shout brought the crew to life. Almost immediately identified as Nakajima single-engine fighters, the enemy "Oscars" promptly broke formation, six starting a swift upward spiral under the bomber and six continuing in tight echelon toward the Hump. Reaching the bomber's altitude, the fighters struck a triple tandem on each side of the giant aircraft and well out of range. The minutes ticked off as the B-29 held true on course at 220 miles an hour. The green gunners tensed at battle stations, hypnotically tracking their first enemy targets.

Slowly the six Oscars reassembled fen the starboard or sun side of the streaking dreadnought, still cruising cautiously out of range and still studying and perhaps photographing America's amazing new aircraft.

The taut stalemate seemed endless. Then at 3:10, fifteen minutes after the simultaneous sightings, the lead fighter suddenly broke formation, barreled back in a low dive at 4 o'clock. Guns winked and flamed at 1,000 ... 800 ... 600 yards. Then a Nip burst stitched the bomber's waist, and a scream from side-gunner Sergeant Walter W. Gilonske told the crew he had been hit. Three top turrets went out and remained inoperative. The tail .50s jammed but were immediately cleared. The 20-mm. tail cannon failed to function, for the spring-loading mechanism had not been wound.

Then a second fighter and a third roared in at 5 o'clock level, breaking away in low dives and firing wildly. A fourth pursuit, swinging in toward the tail, caught a burst from Sergeant Harold

Lanhan's guns at 90 yards, dove smoking out of sight into the overcast.

One after another in half-hearted succession, the pursuits attacked from below, but after the opening volley none ranged closer than 900 yards. No frontal or overhead attacks were attempted, no aggressive close-range fire pressed. In all, 12 single passes were made with the apparent purpose of testing the great ship's armament, and fay 3:35 the six Oscars had vanished as quickly as they flashed into view.

When the smoke had cleared, the crew added up the score. Sergeant Gilonske was the first member of the Command to earn the Purple Heart, while Lanhan, with the confirmation of three crew members, listed the smoking Japanese plane as a probable kill, to become the first B-29 gunner to draw enemy blood. The Superfort, hit by eight explosive shells, continued to Chengtu at 25,000 feet, arriving without further incident.

Upon its return to its Indian base the crew members had the first B-29 combat story to tell: "We could've shot 'em all down if they weren't so damn careful."

"I guess they had a time for themselves trying to figure out what we were flying."

For a brief interlude, morale rose throughout the command. The plane had met the enemy and had probably accounted for one kill. There were boasts of how many more would soon follow.

But the gasoline had to move. General Wolfe ordered full steam ahead in filling the gas tanks. Back in Washington General Arnold and his aides were plotting the first Chengtu—based B-29 raids—with D-Day scheduled for June. Every facility was strained to the breaking point to meet the cry for supplies, but Hump tonnage lagged.

The crews soon forgot the story of aircraft 42-6330 in their dreary and dangerous assignment. With increasing frequency a B-29 manned by a freshman crew would send out a frantic message of distress from somewhere over the Hump: "Engine burning—altitude 22,000—abandoning ship—we're jumping into God knows what ..."

Then silence; unbroken silence.

And men, growing lonely and afraid in this strange land of unbearable heat and ice and snow, would sit glued to their makeshift seats in the ready shack waiting for word—any word—of the missing crews. Often there was no further word from the great Himalayas. Or if the plane cleared the mountains and landed in the jungle there was a chance—a million-to-one chance—that the survivors might make it out. They had to beat their way through unmarked jungle and dodge Chinese bandits who earned 300 rupees a head for captured Yanks—dead ones preferred.

Day after day came reports. Captain W. S. Ball and eleven airmen abandoned their gasless Superfort over jungle-dark South China, and with the help of friendly Chinese walked five days to reach Yunnani—and rescue—on the Burma Road. The B-29 tanker of Captain John R. Simpson, starting its 15th Hump hop, caught fire at a low altitude, and Simpson, watching his crewmates jump one by one, finally leaped through the nose well himself at a scant 300 feet—and lived. First Lieutenant Leslie J. Sloan and nine haggard survivors walked out of the wilderness of China twenty-nine days after their "Esso Express" had exploded over the Hump, and the missing flight crew had long since been given up for lost.

Said Colonel Charles E. Moore, who arrived in India as staff supply officer at the height of the Hump crisis:

"Our operations in this theater were complicated by the sorriest web of difficulties ever to plague an Air Force. The greatest of these were the distances and difficulties of transportation. And the chief cause of them was the implacable Hump, a barrier we never did quite lick, and which exacted to the bitter end a terrible toll of men and supplies."

What the Colonel left unsaid was that morale continued to tumble. The 20th Bomber Command was "just a goddamned trucking outfit," and not a safe one at that.

Rodeo Over Bangkok

On June 1, 1944, a rumor spread through the newly completed Bengal installations at Chakulia, Kharagpur, Piardoba and Dudhkundi. Twenty thousand Americans, numb from overwork and the frightening Hump rounds, heard it. And soon it was more than a rumor passed from adobe barrack to thatched-roof mess hall to ramshackle briefing room. Something big was in the wind.

Crew chiefs and their assistants hurried to ready the planes. Gunners carefully checked their stations; radio men took apart their sets, then put them together again. On June 5 the 20th Bomber Command was finally going into action.

The "Old Man" personally selected the 100 planes which would participate in this first bombing mission. His selections sent the waning morale of the entire command soaring. For while no man is eager to fly to possible death, the pilots, navigators, mechanics, and gunners knew that the sooner Japan was reduced to smoking ruins, the sooner they could go home. At this point, home seemed to be only a word in the dictionary. But more than one man thought of home as he sat in the briefing room that morning and heard General Wolfe say, "This marks the beginning of the organized destruction of the Japanese industrial empire."

On the afternoon of June 4, crews were assembled for a general briefing of the next day's job. Twelve hundred Americans heard an operations officer announce that the target would be Bangkok in enemy-held Thailand.[11] There wasn't a sound as Major Charles McReynolds, a Command intelligence officer, took over to describe in detail every phase of the operation.

"The weather covering the 2,000-mile flight will be..."

"Rendezvous at..."

"Approach target from..."

---

[11] The Kingdom of Thailand was neutral during the outbreak of the war. However, later the Thais granted invading Japanese troops passage into Burma. It was a fruitless bargain made in return for Japan's promise to help the Thais later reclaim former territories of French-Indochina from the West.

Slowly and carefully, officers assigned to brief the crewmen covered their respective fields. No phase of this first mission was overlooked. And then, as the crews silently digested the information, Blondie Saunders stood before the men.

"Hit those Japs and hit 'em hard," said the General, and then he walked from the room.

There were no cheers. In the minds of the men ran one phrase: "Take 'em out, drop 'em, and get 'em back home."

Colonels Harman, Englar, Carmichael and Harvey, in briefing their respective Groups at the predawn Monday meeting, revealed more details of Bangkok's sprawling Makasan rail and shipyards, the Command's first bombing objective. The airmen sat soberly, some taking notes, some studying the big wall maps outlining the target and route, as the speakers explained the strategic, tactical, and logistic factors in the target's choice.

Bangkok made an excellent target for a practice mission: the flight could be staged from the Kharagpur area without using a drop of the fuel supply that had been so painfully flown over the Hump to Chengtu. Its distance, a 2,000-mile round trip from the Bengal bases, would provide a test of the operational capacities of the B-29. It would be an overwater haul with Burma land approaches, a pattern foreshadowing future operations against western Japan, with a route that would entail limited flight over enemy-occupied territory.

Bangkok was the land funnel for Japanese military freight moving to the Burma front. The Makasan railway shops were to be the primary target. Damage to the shops at Insein and the related campaign against rail communications had made these Makasan shops especially important. In addition, their isolated location would permit an assessment of the damage inflicted by the Superforts on their first mission.

General Wolfe had wanted his first bombing mission to be made at night to help overcome what he felt were serious gaps in his training program. The hours his men had spent flying the Hump had not increased their skill in high-altitude flying, rendezvous, gunnery, and bombing, all vital elements of a successful combat mission.

But he was overruled by General Arnold in a message that said:

"The limited number of operations which can be conducted from your forward bases because of logistic difficulties make it mandatory that maximum results be achieved from each operation. This requires destruction of primary targets by daylight precision bombing. The shakedown operation should contribute maximum training and test for this kind of mission. Hence, it is directed that the attack on Bangkok be planned as a daylight precision bombing mission. Your present difficulties are fully recognized, yet the entire bomber program is predicated upon the B-29's employment primarily as a visual precision weapon."

Based on this message, a field order for the June 5 mission was drawn up and sent back to Washington for approval. The reply from General Arnold was an immediate "Mission plan approved." Appended to the message was a personal note to Wolfe, who had requested permission to participate in the Bangkok mission:

"Sorry," said General Arnold to his commander, "you are not to accompany the shakedown raid."

By 5:30 A.M. that Monday, 100 crews were seated in their planes. The engines were turning over, each craft's wing and belly tanks were loaded with 6,846 gallons of high octane; bomb bays were rigged with 10,000 pounds of high explosives and incendiary clusters. The planes lumbered slowly down the traffic aprons, lining up on the edge of the runways. All was ready.

Ground crews, after a final 24 hours of myriad engine changes, fuel pumpings, electric installations, and mechanical checks, sank in tense, exhausted knots along the night lines. General Wolfe, accompanied by Generals Saunders and Upston, suddenly appeared on the Kharagpur line. They stood squinting into the orange sunrise as the bombers headed eastward.

At Dudhkundi at 5:45, the first of Colonel Alva Harvey's 444th Group rumbled down the 7,500 feet of runway, cleared the fringing trees and banked in a slow arc toward the southeast.

At Chakulia, Colonel Jake Harman, leader of the Bangkok mission, started down the runway and eased the first of the 40th Group's 38 bombers into the air.

Three—five—ten—twenty—thirty-two bombers strained into the air at one-minute intervals from each of the four fields.

Ninety-four—ninety-five—ninety-six swung out in long low arcs through the sun-drenched mist to reassemble in four-plane formations and set their course 142 degrees southwest to Bangkok.

One plane of Colonel Carmichael's 462nd Group, aborted because of a mechanical failure and never left the ground.

At Chakulia, base of the 40th Group, one of the B-29s crashed on take-off. Midway down the runway its nose wheel was lifted and remained up for the rest of the run, causing the tail skid to bump repeatedly. After using up 7,000 feet of runway, the plane began its rise in an apparently normal manner.

Suddenly the left wing dipped, but was quickly righted. Again, it dropped. Swiftly the Superfort plummeted earthward, struck ground with a tremendous explosion, and spun in a flaming cartwheel through the air. Three 500-pound general purpose bombs in the forward bay exploded, blowing the fuselage to pieces. First Lieutenant B. A. Eisner, copilot, dragged from the blazing ruins, was so badly crushed he could barely murmur, "The Number 2 engine failed." The ten other crewmen died in their flaming Superfort. Two minutes had elapsed from the time of take-off.

Led by Colonel Harman, the airborne echelons climbed to 5,000 feet and proceeded on their briefed course, holding to a cruise speed of 210 miles per hour. Crew members remained intently at their stations, not only because visibility was bad and becoming worse, but because each pilot, navigator, engineer, bombardier, gunner, observer and technician felt the gnawing fear that comes to all men who are about to face an adversary—and possibly death. Their plane was an unknown quantity—their enemy dangerous and deadly.

But as the 98 Superforts moved through the heavy skies, one by one formations broke. Eighteen planes developed mechanical failures and turned back to their bases, unable to continue. In the remaining 80 planes, crews sweated over their equipment, their fingers crossed in hopes their plane would not only continue to the target and drop its bombs but would hold up for the return journey.

Formation flying grew increasingly difficult as late morning mists increased and visibility sank to zero. Many of the 80 remaining planes were unable to continue the flight in formation, and proceeded on their own to the initial assembly point—three tiny islands southeast of Bangkok. As they approached the islands, the planes climbed to 20,000 feet. Tense crew members pulled on flak suits, again tested the guns, and turned on the radar to screen the Gulf of Siam islands.

In the pressurized cabins men began to talk nervously—more to themselves than to their comrades… "Can't see a thing in this damn soup… How can we make rendezvous when we can't even see another plane?"

"Who's going to follow who to target?"

The bombardiers had their own problems. Would they plant their bombs on target? Could they spot their target if this soup[12] didn't lift during the final 500-mile lap?

Men grown old in combat with other air forces and other comrades sweated out H-Hour with their freshmen crew members. They were 1,300 miles from India; 15,000 miles from home. Would they ever see either again?

In the thick soup three more Superforts, their engines suddenly coughing, turned back toward India. Now there were seventy-seven.

The B-29s rose to 25,000 feet and, cruising at 200 miles per hour, swung up the Siam Gulf, into the seven-tenths overcast above Bangkok. With the Makesan rail shops covered by cloud, most of the planes made rapid adjustments for radar bombing. A steel bridge, some distance up the river from the workshops, returned the strongest radar rays, so it was used as an offset aiming point over the target.

Bomb bays flipped open: explosive and firebombs started to fall. Up barreled the back-tipped fighters; up came the black-red bursts of flak. The Battle of Bangkok was on. The big bombers dipped, dodged and soared in separate attack sallies, bungled and bombed from 17,000 to 27,000 feet.

A navigator, his job over for the moment, looked down through a break in the clouds. "Looks like Saturday night on Coney Island," he said.

B-29s shot in for their bomb runs from all directions. Only nine enemy aircraft attempted to stop them, and their attempts were feeble as the pilots warily stayed far out in the mist during most of the time they were aloft. Gunners, calm now that they

---

[12] Fog. From British slang, 'pea-souper,' in reference to the soup's thick, murky thickness.

actually were in combat, waited for the Nips to attack, but only rarely were they able to fire. One "probable" and two damaged Nips were confirmed. Flak was heavy but inaccurate: a single B-29 received minor flak damage to the tail.

Bomb runs lasted from twelve seconds to six minutes. The first plane reached the aiming point at 10:52 A.M.; the last departed at 12:32 P.M. Seventy-seven aircraft bombed the general target area, 48 utilizing radar.

The first trial by fire and flak was over, and the long trip back began. The fear of sky battle and bullets faded to be replaced with the fear of engine failure. The scattered B-29s swung back over the Gulf of Siam, over the Malay Peninsula and the southernmost tip of Burma to the Bay of Bengal and then started the 800-mile overwater trip.

In the lead once again was Jake Harman. As his plane headed into dark clouds that loomed ahead, he turned to his copilot. "Well, that's the first 10,000 pounds of bombs out of a B-29 to strike the enemy."

"Yes, sir. But this round trip is only half over, Colonel."

"Don't I know it! We could lose the whole force in that weather ahead. Those are the damnedest, darkest line gales I've ever seen."

Most of the planes, running low on gas, dropped down to within 1,000 feet of the ocean as they sped for home. Although 23 planes had failed to reach Bangkok, only one plane, the B-29 that had gone up in flames during the take-off at Chakulia, had been lost so far.

Back in India, at the approach of 4 o'clock, the earliest possible hour of return, the men at the weather-whipped bases gathered in groups around control towers, along the runways and near the crash trucks idling in the humid heat. The sky blackened, the rains came, and the wind blew.

Hundreds of miles away, the casualty toll started to climb.

"Aircraft number 42-6361—678th Squadron—444th Group—calling Salua, calling Chittagong—low on gas, changing course over Bay of Bengal and heading for Kunming in South China... That's all."

That was all, indeed, for alerted American operators glued to their headquarters radio headphones. But it was not all for Major Booth G. Malone and his crew, struggling with two malfunctioning engines, hacking and chopping to jettison equipment from the slowly sinking aircraft, straining to squeeze power from the failing fuel supply. It was not all for the Chinese peasants near Yuchi who looked up from their rice paddies as they heard the four engines die one by one in the sky. They watched the B-29 plummet down to bury itself in the soft black loess, 60 miles from Kunming. Ten of the crew had parachuted safely.

At the identical hour, a second aircraft of the same group, running out of gas and with one engine feathered, crash-landed at Dum Dum, a British base north of Calcutta. The crew escaped unhurt.

Over the Bay of Bengal, limping toward the brown Bengal shore, two more Superforts were in serious trouble. They radioed that they were preparing to ditch in the sea. The B-29 piloted by Captain J. N. Saunders, attempting to reach Chittagong on the Bay's northeastern shore, ran out of fuel 100 miles from base and glided to a smooth landing on the whitecapped waves. Although the big bomber revealed surprising buoyancy and remained afloat until it came to rest on a sand bar, two crewmen, either stunned or trapped, lost their lives in the wreckage. The nine remaining airmen, including Captain Sanders, escaped in life rafts to be picked up 45 minutes later by Spitfires and launches of the Royal Air Force Air-Sea Rescue Service.

The second ditching of a Bengal-bound B-29 occurred almost simultaneously on that squally afternoon of June 5, 1944. Aircraft "304" of the 40th Group had almost gained the coast of India when the last of a series of fuel transfer failures doomed it to a dead-stick landing on the water. The plane first radioed trouble two hours after leaving the target, when the fuel transfer system went out. Repaired three times by the flight engineer, 1st Lieutenant J. E. Phalon, the faulty system finally burned out completely, leaving hundreds of gallons of unused gasoline in the auxiliary tanks. At 3:30 P.M., the plane lost an engine and began to fall. Major A. N. Zamry, the pilot, increased power in the other three engines to maintain a 180-mile-per-hour airspeed, but the plane continued to lose altitude at the rate of 200 feet per minute.

Low on fuel and settling under 10,000 feet, the bomber had a fifty-fifty chance to make an auxiliary base when suddenly the Number 3 engine cut out. Indicated airspeed dropped to 150 miles per hour. As the plane dropped slowly toward the sea, Zamry ordered the remaining gas jettisoned and crewmen to their ditching stations. Heat and gas fumes in the cabin were nauseating. The men braced themselves and waited. Then the Number 4 engine quit, and Zamry cut all power and prepared to ditch. With airspeed barely 100 miles an hour and with full flaps dragging the sultry air, the big bomber struck lightly tail first, bounced off the slight swells, struck again, lifted momentarily over the waves, then crashed into the bay. The tail assembly broke off, the nose section split, glass splintered through the cabin, water poured into the forward compartments. Major Zamry and Corporal J. W. Harvey, the radio operator, were killed instantly.

The other ten men in the plane, after spending two days floating in emergency rafts, beached on a small island at the mouth of the Ganges. They were picked up the following day by a PBY patrol bomber. In all, 73 Superforts of the original 100 scheduled for the mission completed the round trip. Singly and in groups they landed 10 to 12 hours after take-off. They landed at Kharagpur, Chakulia, Piardoba, and at Dudhkundi. And others, blown off course by the raging monsoon, came to rest at Calcutta, Dum Dum, Charra, and nine other English bases.

The first mission was over. General Wolfe, shortly after the last plane landed, said, "This Command, in the person of its officers and men, is determined that come heat, rains, politics, failures, the enemy, death or hell itself—its job shall be done."

And in Washington two weeks later General Arnold told reporters, "This first employment of the B-29s makes possible the softening-up attack on Japan very much earlier than would be possible with aircraft hitherto known to combat."

The men of the 20th Bomber Command had come through. But 15 airmen had died in the ruins of their smashed aircraft. In all, five of the million-dollar Superforts had been destroyed, and 23 had failed to reach the target.

As the men sat around their barracks resting up from the Bangkok mission, their thoughts turned to the planes that did not complete the trip, and to the jinx that seemed to be dogging their every move. The jinx prevailed: a few days later reconnaissance planes returned with photos showing that all principal units at Bangkok were still operational, despite the 700,000 pounds of bombs dropped. The crews were bewildered; they had done their job. What had gone wrong?

"It was just like a rodeo," said one old combat man. "We gave them a hell of a show, but nobody got hurt."

"Nobody but us," someone replied. "And where do we go from here?"

DING HAO!

WHERE DO WE GO FROM HERE? It was a good question, and one the Joint Chiefs of Staff in Washington had already answered.

The day following the Bangkok raid, AAF Headquarters requested information as to the weight of an attack that could be mounted against the Japanese homeland between June 15th and 20th. Planners figured that such a strike would relieve pressure in east China and would also coordinate with the important Marianas operation in the Pacific.

To strike the islands of Japan the Superforts would have to stage out of China; and this meant biting deep into the stockpile so laboriously built up during the continuing Hump operations. General Wolfe, after considering all factors, reported back to headquarters that 50 B-29s could be put over the target on June 15th; 55 would be available five days later.

To the Joint Chiefs, this seemed too little, so on June 7 they issued a directive ordering a minimum strike of 70 planes on June 15; the primary target was to be the Imperial Iron and Steel Works at Yawata.

But what of the bases in China?

AAF engineers had encountered myriad problems in the building of the Superfort bases in China. The basic purpose behind their construction was purely strategic: the conquering of distance. For the B-29 to reach Japan, a great staging area had first to be set up in central China to be the connecting link between the rear area bases in India, some 1,200 miles away, and targets in Japan proper and in Manchuria.

In China there was a massed mingling of the old and the new. The Americans approached the task with pride in their new technology. The Chinese, equally proud of their ancient heritage, responded with a hundred assurances that the old ways were best. Yet, with a humor characteristic of both nations, they managed to cooperate and to create in the rich valley of Chengtu a project ranked by some as the greatest engineering accomplishment since the building of the Great Wall of China.

The city of Chengtu, capital of the province of Szechwan, was often referred to as the last outpost of Chinese civilization. Lying in the shadows of the wild western mountains, not far from remote, towering Tibet, the city dominated a rich farming valley with an irrigation system that dated back nearly two thousand years. It was a valley of lusty, red-cheeked peasants; soil-bound people with an earthy sense of humor.

Among the first to "invade" Chengtu was Lieutenant Colonel Waldo I. Kennerson, who approved preliminary plans for the bases on December 12, 1943, a month after the original commitments had been made between the Chinese and U. S. governments at the Cairo conference. Before this, Colonel Henry A. Byroade, under the direction of General Chennault and General Covell, had taken a small group of American Army officers to Chengtu to select the airfield sites and prepare designs, specifications, and requests which were submitted to the Chinese government.

Heavy bomber fields were to be located at Pengsham, Kwanghan, Kiunglai, and Hsinching. General Chennault, who was responsible for air defense, asked for fighter fields at Fenghuangshan, Shwangliu, Kwanghan, and Pengchiachiang, with an outer arc of smaller strips. The actual construction work was to be directed by Chinese engineers with Americans doing the planning and supervision.

Original estimates called for a labor force of 240,000. The governor of the province issued a decree calling up the men, and within two weeks 200,000 had appeared and work had begun on most of the fields. The workers came from a radius of 150 miles, literally drafted from the soil itself. Later conscriptions increased the number of workers. The total number of men who worked on the Chengtu bases is not known exactly, but it may have reached as high as a third of a million.

Loading their hoes and hammers and food supplies into squeaky, archaic wheelbarrows, they said farewell to their families in the little mud huts and compounds and moved out to the airfield sites in armies, as many as 100,000 working on a single field. There were all sorts of complications at first. With the Chinese New Year coming up within the month, many of the peasants wanted to remain at home to celebrate the festival with their families, a celebration which customarily ran for days. No sooner was this threat eliminated than an endless series of squabbles over land values and ownership began. The Chinese, with their traditional love of bargaining, were simply appalled by the speed with which their land was appraised. In some cases, engineering forces moved in even before negotiations for purchase had begun. And among the tenant farmers, who enjoyed no actual ownership but possessed only the "human claim" that their families had worked over this land for generations, the outcry was even greater. Only the Americans' willingness to pay promptly and fairly prevented a great uprising. As it was, the graft and unnecessary delays in the local magistracies resulted in much suffering among the poorer people.

Generally, the Chinese were eager to cooperate with the Americans. They smiled their smiles of curiosity and genuine good-fellowship at the few Americans they encountered and were always ready to show the thumbs-up sign and cry "Ding Hao." To explain the reason for the sudden upheaval, propaganda units arrived from Chungking and did much to counteract rumors and instill in the peasants a feeling of patriotism.

During the early days while the laborers were being gathered, Colonel Kennerson spent most of his time explaining to his Chinese assistants the reasons why the runways had to be of such great thickness and length; he understood their handicap in approaching such a gigantic undertaking with hoes and hammers and ancient stone rollers.

By January 24, preliminary work had begun on most of the project sites. Since the greater portions of the fields were to rest on rice-paddy land, the first move was to break down the paddy walls and let the impounded water drain off into the irrigation ditches. Then special roads were constructed to make the sites more accessible to heavy traffic. Sites had purposely been chosen close to rivers, making available such natural deposits as sand, gravel and water-rounded stones.

However, the materials needed for the construction of base buildings placed quite a strain on the Chengtu market. To establish a price ceiling on these materials, the Chinese engineers contacted General Chang Chum, the governor, who in turn appointed a negotiating board consisting of the Chengtu mayor and representatives of the larger building supply syndicates, with the result that an unfluctuating price was set and a steady flow of materials assured.

The majority of the peasants were housed in native barracks under the control of the Chinese government and were paid from 25 to 40 cents a day by the U.S. Army. As labor armies go, they were an exceedingly cheerful lot, continuing to the very end to greet the passing Occidental with their lusty cries of "Ding Hao!" Matching their cheerfulness was a plodding industry which never failed to amaze the Americans.

As Colonel Kennerson said later, "I doubt very much if we could have completed a job of similar magnitude in the States within the time allowed, even with the skilled labor and mechanical equipment available there."

One characteristic of the Chinese which was especially puzzling to the American was their attitude toward death. The first day, one of the peasants was crushed under a stone roller, and the Americans expected trouble. But instead the Chinese gathered around pointing and laughing at the unfortunate victim as though it were a great joke. More than 80 Chinese workers lost their lives in construction accidents. The most gruesome of these deaths were caused by the 10-ton rollers, which could not be stopped quickly. An unlucky worker stumbling into the path of one of these rollers was squashed into a bloody pancake.

There were other things that caused delays. One morning an American engineer pushed back his cap, looked over the field at the thousands of coolies with their thousands of squeaking wheelbarrows and said, "Goddam, I can't stand this racket a minute longer!"

So, when the coolies knocked off for lunch, the engineer called in his men and they set to work greasing all the axles they could lay their hands on. "This will stop that racket," said the engineer. But when the coolies picked up their wheelbarrows and discovered no squeaking sounds, they walked off the field en masse, mumbling something about going home.

Baffled, the engineer ran for his interpreter. "What's going on here? We do them a favor, greasing their wheelbarrows, and they walk out on us."

The interpreter grinned at the engineer: "No squeak in the wheelbarrows means the devil will get them. So long as the squeak comes, it keeps the devil behind them, and they can work. But no squeak, lots of devils, and no work."

The engineer slapped his head in disgust, and a few moments later he and his men were back at the wheelbarrows, laboriously rubbing the grease from their axles.

The sheer number of Chinese was sometimes terrifying to the Westerners. They would come down the field, hundreds of them pulling at a stone roller, their weird labor chants rising above their grunts and groans; and on all sides of them would be the thousands of men, women, and children, pounding the rocks with their little hammers, carrying the pails of sand on their shoulder-borne tandem baskets, their blue peasant garments merging into one great mass of power-patience, until at last it seemed that if the command were given to move a mountain, the mountain would be moved.

By the middle of February, with the deadline approaching, it was apparent that the workforce, gigantic as it was, would have to be augmented with another conscription. Several conferences were held with the governor on this subject, whereupon he agreed to conscript an additional 60,000, bringing the number of coolies employed on the project to approximately 300,000. These figures represented only conscript labor; an additional 10,000 were working as contract laborers.

Finally, on April 24, they were ready to receive the first B-29. It was a strange conglomeration of people who gathered at Kwanghan that day. There were Generals Chennault and Gilkeson, commanding generals of the Fourteenth Air Force and 312th Fighter Wing, respectively; American and Chinese engineers; Chinese officials in their formal garb, and in the background the ever-present, ever-inquisitive Chinese coolies, some 75,000 of them.

Suddenly, a great cry went up as the B-29 was sighted. Slowly it circled the field, then slanted down toward the runway, its wheels at last touching the strip which had been completed that very day. Out of the plane stepped General Saunders, bringing with him several staff officers of the 58th Wing.

On April 25, Pengshan Field was opened to air freight; two days later Kiunglai Field was functioning, and by May 1, all four airstrips were ready for traffic.

The Chinese government had been busy building barracks at its own expense for the American airmen who were soon to fly over the Hump to prepare for the coming bombardment operations against the Japanese. Here was to be an example of reverse lend-lease.

In China, troops of the 20th Bomber Command were to live in hostels maintained by the War Area Service Corps, a special project of Madame Chiang,[13] with each soldier being a personal guest of the Chinese government.

As the advance area staffs of the Command and Wing merged informally under the command of Colonel Claude E. Duncan, the status of the area gradually resolved itself. The plan was to use the forward area primarily for the staging of missions against Japan's inner zone. With the bulk of staff work, maintenance and supply handled at the rear bases in India, the forward area in China was to be confined to storing the fuel for missions, making small-scale repairs, establishing and maintaining liaison with Chinese agencies, organizing search and rescue work in China, and providing the bases with fighter cover. With this plan in effect, the B-29s could arrive one to three days before D-Day, go out on their mission after gassing up and receiving final check over, return to the forward bases for repair and additional gas, then fly back promptly to the rear area.

Enthusiasm among the officers and GIs assigned to Chengtu started off at fever pitch. Dropped suddenly into this ancient valley, seeing the peasants at work with their archaic tools and strange methods, the Americans found Chinese life enjoyable and interesting. They journeyed to the nearby villages, purchasing curios and knickknacks, and visited the old city of Chengtu, the cultural center of Szechwan province.

But as the novelty of a new land soon wore off, even the coming of Captain Henry (Hank) Greenberg, the Detroit baseball star, as special services officer failed to lift sinking spirits. Soon Chengtu had produced a full complement of local GI gripes:

"A guy can't even get a drink out here."

"New, aren't you? Unless you got a hundred dollars for a bottle of Scotch, just hop down the road and swallow some of that rice wine. It tastes like hell—but it's wet."

The mess halls came in for most of the criticism:

---

[13] Madame Chiang Kai-shek or Madame Chiang, First Lady of the Republic of China.

"Pork and eggs—pork and eggs—don't they eat anything else around here?"

"Sure—eggs and pork, and when you're here long enough you might get a fresh tomato. But give it a good going over in the boiling pot first. There's more germs on those tomatoes than there is in a whole hospital."

And on and on. Mail was always late, and new PX supplies rarely arrived. Men became finicky about their food—and with empty bellies, their tempers flared. Something had to happen, and soon.

And on June 13, 1944, it began to look as if something were going to happen. For suddenly B-29s began dropping out of the China skies. Two days later, it happened.

BETTY OVER TARGET

IN A SMOKY LITTLE OPERATIONS ROOM deep in the mountains of western China sat three Air Corps generals: George Stratemeyer, K. B. Wolfe, and John Upston. For hours they had been moving in and out of the room, chain-smoking and drinking black coffee as they waited for the all-important message.

Then, like a new father, Colonel William Blanchard came rushing in from the aircraft control room, enthusiasm unmistakable in his weary face.

"Sirs," he cried, "I have the pleasure to announce it's 'Betty' over the target!"[14]

The three generals came to their feet as a man. In a moment the tension was shattered, and they were all talking excitedly. For behind the simple message of "Betty!" lay the revelation that at last the Superforts had bombed Japan.

Quickly the excitement spread to other sections of headquarters. It was explained over and over again that "Betty," the name of the wife of Colonel James Garcia, Intelligence chief who accompanied the mission, was the radio code symbol released immediately upon the dropping of the first bombs over Yawata.

Corporal Paul Turner, the radio operator who had intercepted the message, pulled a snapshot out of his wallet and said, "That's for you too, honey." The picture was a snapshot of his girl, Betty Gorham.

The men of the 20th Bomber Command eagerly awaited the count of planes that had returned from the raid, of the planes that had been unable to reach the target, and finally, of the number of losses. They remembered well the numerous mechanical failures of the Bangkok mission; they were wondering if this time their B-29s had been able to shake the jinx. Twice they had gone out to bomb the Japanese—and the Japanese had not been nearly as tough as they had feared. But their plane—that was a question they still couldn't answer.

---

[14] Not to be confused with a 'Betty' plane; Japan's Mitsubishi Navy Type 1 attack bomber.

Behind the Yawata mission lay months of intensive toil and planning. Until the headlines screamed "Yawata" on June 15, few Americans had even heard of the city in the northwestern corner of Kyushu. Only the target experts were aware that here was the site of the Imperial Iron and Steel Works, the number one steel target of the Japanese empire, with a yearly production of more than two million metric tons, some 24 percent of the total for all Japan.

Since the early days of February, the Command had been busy building up gasoline reserves in the Chengtu staging area. The Bangkok shakedown mission had tested the planes in action and given the crews some much-needed combat experience. But when the June 7 mission directive came in from AAF Headquarters calling for 70 planes to go to Yawata on the night of June 15, staff officers in the sweltering, oozing heat of the 20th Bomber Command's rear headquarters shook their heads. Washington was going crazy, they told themselves.

General Wolfe had estimated that he could put only 50 planes over the target by that date. Stockpiling was lagging behind schedule, but it wasn't just a matter of fuel. The Superforts would have to be equipped with bomb-bay tanks before they could undertake the long flight to Japan.

But this was to be no token raid; it was coordinated with the crucial invasion of Saipan, and the Washington order held. General Wolfe began at once to get ready for the mission. Working around the clock, his bald head beaded with perspiration, he contacted forward area bases in China, ordering each field to use no more than one motor vehicle. Meanwhile, Hump transport was stepped up to its very limits.

Calling his staff together, Wolfe said bluntly, "I'm going to screen personally the requests of every section head who hopes to go on this job. Only the most essential personnel will be allowed to take the trip to the China bases."

Then, turning to Colonel Garcia, he added, "We can put more planes over the target if we cut down the fighter defense sorties in the forward areas. What are the capabilities of the Japanese Air Force to execute a counterstrike at our Chinese bases?"

"Do you mean, sir, you are intending to delay the return of the '29s to India, holding them over in China after the mission?"

"Exactly!"

"For how long, sir?"

"Long enough for them to get enough gas to return home," said General Wolfe with a sardonic smile.

It was a grim decision. Discussing the problem in detail with Garcia and other staff officers, General Wolfe realized that if the Japanese struck at that time, they could endanger the immediate B-29 operational program. But the radio messages from Washington were growing more and more imperative. Wolfe finally decided to take the risk.

It was to be a night bombing mission by single-plane elements, with bomb release from two altitude brackets. To disrupt interception capabilities of the enemy, the 14th Air Force would strike at airfield concentrations around Hankow, China, as the bombers returned from target. With luck, the ordered total of 70 planes might get airborne out of China. Two Pathfinder aircraft from each group would take off five to six minutes before the other planes, surprising the enemy before it could organize its defense, and starting fires for the planes that followed.

Movement of the planes from India to China began June 13 and was completed on the 15th. Colonel Garcia, who rode as a combat observer in the plane of Lieutenant Colonel Winton Close, reported typical difficulties:

"Halfway over the Hump, engine trouble developed, and we had to turn back. We landed at Texpur in bad weather, after jettisoning our bombs on an island in the river. The crew worked all night repairing the plane. They had the necessary parts flown in from Charra. The next morning, we took off and went to the forward area, landing at Kwanghan. The rest of the afternoon and throughout the night and the next morning we worked on the airplane to get it in shape for the mission the following day. The entire crew worked on it."

High-ranking officers worked shoulder to shoulder with buck privates. At Hsinching, eight general officers arrived in three days, bulging the inadequate staff officers' quarters. Security by this time was nonexistent. The base intelligence officer threw up his hands and walked off in disgust, unable to control the swarms of Chinese, some of whom had already set up peanut stands to cash in on the sudden invasion.

Again, the take-off for combat caused concern. Eighty-three B-29s were in the forward area, 75 of which were to participate in the raid. Sixty-eight planes finally managed to get airborne on the afternoon of June 15, leaving around four o'clock from four China bases. At Pengshan, forward base of the 468th Group, the sixteenth ship crashed and burned on take-off. Command Chaplain Lieutenant Colonel Kenneth G. Stack wrote of the crash:

"The Commanding General of the 58th Wing, General Saunders, asked me to bless his ship, 'The Lady Hamilton,' which was piloted by Colonel Howard Engler, Group Commander.

Inasmuch as this plane was the first ship to take off in the 468th Group, the blessing was for all the crews and all the ships in that Group. It is interesting to note that the sixteenth ship to take off crashed and burned just before it was airborne and that not one of the crew was even scratched. This certainly seemed a direct answer to our prayers because not one of the crew could explain how he had escaped from the ship. The exploding bombs, gasoline and ammunition convinced everyone who saw the crash that the hand of God was evident..."

Of the 68 planes to get into the air, four were early "aborts" and 16 failed for various reasons to bomb the primary target. Of these 16, six had mechanical difficulties in the target area and jettisoned their bombs into the sea; three failed to reach the target because of mechanical difficulties or navigational errors; another pair hit Laoyao, the secondary target, and five bombed targets of opportunity.

For the planes destined to reach Yawata it was a long, tense, eager flight. As Theburn Wiant, Associated Press reporter, described it in his dispatch filed the next day:

"We have been calm, intent on reaching Japan, but our hearts are pounding now, partly from natural fright, mostly from anticipation of the big moment we have been waiting for since Doolittle hit Tokyo. We are in the forefront of scores of Superfortresses, concentrating tonight on Japan's biggest steel and coke works... As Colonel Harman, commander of the 'General Billy Mitchell group,' told us before take-off, 'If ever there was a juicy target this is it.'

"Our Superfortress is piloted by Lieutenant Colonel Warren Wilkinson and is running smoother than a watch. Already Captain Dean Delafield has navigated us in pitch darkness through storms farther than from Los Angeles to Kansas City. By the time we return we will have established a world's record for long-distance bombing.

"But now we are only five minutes from the Imperial Iron and Steel Works and searchlights are frantically sweeping the sky. At least one of the Superforts beat us to the target because we see several bomb bursts. Wilkinson shouts into the interphone, 'It's all yours,' and Captain William C. Goldstein and 2nd Lieutenant Glen Berkihiser prepare to drop their bombs.

"The target is now only seconds away, but those seconds are like hours. 'There they go smack into their damned steelworks,' yells Goldstein. Wilkinson, aided by 2nd Lieutenant Delmar Stevans, copilot, sharply turns and dives in the direction of home. We look back on a firebug's dream. Flames are shooting at least 2,000 feet high from two huge fires. Several smaller fires are blazing up rapidly.... Sixty miles from Yawata the fires are still plainly visible. Sergeant Morris Kramer, gunner, confesses over the interphone, 'If I said I was not scared I would be a liar, but I wouldn't have missed this for anything.'"

The bomb run over Yawata was a montage of searing searchlights and bursting flak. The lights would cling to the ships as they entered the run, blinding the crews, seeming to hold back time until a second became a minute and a minute became an hour.

Radio correspondent Roy Porter, flying as an observer, reported:

"One full battery caught us in its fierce, savage beam—and from that time until we outran the beacons, our whole cabin was lit up like Madison Square Garden on hockey night. When the bombs had dropped and we turned away from the target, the seconds which had seemed hours beforehand became days in proportionate length. The ship pointed her nose upward; it seemed to take an hour, but the speed gauge showed a remarkable figure. Still the searchlights held on—and there were some words used in the cabin of that plane that expressed exactly the idea of the moment. Still the lights blazed—and though we dodged and dipped, we could not avoid them. We climbed a bit—we dropped a bit—and all this time the cold steel was spattering against the outside of the cabin. Then, suddenly, as if nothing at all had happened, the pilot leaned back and said, 'We are very well out of that,' and as he spoke the lights died away—the plane picked

up speed—and we roared away into the darkness toward the west—toward China—and safety."

Down below the Japanese were having their troubles, too. A Yawata newspaperman reported:

"Now all the city is black. Suddenly in the north we heard the sound of plane engines. The orders were flashed everywhere and all the sounds on the street stilled. The propeller noise of the enemy planes spread over the whole sky. Minute by minute the noise approached. At this moment there was a shot, like a skyrocket, into the air. Several tons of shots. I could see clearly the figures of the enemy planes. At once antiaircraft began to shoot. The guns shouted like lightning. But the hateful enemy planes flew on. Suddenly, fire dropped from them... one, two, three. These were the flares. The whole city could be clearly seen in reddish light. Then came big black things from the white bodies of the planes. Bombs! And BOOM! BOOM! BOOM! The devils, the beasts! Again, BOOM! BOOM! BOOM!"

THE PSYCHOLOGICAL EFFECT OF THE MISSION was overwhelming. Hardly had the planes turned away from the target before word was reaching the distant points of occupied China. It was a shot in the arm for the sagging Chinese armies and to the guerrillas and peasants living in the shadow of Nip terror.

All over China news spread that at last America had struck. From the shores of the Yellow Sea down the coast and far inland, the Japanese suddenly found themselves confronted with rebellious peoples.

Japan immediately attempted to offset the reverses of that day: the invasion of Saipan, and the bombing of home islands. Through espionage they had gained the names of certain high-ranking American officers, and immediately a radio announcer took to the air, claiming that B-29 after B-29 had been shot down, one of which contained no less than five lieutenant colonels and a major: Lieutenant Colonel Edward C. Teats, assistant A-2, 20th Bomber Command; Lieutenant Colonel Louis E. Coira, deputy commander, 40th Bomb Group; Lieutenant Colonel James V. Edmundson, commanding officer, 792nd Squadron; Lieutenant Colonel James Ira Cornett, commanding officer, 44th

Squadron; Lieutenant Colonel Walter Y. Lucas, commanding officer, 395th Squadron; Major William O'Malley, 58th Bomb Wing navigator.

It made a good story while it lasted; that is, until American counter-radio informed the listening Eastern world that only two of the officers, Lieutenant Colonels Edmundson and Cornett, had even been on the mission, and both had returned safely.

Perhaps the best example of Japanese reaction to the raid was in the fury with which Nip airmen raked the gutted plane of Captain Robert Root. Forced down with engine trouble at Neihsiang, China, Root and his crew were working on their craft when they heard the sound of approaching planes. Time's combat correspondent, Harry Zinder, who had flown the mission on Root's plane, reported the attack:

"Two fighters were streaking across the low mountains. We saw the Rising Sun on their sides. We yelled to Root, Doolen and Robinson and rushed for a shallow ditch 50 yards away. The fighters roared across, pulled up and then turned down on our ship. They spattered bullets across the fuselage and wings, then started a little fire on the left side. We hugged the ground closer as bullets kicked up dust and grass alongside the ditch. They made many passes. When the fire was fully blazing, they left. We went to see what had happened to Root. By the time he joined us from inside the B-29 we heard more planes. There were 15 this time; six bombers and nine fighters. The fighters peeled off first and did a strafing job, and then the bombers went to work and finished the job. We were in the ditch again, renewing our prayers. We felt sure they must have seen us because we could see their bomb-bay doors open, see their bombs fall on the ship and around it. We decided to spend the rest of the morning in the ditch. There was nothing we could do for '293.' We covered ourselves with grass, leaves and tree branches. Through the next three hours more and more Jap planes came over, strafing and bombing, and just as suddenly as it started, it all stopped. The sky was quiet. But '293' lay dead and gutted, finished on her first trip..."

To the men who viewed this strangely prolonged attack it seemed the Japanese were doing more than merely destroying a downed aircraft. It was as if they were slaying a phoenix that might rise again from its own ashes. Early news accounts of the

Yawata mission were enthusiastic. Many made sentimental reference to the Doolittle raid of April 18, 1942. The correspondents who had gone along described Japan's Pittsburgh as "a glowing mass of ruins." Another waxed poetic: he wrote of Japanese ack-ack, "winking like little mirrors on a night club dancer's costume." All seemed convinced that Yawata had been, "reduced to a huge rubbish heap."

But Colonel Alan D. Clark, combat observer on a B-29, made an intelligence report that summed up the raid far more accurately:

"The results of the mission were poor. Of the bombs dropped on the Yawata area, only a very small proportion came within the target area, and some were as far as 20 miles away. The reason was that our radar operators had not been trained to do blind bombing (bombing by radar). As a result of this mission, the 20th Bomber Command put in a training schedule for radar operators, and radar bombing improved somewhat in subsequent missions."

The cost of the mission in aircraft was seven; high from the strategic point of view. It would have been higher if Japanese antiaircraft had tracked the planes more consistently. Although only 68 had been airborne, the mission so depleted the gasoline stockpile at Chengtu that not all could return to their India bases immediately; it took stepped-up operations over the Hump to fuel the last of the Superfortresses for the journey home.

Summer Operations

WITH THE YAWATA RAID AND the invasion of Saipan came the first public announcement of the existence of the strategic Twentieth Air Force, the first truly global bombing unit, which was to operate under the personal supervision of General Arnold and the Joint Chiefs of Staff. It had been activated on April 4 but remained a closely guarded secret until the June 15 attack on Japan. General Arnold was named commander and each member of his staff was assigned to the new organization as well as to headquarters. Because they could not devote all the time to the Twentieth Air Force that was necessary for such a new and important operation, groups of deputies made up a working staff by Brigadier General H. S. Hansell, Jr.; Hansell had played an important part in working out the Matterhorn plan and was one of the leading exponents of strategic bombardment.

The 20th Bomber Command in India was assigned to the new Twentieth Air Force, which was to make all the major decisions on deployment, missions, and bombing targets. General Stilwell, who once had been slated to have the Bomber Command under his direct control, was responsible for coordinating B-29 operations in the CBI; in an emergency he could divert the B-29s from their primary mission, but full control would remain in Washington. This was a new system, a radical departure from command through general directives by Washington with the theater commander free to work out the details. And most of the theater commanders didn't like it.

Operating from the China bases, the missions flown by the 20th Bomber Command in June, July and August 1944, were primarily individual medium-altitude night attacks. Behind and between each of these missions were hours and days of backbreaking labor to overcome the mechanical difficulties that seemed endless. And between combat missions the Superforts found themselves flying vital fuel supplies over the Hump to build up the stockpile at Chengtu for additional operations.

On June 4th, the Japanese had started their long-anticipated drive for the Canton-Changsha railroad. General Stilwell immediately diverted the Hump tonnage meant for the 20th Bomber

Command to the Fourteenth Air Force. The Joint Chiefs of Staff approved this emergency measure, and directed that the tonnage be repaid as soon as conditions permitted; but when General Wolfe, at this time attempting to build up supplies for the June 15 raid against Yawata, tried to get back his badly needed gas, he locked horns with General Chennault. They kept at it for more than a month, until the crews on the Hump run finally started to get ahead of the combat crews.

To the men of the Command, home seemed to be moving farther away daily. Their efforts seemed far too feeble to defeat a war machine built up over a period of years. It wasn't only the endless overhauling of planes and the death-dealing flights over the Himalayas that discouraged them; it was also the results of their combat missions—results that continued far below expectations.

Back in the States radio commentators reported:
"Yesterday, 70 B-29s hit the Japanese home islands..."
And listeners were impressed.

But in ready shacks, mess halls and barracks in India, combat crews shook their heads over the results shown in reconnaissance photos.

"I can't understand it," said one intelligence officer who had flown as an observer on a raid. "The whole damn place looked like an inferno when we went over. Then I see the photos, and damned if every target we bombed isn't in full operation the very next day."

Missions were conducted against iron and steel works in Kyushu and in Manchuria; ports, shipping facilities, marshaling yards, aircraft plants, supply dumps and fuel storage areas were hit. Operations were also conducted against Palembang in Sumatra from an RAF base on Ceylon.

Activities in the Command during this period produced one of the most famous of the B-29s, the "General H. H. Arnold Special." The plane received its name in January 1944, when General Arnold visited the Boeing plant in Wichita during the all-out effort to complete the initial complement of B-29s that the 58th Bombardment Wing was to take to India. Walking along the assembly line, the General stopped in front of one of the planes in the process of assembly. "This is the plane I want, right here!" he said, as he picked up a black grease pencil and scrawled "H. H. Arnold" on the side of the airplane.

That Superfort immediately became known as the "General H. H. Arnold Special." It was delivered to a Boeing flight test crew and then flown to Smoky Hill Air Base in Kansas. On April 13, 1944, it left Kansas on the 12,000-mile journey to India. It was the first plane over the target in the exploratory raid on Bangkok and took part in the Yawata attack on June 15.

The "Special" returned to its base at Kharagpur from the Yawata raid on June 17 and began a period of routine formation flying training and ceaseless maintenance made more difficult by the intense heat and the ever-present dust.

On July 4th, the B-29 was poised for its third combat mission; this time the target was Sasebo, the naval bastion on Japan's west coast. Just before take-off, an official order reached Colonel Sullivan, the aircraft commander, that directed his crew to remain behind while an alternate crew, headed by Captain Weston H. Price, took over.

The mission, a night attack, took off from its forward base on July 7; in the copilot seat was John Flanagan, while Colonel Ted S. Faulkner flew in the "Special" as command pilot. Fifteen hundred miles later a blaze of searchlights marked their arrival.

"We hit the target right on the nose," said Lieutenant Melvin Scherer, the navigator.

"I hope so," added Lieutenant Edwin Morrison, the bombardier.

"Hey," yelled Technical Sergeant David Pletter, the radio operator, "I can see the lights in the Admiral's outhouse."

"The flak was light and inaccurate as in the first two raids," reported Lieutenant E. P. Rutherford, flight engineer.

The gunners had little trouble driving off the few Jap interceptors that were airborne during the raid.

Other units participating in the raid struck Yawata, Gmura, Tobata, Laoyao, and Hankow, and again the skies were filled with planes forced by engine failures to turn back before reaching their target.

Once more the Special returned to Kharagpur. Seemingly none the worse for wear, the big bomber again went from blue-ribbon trotting to heavy trucking: two more Hump trips ferrying two more loads of gasoline and replacement engines from the Bengal bases to Hsinching. After three weeks of freight hauling, the China stock was sufficient to mount Mission Num4. Colonel

Sullivan and his crew returned for this one and flew their plane to Chengtu. On July 29 they took off on the first of a series of daylight strikes against Anshan, a center of enemy steel production on the Asiatic mainland and site of the notorious Kamikaze school.

Fifty-six aircraft, including the Special, hit the steel city with 160 tons of high explosives. Bombing was by visual means, and for the first time Intelligence could report: "Coke ovens destroyed for the duration." Two B-29s were lost. The Special, carrying its first combat observer in the person of Colonel P. S. Emrick, flew the 1,350 miles to splatter its bombs squarely into an already blazing target. Captain Suberman reported black smoke columns visible 75 miles after leaving the bombing run. No Nip fighters attacked the bomber, and no flak fire pierced its fuselage.

Next for the General H. H. Arnold Special was "Operation Boomerang," the long-projected strike against Palembang in southern Sumatra, the source of 78 percent of Japan's aviation gasoline and 22 percent of her oil. A mission of 3,800 miles, it was to be the fifth for the Special and by over 500 miles the longest to date for the 20th Bomber Command. Nearly six months had gone into the planning of what was to be a twin blow against Palembang and shipbuilding works in Nagasaki, Japan's twelfth largest city.

These targets were as far removed from each other as the Panama Canal and Hudson Bay; the strikes were synchronized for psychological reasons. The mission against Palembang had at first been planned as a daylight mission at maximum strength, but the tremendous distances involved, and the lack of adequate staging areas directed the running of a night mission with a minimum of 50 aircraft. Switching to a night mission increased the operational safety margin, as well as minimized such hot-weather hazards as overheating of engines.

The staging area for the raid was China Bay, a RAF field in Ceylon; earlier plans to use four Ceylon fields had been abandoned when construction lagged. At China Bay the runway had been extended and extra taxiways and hardstands built; on August 4 the field was judged operational for the B-29s.

On August 9, fifty-six B-29s, among them the Special, flew the 1,100 miles from Bengal to Ceylon. Vehicles, food, and other supplies had preceded them. At China Bay hundreds of British spectators watched the Superfortresses sweep in from over the sea and park for their overnight stay. It was the largest armada of B-29s ever assembled at a single overseas base. The next afternoon, even as 2,000 miles to the north 29 Superforts were taking off to bomb Nagasaki, 54 of the China Bay bombers were airborne between 4:15 and 5:39. They swung in a low arc out over Tambalagan Bay, and disappeared against the sun-etched headland east-southeast.

Pacing the pack, the Special led the 468th Group into the air. This time only one plane failed to take off because of engine trouble. With Captain Price's crew at the controls, the Special flew on a straight track from China Bay to a point south of Siberoet Island off the west coast of Sumatra.

The first of the three groups assigned to bomb Palembang roared in over the target a few minutes after midnight on the morning of August 11 to find complete blackout conditions prevailing. In the next three hours, 31 aircraft dropped a total of 102 500-pound general-purpose bombs, 40 flash bombs, and 17 incendiary clusters from altitudes of 8,000 to 18,000 feet.

Once again, the overall results were far from satisfactory. Some placed the blame on the severe blackout; others said it was the cloud cover over the target plus the forced early return of the plane assigned to illuminate the target with parachute flares. Fifteen of the planes that reached the target bombed by radar, while 16 bombed by visual release.

Enemy antiaircraft fire was weak but included some ground to air rockets. While the Special plotted, bombed, twisted, and headed for home unmolested, eight companions fought off 26 single and coordinated pursuit attacks which continued some 350 miles along the return route. Three-quarters of the attacks were broken off short of 500 yards with the result that no B-29 suffered damage and no fighter planes were officially recorded as kills.

Eight B-29s successfully mined the Moesi River channel between Palembang and the Bangka Straits, and several aircraft struck the secondary target, the Pangkalanbrandon oil refinery located on Sumatra's northeast coast. Of the 54 airborne aircraft, 39 bombed the specified primary targets, three bombed alternative targets, eight returned without bombing at all because of mechanical difficulties, three were unable to locate the target and returned because of a shortage of fuel, and one failed to bomb because of a bomb-rack malfunction.

By mid-morning of the eleventh, 53 aircraft of the three participating groups, including the Special, had made it back to China Bay. One B-29 of the 444th Group ditched 90 miles northwest of the base and lost a gunner in the crash. A plane of the 40th Group, taking off two hours behind the main group, lost an engine before reaching Sumatra and a second on the way home, but with props feathered, excess equipment jettisoned, and fuel setting lowered, made it back to Ceylon on two engines—three hours behind estimated time of arrival and with barely 200 gallons in its cavernous tanks.

On August 12, the Special returned to its 468th Group nest at Kharagpur. To date, the crews of Colonel Sullivan and Captain Price had alternated in flying the big plane to and from five major missions. Now, with a daylight raid on Yawata planned as the Command's seventh strike—Nagasaki, run off concurrent with the Palembang bombing, was entered as Mission 6—Colonel Sullivan's group was disbanded, and its members scattered among other crews to distribute the weight of their combat experience. And simultaneously the Arnold aircraft got a brand-new crew, fresh from the United States. At the controls for the first time, when the plane took off August 18 for Chengtu's Hsinching Field, was Major Boyce C. Anderson, with Lieutenant Frederick N. Corvinus as copilot and Lieutenant Charles Moresi as navigator.

Bombed and gassed up and setting on the Hsinching paddy plain, the Special was warming up for take-off late the evening of August 19. It was crowding midnight and time to go, when the No. 1 engine began to balk. With oil pressure dropping, the flying freshmen sat and waited, strained and apprehensive.

"Finally," as Major Anderson reported later, "after consulting with the engineer, we decided the gauge was faulty and took off. We used only three-fourths of the runway to get off with our heavy load, then we circled searching for the formation, and soon caught up with the others. We took No. 3 position in the formation. About an hour out the oil pressure on No. 1 came back to normal and it was smooth sailing to the China coast.

"We crossed a convoy of Japanese ships in the China Sea and they threw up a lot of antiaircraft fire, but it was too weak to reach us. Lieutenant Moresi missed his estimated time of arrival over the target by one minute. We razzed hell out of him for his 'inefficiency;' an error of one minute for a flight as long as that is as near perfect as I'll ever ask.

"Nearing Yawata we saw a burning B-29 go down on a small island and noticed some parachutes blossom out. It looked like a Jap fighter crashed also. We looked out the window and saw two Jap Tonys[15] sitting level and a little above, doing acrobatics like flying stool pigeons. They were undoubtedly flashing our altitude and speed to the antiaircraft batteries below for when the gunners opened fire, the Tonys rolled away.

"Three B-29s passed about 100 feet below us from another direction; our gunners reported seeing their bombs hit and destroy oil tanks and other installations in the target area. Flak followed us right in on our bombing rim. It was a thick black apron which jolted the plane, but none of it hit us. The bombardier was busy training his gunsight on two Jap fighters we thought might attack us, so copilot Corvinus toggled off the bombs.

"We turned away from the target and then the fighters came, fit up like Christmas trees with pinpoints of flame blinking at us. The tail gunner got some bursts at two Nicks which were diving at other B-29s. His shots went into them and they turned away. Another came in shortly afterwards and the top gunner got in a few licks. A Tojo[16] passed directly under the formation but did not fire. Then Moresi shouted to Stillons, the bombardier, to 'get that Nick!'[17] The Jap was coming in from below and was getting too close for comfort. The left gunner also answered the call and poured out lead. 'Those Nicks are faster than hell and climb like nobody's business,' he said after it whirled past. More attacks were forming. Stillons stood up in the nose and shot straight down, firing at an Oscar and a pair of attacking Nicks, He hit one. They came from everywhere—a gunner got a shot at an

---

[15] 'Tony' was US Naval code for the Kawasaki Ki-61 Hien, so-nicknamed because Allied spotters initially believed the aircraft was of Italian design. The Hien appellation was bestowed by the Japanese, and means "flying swallow."
[16] 'Tojo' was the reporting name for Japan's Nakajima Ki-44 fighter.
[17] 'Nick' referred to the Kawasaki Ki-45 'Toryu' ('Dragonslayer') twin-engine fighter.

Oscar who made a poor pursuit curve toward us, but he was too far out to hit. A Nick at 10 o'clock came under the plane—we saw tracers go into his fuselage. Nicks and Tonys cruising alongside were given short bursts. A Nick followed us for a long way, but we kept him at a safe distance by firing frequently. When we were about 30 miles from the target and were just beginning to relax, a single enemy tighter came wheeling out of the sun and made one pass at us. He came in damned close but did no damage.

"We left the formation in about half an hour and headed for home, passing through a rough electrical storm. Our plane was outlined by an aura of St. Elmo's fire. Moresi did another swell job and brought us in right on course, missing his ETA again by one minute."

This Yawata mission had been rough; the roughest on the record. For the first time, the B-29s met strong fighter opposition and heavy, accurate flak. Fifteen Jap fighters were destroyed, and another dozen listed as probables, but four Superforts were lost to enemy action; more than on any mission up to that time.

With three crews and six missions under its belt, the Special now held all the records in the Command. During its first five months in the CBI Theater, from April 13 to August 20, this Superfort had flown almost 400 hours and spanned 75,000 miles, or thrice around the world at the equator. It had amassed more flying time than any other plane in the 468th Group; it had hurdled the death-dealing Hump seven times; for the first time in history it had made land-based air attacks against Japan proper; three of its six missions had been pressed against Jap targets in daylight: the first Yawata raid, Sasebo and Palembang, the longest mission in military annals.

By early fall, both the Special and the Command began a performance which would reach a triple-strike climax in November, Resuming the offensive on September 8, the Special sparked the second attack on Anshan's Showa Steel Works, fought its way through the Japs to hit the primary target and got home. It was a rough 3,000-mile ride, but, as summed up by Anderson's copilot Lieutenant Corvinus, "Flak bursts were not nearly so intense or accurate as over Yawata; only three planes attacked us and without success, and our biggest worry, really, was sweating out the fuel supply back to Hsinching."

Mission 7 was in the books. Crew Chief Hague painted the seventh black bomb on the Special's mighty nose.

Again, on September 26, the 20th Bomber Command attacked Anshan. For the first time in eight tries the Special failed to make the grade; and in the tense moments following a heavily loaded take-off only Major Anderson's skill and heroism saved the crew and airplane. As the big bomber climbed for altitude, No. 4 engine blew a cylinder and caught fire. Swiftly the entire wing was enveloped in flame. Black smoke and fire streamed backward along the fuselage and beyond the tail of the aircraft.

It was at this point, according to the official citation awarding the young Texas pilot the Distinguished Flying Cross, that, "Major Anderson by skillful piloting, initiative, and judgment succeeded in maintaining control of his aircraft and gained sufficient altitude to enable certain members of his crew to parachute to safety. Major Anderson then saw that the fire was brought under control. In addition, so as not to disrupt the sequence of take-offs and delay other B-29s on the mission, he continued to circle his home base on three engines at an approximate gross weight of 130,000 pounds until all other B-29 take-offs had been completed."

A minor mechanical mishap had caused a near disaster and the plane's first and only aborted mission. Operations were stepped up: in September 217 B-29s were airborne as compared with 115 and 117 for July and August. The stockpile at Chengtu began to grow. On October 14, the first day of a strike against Formosa,[18] Hap's Big Boy tried again. Flown by Captain Price and his crew, the Special was one of 117 B-29s airborne in a strike designed to reduce the usefulness of Formosa as a staging base for Japanese aircraft on their way to the Philippines. It was the maximum effort to date and was the first of a series of strikes coordinated with Navy carrier-based aircraft cruising off the Formosan coast.

B-29 airmen agreed that the best precision bombing results were obtained on "milk-runs," the long uneventful missions highlighted by perfect coordination of men and machines, light opposition, successful bomb run, no mechanical difficulties. But

---

[18] Taiwan.

a better test of a crew's skill and initiative came when foresight faltered, and things went wrong. Such a mission was now mounted, as the Special moved against Formosa.

"There was a sudden loss of power on No. 4," explained Captain Price later. "The supercharger was shot. We couldn't possibly keep up with the formation. Disappointed, we turned and headed back. Formosa was just 30 minutes away. And we had to quit.

"Lieutenant Scherer, the navigator, gave us the two secondary targets on which we had been briefed. The bombardier, Lieutenant Morrison, chose Swatow as having better weather.

"After reaching the target we turned and circled to get on the best approach heading, and made a bomb run.

"Over the target the intercom crackled: 'Bombs away!' 'Keep a watch for hits!' 'Get those pictures!' 'Bomb-bay doors closed.'

"Lieutenant Morrison stretched his neck to see where the bombs hit. 'One of 'em hit a boat,' came from the right gunner, Staff Sergeant John Bardunias. 'It's burning. And you hit two docks!'

"'That's right, hey, that's pretty good,' said Sergeant Larkin. A moment later, he added: 'There are four bombs left in the bomb bay back here.' 'And there are four in the front bay, too,' reported the radio operator, Technical Sergeant David Pletter."

"Lieutenant Morrison turned to me and said, 'Boy, I got some good hits.' Then he went back to check the remaining bombs. His report was far from good. 'Six are hanging okay, but two are on a shackle that has tripped. It's broken and they're just hanging on by imagination.'

"However, he decided they would hang all right until we were low enough to depressurize. The trip home was an anxious one. We were behind enemy lines with No. 1 engine smoking and vibrating like hell. We had only partial power on No. 4 and no nose guns in case of attack—and bombs hanging precariously in the bomb bays.

"Morrison opened the bomb-bay doors, slid out of his parachute harness and lowered himself into the open bays to defuse the bombs and cut loose the two dangling ones. It was dangerous work. It's pretty breezy back there, and a slip would have meant he'd bounce hard a long way down. We breathed easier a few minutes later when he clambered grinning through the hatch and gave us the okay sign.

"When we had flown well into friendly territory, we searched for an emergency landing field. Through a break in the undercast we spotted an airport at Paishihui, China, into which we could fit nicely. That night was spent comfortably with the Chinese-American Composite Wing of the Fourteenth Air Force. Next morning, we repaired the Special, flew on back to our base and began preparation for the next.

"The strike photos again were not satisfactory, but news came from Intelligence reporting a 500-ton Jap freighter sunk in the harbor after receiving a direct hit. And we knew there were a couple of docks that needed a lot of repairing before the enemy could use them again."

After the blasting of the secondary Formosan targets (the primary was the Okayama aircraft factories), on October 24, the Special again flew the Hump to Hsinching. The following day, with 77 accompanying aircraft, it flew 1,500 miles to drop 150 tons of high explosives on the Omura aircraft assembly plants on the Jap home island of Kyushu, and all B-29s returned to their Chengtu bases.

Skipping the Rangoon raid on November 3, the Special was ready to go two days later when a force of Superforts took off from northeastern India on the historic Singapore-Sumatra mission. The longest daylight run in the Command's first six months of operation; the Singapore naval bastion stood nearly 2,000 miles from the Bengal bases. As the primary force pounded the naval docks and warships at Singapore, the Special led a secondary formation over the Pangkalanbrandon oil refinery. Flak exploded in black-red coils under the wingtips and along the fuselage during the bomb run. Skillfully flown by Major Gordon L. Eaton, replacing Captain Price who was ill, the Special took a sudden evasive turn over the target, and crewmen saw heavy flak explode down its previous flight path.

Tropic typhoons and Nip fighters buffeted the bomber starting its long trip home, but Major Eaton poured on the coal to outdistance both storm and steel. Seventeen hours after take-off, the Special was back at Kharagpur, and mission No. 9 was on the record.

Then came November 11. The target was Omura with its aircraft assembly plants. For the 20th Bomber Command it would be the seventeeth strike in six months; for the Special, with

Captain Price again in command, it would be the tenth—and last—mission. The Command had girded for a maximum effort.

Night take-offs from rain-sodden China fields caused the fiery pile-up of two aircraft. After a slow, sluggish rise, 96 B-29s went winging out toward the China Sea. Shortly after daybreak, 29 aircraft, including the Special, flew in to bomb Omura through a 7 to 10/10 cloud cover. A total bomb load of 150 tons was dropped at altitudes of 19,000 to 23,400 feet. Thirty-five Superforts hit secondary targets at Shanghai and Nanking. Enemy fighters, attacking aggressively from above and below at Omura, barreled through the formations in death-dealing dives. One B-29 slowly spun over and went down flaming over the hard-hit industrial center.

Others, with gaping holes in wings and bodies, with engines smoking and props feathered, turned from the bomb run to head for home or a haven of safety. Not the least of these was the Special. Breaking radio silence, the peerless Special and a dozen other Superforts of the 20th Bomber Command dot-dashed SOS and their exact locations. One crashed near Tenghsien on the China Coast. Another went down barely 20 miles from the field at Pengshan. Still others crash-landed at various emergency fields of the Fourteenth Air Force. In all, five B-29s failed to return from the mission.

Among them was the General H. H. Arnold Special, which had been unable to bomb the target because its radar equipment was out of order. After flying over what they thought was Omura, for thirty minutes unable to pick up any images on the radar scopes, the crew turned around and headed for home. At the end of five-and one-half hours they finally broke out of the overcast to discover that due to a 155-mile-an-hour headwind they were 900 miles short of the navigator's estimated position. Also, they were just off the southern tip of Korea, 100 miles north of their course.

There was now no question of reaching their command base. Their dwindling fuel supply limited the choice to crashing in enemy-held China or landing at Vladivostok, Russia. They headed for Russia. The General H. H. Arnold Special was swallowed up in the Soviet mists and it was not heard from again for months. Then on February 1, the entire crew, after having been interned in the "Asiatic Theater," was turned over to the Allied Military Control. They were later flown back to the United States.

It wasn't until early 1947 that the story of Captain Price and his crew, as well as that of Lt. William J. Mickish and the crew of the "Ding Hao," which headed for Russia after the November 21st raid against Omura, was released. The 1944 official report was the terse statement that "Two crews are listed as 'Missing in Action.' They are the 'General H. H. Arnold Special' and the 'Ding Hao.' It is believed that these crews are safe."

This report was issued within a matter of days after the "Ding Hao" was lost.

A highly secret matter during the war, the story of the airmen who fled to seek sanctuary in Siberia appeared for the first time in THE NEW YORK TIMES on February 14, 1947, under the byline of Sidney Shallett. According to the Times story, four B-29 crews were known to have been interned by the Russians; three of the Superforts were taken over by the Russians and never seen again by their crews after they landed in the vicinity of Vladivostok; the fourth, badly damaged in a raid, crashed on Soviet soil after its crew bad safely bailed out. These B-29 crewmen joined a list of Navy and AAF men (many of the latter from the Aleutian and Alaskan-based Eleventh Air Force) in an internment camp at Tashkent in south-central Russia. At one time, there were 131 men in the closely guarded camp, some of whom remained there for more than a year before "arrangements" could be made to smuggle them out via Iran and then back to the United States by various secret routes.

The number of B-29s that went down in Russian territory is still undetermined. The first known to have landed on Soviet territory was piloted by Major Richard M. McGlinn, whose plane developed trouble after an engine was shot out during a raid on Yawata in July 1944. Forced to bail out east of Khabarovsk, the crew saw their plane crash into the ground and spent several days lost in a Russian forest before they were finally rescued.

Later that same month, a second B-29, running low on fuel after bombing the Showa Steel Works at Anshan, Manchuria, landed 30 miles north of Vladivostok. The crew was eventually sent to Tashkent.

There is no record of any Superfort going into Russia during August, September or October 1944, but on November 11 the Arnold Special ended its career a few miles from Vladivostok; its crew also was sent to Tashkent. Ironically, just a few days prior to this last mission, the Arnold Special had completed a 17-hour flight over the Pacific in search of another Superfort lost on the November 5th raid against Singapore. Ten days later, on November 21, the "Ding Hao," with Captain Mickish at the controls, made its forced landing on Russian soil.

The crews of the three B-29s discovered that conditions were far different from what they had expected: Two of the planes were fired upon by Russian aircraft while they were searching for a landing place; and one was forced to fly into flak, sent up in broad daylight, as it came in to land at an airport. The pilots had no idea what actually would happen in forced landings in Russia, but they believed they could get needed repairs there, and they would be permitted to return to their base. There was no way of knowing whether previous flights listed as "Missing in Action" had actually gone into Russian territory, or been lost over the long stretches of water.

And just as the airmen had no idea of what would happen on forced landings in Russia, they also knew little of the conditions existing within the country. Upon landing, they were forced to give up their arms, including knives, and undergo a severe interrogation. Then, usually on the first night, they were wined and dined. However, they soon discovered that the Russian people were existing under the severest conditions; their land, ravaged by the Nazi war machine, was producing only the very essentials. In the subsequent days and months of their internment, the men realized that while their fare was poor, it was no worse than the food the Russians were eating. They also realized that they were being held virtually as prisoners because Russia, although our ally in the war against Germany, remained at peace with Japan during this period, and was following a rather strict interpretation of international regulations relating to belligerents. But they were hard put to reconcile themselves to the fact.

Equally hard to accept was the loss of the aircraft. The crews knew how urgently each B-29 was needed, how few replacements and additions were coming through. To men who were fighting a long-range war in which their few aircraft were required to fly many miles over extremely dangerous routes, the loss of even one B-29 was keenly felt. And they were never to see their Superforts again.

A British journal, THE AEROPLANE SPOTTER, made the first public disclosure of what had happened to the planes. In 1947 one of its sharp-eyed writers noticed that Russian newsreels on view in London theaters featuring the new Tupolev TU-70, a 72-passenger transport, showed a plane that looked very much like the B-29. He had clips made of the film and sent them to Boeing. Boeing engineers compared the Russian plane with their B-29 and concluded that they had given Mr. Andreas N. Tupolev considerable help in designing the TU-70.

From the pictures Boeing designers were able to recognize more than twenty parts that were copied exactly from the B-29; among them were the wing, the nacelles, the cooling air intake, the cowl flaps, the main landing gear, and the propellers. The tail surfaces of the Russian transport also came from the Boeing engineering department, including a patch which had been installed on the vertical tail of one of the downed planes after a minor change was made. The Russians had copied the patch and it was easily identified in the TU-70 pictures. Tupolev did design a new fuselage for the TU-70; it sat higher on the wing and was a little larger.

There had been hints as early as Armistice Day, 1946 (exactly two years after the disappearance of the General H. H. Arnold Special) that the Russians were producing copies of the B-29 in the Far Eastern Ural state aircraft factories. United States observers at the 1947 Soviet Aviation Day parade at Tushino Aerodrome in Moscow reported seeing "several B-29s." The number was described by General Spaatz as "definitely more than they came by from us." He later disclosed that in 1946 Russia had tried to place an order with an American rubber company for tires, wheels, and brake assemblies of the B-29.

While Russia's adoption of an American bomber indicated that she had no satisfactory long-range weapon of her own, it also shed a new and interesting light on Soviet technological progress. The translation of an airplane back to its production breakdown required considerable engineering skill; the TU-70 had a background that was unique in aviation history.

An account of what happened to the B-29s as they came in for a landing at what they had assumed would be a friendly field was given by Captain William J. Mickish, pilot of the "Ding Hao," which landed at Vladivostok ten days after the General H. H. Arnold Special.

"When we were forced down it was 3 o'clock in the afternoon. Broad daylight," reported Captain Mickish. "First the antiaircraft batteries started sending flak around us, although they could see we were an American ship and that I had my flaps down for a landing. Then six fighters came up and the leader began spraying tracer bullets around our nose. My boys didn't like it. I had a hard time getting them to keep their trigger fingers off their guns."

The "Ding Hao" flew over Vladivostok at about 5,000 feet, giving the international radio signal for "friend." For ten minutes, Mickish searched for a landing strip. The weather was bad, and getting worse and he knew that he would have to set down soon. He had about decided to head for a small naval airfield just to the south of the city when his bombardier reported that there was a B-29 on the ground directly beneath them. Mickish later discovered the grounded plane was the Arnold Special.

Discarding the smaller field, the pilot decided to land beside the first B-29. He proceeded with his landing preparations, which could not possibly be mistaken by anyone familiar with aircraft, and had just lowered his landing gear at 500 feet when antiaircraft fire started from the field below. Despite the flak and the six Russian fighter planes, Captain Mickish completed his landing, the fighters still firing tracers across his nose.

The 11-man crew dropped to the ground, bewildered by their unexpected reception, not knowing what was coming next.

"We were puzzled by their attitude," said Captain Mickish. "We felt they (the Russians) should have been friendly, but somehow they didn't seem friendly."

The men were taken to an administration building on the naval field. They were then told to give up their sidearms and ammunition, including knives. Eight Russians interrogated the entire crew.

Then came a break for dinner, and the Americans were taken to the officers' mess where they found plenty of food and vodka. When they had finished, they were returned to the interrogation room; the questioning continued, this time with a three-star general in charge. The general was very active in the interrogation, repeatedly asking Mickish why the United States had not given

Russia any B-29s under the lend-lease arrangements then in force. The captain explained patiently that he was sure it was because we were so short of the Superforts ourselves.

Shortly after the crew had left their plane, they had asked to see the American consul general at Vladivostok and were assured that he would be over "soon." The term "soon" stretched into three days before O. Edmund Chubb, the consul general, came to see them.

"We asked him if we were going to be able to get our plane repaired so we could get back to the war," said Captain Mickish. "He said, 'No, you'll never see your plane again.'"

The entire crew, meanwhile, had received heavy clothing, so necessary in the severe Russian winter weather, and had been assigned a Russian lieutenant to act as their interpreter. On December 3 they boarded a train, and twenty-four hours later arrived at Khabarovsk, where they were quartered in an unoccupied hospital building. And there they found Captain Price and the crew of the Arnold Special.

On December 6, the 22 Americans began a 12-day trip by train to Tashkent, where they began to get a full picture of their status. All told, there were 131 American fliers interned in a two-acre area that had formerly been an officers' training camp. Lieutenant Commander Charles Wayne of Seattle, as the senior officer, was spokesman for the internees who included B-29 crews, naval flyers who had bombed the Kuriles, and members of the Eleventh Air Force.

Interviewed by Mr. Shallet for the February 14, 1947 TIMES article, Commander Wayne said it was hard for the Americans to reconcile themselves to the "grim" food and quarters the Russians provided at Tashkent, even though some of the older hands recognized that the Russians themselves did not eat and live any better, if as well. Nor could the Americans ever understand why the Russians had to "hem" them in within a two-acre compound and refused to allow them to communicate freely with American officials. Captain Mickish explained, "We were notified that guards were patrolling the boundaries for our own protection, but at the same time we were advised not to try to get out."

Meanwhile, unknown to the internees, an American military mission to Moscow was working with the NKVD (Russian secret police) to release the internees via the Iranian border. Heading this mission were Averell Harriman and Major General John R. Deane.

In December, Commander Wayne led a group of 100 "gloriously happy" airmen on a "cloak and dagger" adventure arranged by the NKVD which was designed to "smuggle" the men over the border to Iran. Traveling for four days by truck and train, the 100 men finally reached the border, only to be turned back. There were no explanations, and there was no crossing. The Americans were sorely disappointed but had no choice. They were unable to figure out what had happened until a letter was received from the United States by one of the Americans which contained a clipping from a syndicated columnist telling the story of how 60 men had been smuggled out of Russia a year before. That ill-timed publicity had canceled out the delivery of Commander Wayne and his party.

But six weeks later, on January 29, 1945, the men were again at the Iranian border, and this time they crossed over and were immediately taken to Tehran where the American Army was waiting to delouse the ex-internees and stuff them with fresh eggs, steaks, ice cream and milk until they could be moved to Cairo and then back to the United States.

Meanwhile, the 20th Bomber Command had had a busy summer and fall. On July 4, 1944, General K. B. Wolfe had been ordered back to Washington for a new assignment leaving General Saunders temporarily in charge at the Kharagpur headquarters. On August 29, Major General Curtis E. LeMay assumed command of the 20th.

Cigar-chewing, tough LeMay was young in years but long on experience. Considered one of the most effective strategic airmen developed in the European theater, the young two-star general had commanded the 3rd Bombardment Division; which was credited with unparalleled bombing accuracy and a low lost-aircraft rate. European veterans knew him as a courageous flyer, the man who had led the famous August 17, 1943, raid against the Messerschmitt Works at Regensburg, Austria.

General Arnold knew his record, and to replace Wolfe, who was a production expert, the commander of the Twentieth Air Force had picked LeMay, the heavy bombardment specialist, to lead the B-29s on their strategic mission.

The Hard Way Back

In July 1944, the 20th Bomber Command finally achieved self-sufficiency: the 3,000 tons its planes hauled over the Hump that month just about supported the 115 sorties it flew against the enemy. However, the 115 sorties were only half the number that had been anticipated, and it was obvious that the system of supplying the B-29s in China would have to be revamped. In the meantime, the planes of the 20th continued in the transport business between missions flown from its bases in China and India.

The route over the Hump was a dangerous one with jagged mountain ranges, uncertain weather, and the ever-present possibility of Japanese fighter attack. But engine failure was still the chief source of trouble. Many crews were forced to bail out. Not all of them survived the landing or the long walk out. Those who finally reached civilization brought with them remarkable stories of peril, hardship, and the strange people of the remote country.

The story of Captain Leslie Sloan and his crew began high over the treacherous mountains of Lololand,[19] on the way back to India after a routine tanking mission to China. Suddenly, Corporal William Shufelt, a gunner, shouted over the interphone that a fire had broken out in Number 3 engine. This was followed immediately by a violent explosion which shook the entire ship. Immediately Captain Sloan pulled back the power, hit the feathering switch. The engine began to slow down, but about four miles later, its prop began to run away crazily. The ship vibrated, trembled, and soon became unmanageable. Sloan was forced to give the order to bail out.

The skipper watched his crew plummet downward feet first, and then, believing he was the last man to abandon ship, leaped himself. But one man, the left gunner, never left the plane. His companions last saw him with his chute on and adjusted; they

---

[19] The Lolos is an old name for the Yi or Nuosuo people. In China, the Lolos live in the mountainous regions of Guangxi, Guizhou, Sichuan and Yunnan. This region is sometimes referred to as 'The Land of the Lolos.'

could offer no explanation as to why he didn't jump except that the plane may have lurched, knocking him unconscious.

Another gunner, Sergeant Virgil Bailey, almost went down with the plane. As he was stepping forth to parachute, he tripped over the rear door exit, and caught by the powerful slip stream, was flattened against the fuselage and pinned there securely, almost as if he were sucked in by a vacuum. The speeding plane was losing altitude and Bailey struggled frantically to free himself. He pushed with his hands—kicked his legs—twisted his feet—he screamed wildly for the left gunner still inside the plane to free him. There was no answer. Finally, a desperate twist and kick did the trick; he tore himself loose, pulled the cord, and floated down.

Ten men reached the ground safely. Sloan landed several miles northeast of the others. As he descended below the undercast, he saw "seven or eight" going down, and that was the last he saw of them for the next two days.

"Hitting the silk isn't as easy as it may look," Sloan said. "On the way down, you have a sensation you're going to float forever. But when you near the earth, you realize you're coming down in a hell of a hurry. I struck a good-sized tree, came crashing through the branches, and finally hung about 15 or 20 feet from the ground. My chute was caught in the upper branches. I pulled myself in toward the trunk of the tree, unfastened the chute and slid down."

Sloan then walked to a clearing atop a little mesa and looked out at the surrounding terrain. It was high, jagged, mountainous country with steep cliffs and slopes, and thick undergrowth. The ground was soaking wet. As he started to walk away, he heard voices. He drew his .45 and fired a shot into the air to attract attention. He then ran excitedly to the side of a cliff, looked down, and saw three Chinese below. One waved at him, whereupon he scrambled down and joined them. He hadn't the slightest idea of his whereabouts or if the people were friendly. None of the Chinese spoke English, so there was no communication other than pantomime.

As the three Chinese led him to a village nearby, Sloan noticed bits of wreckage scattered along the trail, indicating that the natives had found the plane and were carrying off whatever they fancied. As they neared the village, they were surrounded by 12 men, smaller, darker, hardier, with Mongolian-like features, all armed with rifles or pistols of German and American make. They wore cloth pants, tightly bound turbans, and felt capes which draped almost to their knees.[20] The men were members of the Lolo tribe.[21] Sloan quickly hid his watch and two rings. The Lolos grabbed for his .45, but Sloan drew back and didn't yield it. Then one of the Chinese boys exchanged words with the Lolos and the incident ended with Sloan giving up his cartridge clip.

Upon arriving at the village, Sloan was taken to the chief's house where exhaustion caught up with him. When he awoke, the chief gave him food: rice, fat and greasy sowbelly.[22] Sloan supplemented this with some of his own emergency rations. His remaining rations were taken away.

The party then retired to a large room, sat cross-legged around a fire, and opium pipes were passed around.[23] Sloan was invited to join in but politely refused. The opium was in the form of a dark brownish paste which was tamped into a little cup on the end of the pipe and the pipe held over the fire. A small hole on the bottom of the cup allowed the heat to penetrate, and the smokers drew deep puffs and inhaled. The odor was pungent and sickening. Sloan curled up on the floor and fell asleep.

He began the next morning diplomatically enough by giving the chief a pair of cotton mosquito gloves, a gesture which drew a wide, childlike grin and a half bow. After breakfast of rice and sowbelly, he suggested, by sign language, that they walk to the scene of the wreck. The chief made no response, apparently unable to understand the pantomime. However, one of the Chinese, a young man whose name was Saing Tou, informed him with gestures that nine of the crew were safe at another village and that one was dead.

Although slightly befuddled with opium, Saing Tou offered to lead Sloan to the other crewmen. The chief granted permission to leave and gave Sloan a note scribbled in a Lolo version of Chinese characters. (Later, a Chinese translator was unable to read it.)

---

[20] Yi women are adept at embroidery; a skill that raises their social status.
[21] The Yi are the largest ethnic group in China, numbering 9 million.
[22] Essentially, a big, fat, salted slab of bacon.
[23] Probably made of bamboo.

The two hit the trail and reached another village shortly before dark. Saing Tou led the way to the chief's house, and after considerable talking, they were fed and permitted to sleep on the floor. The nights were bitter cold in those high mountains and Sloan wore nothing but a khaki uniform.

The next day, curious natives crowded around him, examined his wings and insignia, felt his shoes, stared at him coldly and strangely. However, he was neither molested nor robbed. He was given breakfast and lunch—rice and sowbelly both times—and the safari continued with Saing Tou and four Lolo guides dispatched by the chiefs as escorts. That night they reached the village; Sloan was reunited with his crew.

The plight of the nine crewmen during the first two days had been more serious than Sloan's. Lieutenant Gray had landed in the middle of the village. He was immediately surrounded, and his knife, pen, pencil, and jewelry were taken away. When he momentarily balked at giving up his gun, a Lolo split his belt with one swish of his knife; the pistol dropped to the ground, and the Lolo quickly scooped it up. The eight other men were not mistreated, but they lost all valuables; guns, wallets, knives, jewelry, silk parachutes. Lieutenant Ray saved his watch, ring, and an AAF wrist chain by slipping them in his watch pocket, a place the natives never thought of investigating.

One of the Lolos took a particular fancy to a cameo ring worn by Corporal Shufelt. Brandishing a vicious-looking knife, he grabbed Shufelt's finger and raised the knife as if to remove the finger completely. Shufelt jerked his hand back quickly, pulled off the ring, and handed it to the knife-wielder.

The nine men were finally brought to the chief's house and given rice and sowbelly. After Sloan arrived, there was a slight variation in the menu; a gruel of cornmeal paste was added to the rice and sowbelly. For eight days, the men did nothing. Two of the crew were allowed to visit the site of the crash accompanied by Lolo guides. The plane was completely wrecked; the body of the left gunner was positively identified, then buried. The exact intentions of the chief remained a mystery. He gave no explanation for holding the flyers. They were not under guard; they took walks during the day and hunted for edible berries; they could have escaped at any time; if they only knew where to go. Saing

Tou was still around but apparently taking his orders from the chief.

The cold and the poor diet soon began to show on the men. They became ill and suffered from dysentery. The big, black fleas, mosquitoes and other bugs infesting their quarters pestered them continually. They wore the same dirty clothes. Day and night, they watched the Lolos puff opium. Flight engineer Robert Casey said, "They hardly did a damned thing all day but eat, sit and smoke."

Under such circumstances, it was remarkable that the men did not crack. With the exception of occasional flare-ups, which ended quickly and were forgotten, their spirits remained amazingly high. They sang most of the time and took particular pride in teaching one friendly Lolo an American song. The native was nicknamed "Joe Sharp," and before the airmen left the village, Joe Sharp had learned the words to the old cowboy ballad, "I Saw Your Face in the Moon."[24]

On the eleventh day after the crash, the chief informed Saing Tou that the visitors could leave, and as a parting gesture, he presented them with three pans of opium to help pay their way. The men estimated that in illegal channels in the United States those three pans of opium probably would bring a small fortune.

After leaving the village, Sloan and his men were able to walk for the next two and one-half days, stopping only to eat and sleep at native houses along the way. They paid for this with opium and with money Captain Sloan had hidden. On the afternoon of the twelfth day, American planes passed overhead, and the men signaled desperately. The planes sped on, disappearing into the overcast. On the thirteenth day, they entered a wide valley blooming with poppies. General debilitation and the injured leg of navigator Frank Holmes, Jr., kept them for the next four days in a chief's house in this valley. The chief's inviting cuisine: rice, sowbelly, goat's meat, potatoes and round, flat pieces of hard

---

[24] "I saw your face in the moon honey/You threw a smile at me/You pretended that you were happy/But in those loving eyes I could see/You were having blue thoughts of by gone/Days you and I once knew/But I could see you smile/And you faded with the blue/When I saw your face in the moon honey/When I saw your face in the moon." Written by Odis Elder. First recorded by Ray Whitley's Range Ramblers in 1936.

brown sugar, which were delicious once the layers of dirt were scraped off. The bill amounted to half a pan of opium.

Before leaving the valley, they were joined by another young Chinese whose name was Shun Wai. The new friend warned them that people in the next town were not to be trusted. He did this by pointing in the direction of the next village, then pointing to a Lolo, then running his finger across the throat of one of the Americans.

When they reached this settlement, they were accosted by six Chinese, one of whom spoke a little English. The Chinese offered to lead them to safety, but the route they suggested was to the south. The Americans suspected the strangers were planning to lead them to the Japanese to collect a bounty. When Shun Wai warned them emphatically "no," one of the Chinese whipped out a knife and threatened to kill him. The Americans brushed past the strangers and walked away, expecting at any time to be shot in the back. Nothing happened, except a pan of opium was stolen while the conversation and pantomime were taking place.

They now set out for Leipo, a friendly Chinese city. As they followed a river, some Lolos fired at them from the opposite bank. The men sprinted for safety and dropped flat on their bellies behind rocks. The firing continued. As darkness settled, one by one the Americans crept away.

In the pitch blackness that soon covered the area, Lieutenants Vincent Casazza, Holmes, and Ray and one of the Chinese boys became separated from the group; they spent the rainy night sleeping under a tree. The others took refuge in a farmhouse owned by two elderly Chinese women, who produced the best meal the men had eaten since the crash—boiled eggs, fried potatoes, and a bowl of Chinese custard. The tab was settled in Chinese yuans. The two groups found each other next morning, and on the twenty-fourth day the tired, dirty, sickly-looking party reached Leipo, an ancient town inhabited mostly by Chinese, but visited often by Lolos on trading trips. The arrival of the Americans was not a surprise to the mayor of Leipo,[25] known as Magistrate Lee. Apparently, a runner had carried the news ahead.

---

[25] In Sichuan province.

Magistrate Lee and a young schoolteacher who acted as interpreter listened eagerly to their story, and treated them royally. They were given a hot bath, and clean clothes while their own were being washed. American cigarettes, and a sumptuous meal of eggs, chicken, peaches, and hot tea. It was at Leipo that the airmen learned of the first B-29 bombing of Japan on June 15. Word had reached Magistrate Lee by runner.

When Magistrate Lee bade goodbye to his visitors, he dispatched an armed guard to accompany them the rest of the way to Ipin. On the second day out of Leipo, the Chinese guard moved ahead by about ten minutes.

As the Americans, along with some local Chinese merchants, were walking along the trail, they were startled by shots. For thirty minutes, a hot skirmish continued up ahead. When they joined the soldiers, they found them standing over two dead Lolo bandits, one with a single bright red ring in his ear. That was the head a soldier chose to cut off. He tied a rope tightly around it, flung it over his shoulder, and the procession walked on. As they passed Lolos along the trail, the soldier would warn them by swinging the head around like a hammer thrower winding up in a track meet. The whirling red ring was the grisliest touch.

The long march continued. The 26th day found them in Pingshan. Here a retired Chinese general, who was both wealthy and hospitable, provided the men with food and quarters for the night, and gave them eight bamboo chairs and carriers for the rest of their journey. The two strongest walked, the others rode. They arrived in Anpienchang on the 27th day, and from there proceeded by boat up the river to Ipin.

On reaching Ipin, Sloan raced for a phone, excitedly put through a long-distance call to his base in the Chengtu area.

"Hello! Hello!" he cried. "This is Sloan! We're here in Ipin!"

"Who?" came the sleepy reply of the night duty officer.

"Sloan! ... Aircraft 314... We went down over the Hump; don't you remember?"

There was a thoughtful pause. Finally, the officer said, "Oh yes, I think I remember hearing about you. I'm a new guy here. Just come over from the States. Where are you now?"

"Ipin!" Sloan shouted. "When are you going to send a plane to pick us up?"

"Soon as one's available. Probably tomorrow. Take it easy." With that, the officer yawned and hung up.

Sloan and his crew didn't take it easy until, on their arrival in Chengtu, they cabled home and corrected the War Department wires that they were "missing in flight." Then, in a 20th Bomber Command hospital, they spent hours taking it easy and telling their friends what had happened.

The effects of the 29-day episode included dysentery, malaria (one case), skin infection, exposure, and insect bites. Loss of weight ranged from fifteen to thirty-five pounds per man. Pilot Sloan estimated that they had walked approximately 250 miles.

The crew rejoined the Command, and after several weeks of rest was again flying against the enemy.

Another crew which survived a bail-out was that of Lt. Colonel H. R. Sullivan, the original skipper of the General H. H. Arnold Special. Sullivan had left the Special to become Deputy Commander of the 40th Bombardment Group. On August 19, he commanded one of three B-29s which took off on a flight over the Hump.

About four hours after take-off, while the plane was flying at 21,000 feet some 70 miles west-southwest of Hsichang, its No. 4 engine started throwing oil. Colonel Sullivan, who was at the controls, attempted unsuccessfully to feather the prop. Matters were getting worse, and after some anxious moments, the colonel told the crew to stand by for a bail-out signal. Bombs was salvoed to lighten the ship; a few minutes later the disabled engine disintegrated, and the plane was down to 18,000 feet. Without further ado the jump signal was given.

The bail-out was accomplished over rugged country which they later found out was a section of Lololand. Colonel Sullivan and two of his crew members landed on the south side of a stream flowing in a deep gorge; nine others landed on the north side, and Lieutenant Shine, the bombardier, came down on a high peak some distance away. The flight engineer landed in a tree and hung there some 20 feet in the air until he was able to struggle out of his parachute and climb down.

When Colonel Sullivan landed, he heard Chinese shouting nearby. Two of the natives, who turned out to be Lolos, ran to him and by means of sign language indicated that the three Americans were to follow them. After walking about a mile, the party arrived at a native farmhouse. The colonel was offered food but declined because the house was so filthy. As the natives were preparing a place for the three Americans to sleep, a procession of torch bearers arrived with a note to the Americans from the Chinese Catholic priest of a small mission a few miles away. The note invited the fliers to spend the night at the mission. It was too late for safe travel, but at eight o'clock in the morning, the Americans set off with a guide on the four-hour walk to the mission.

The crewmen who had landed on the north side of the stream were almost immediately picked up by a group of friendly Lolos. After examining the equipment carried by the party, the leader of the natives, who later turned out to be a Buddhist priest, beckoned the Americans to follow him. They walked a short distance to the Buddhist temple where they spent the night.

Early the next morning, they continued their journey to the Catholic mission. On the way, they picked up Lieutenant Shine, who had spent the night on top of a hill. Thus, the entire crew was reunited at the mission on the outskirts of Lololand.

The priest in charge of the mission read and wrote English, although his vocabulary was extremely limited. He showed the Americans every courtesy, fed them well, and suggested they rest up for a day before making the trip to Te Chang. Colonel Sullivan decided to visit the site of the crash but found nothing of value left. During the day, a large number of Lolos arrived at the mission to see the Americans. While not friendly, they appeared to tolerate the priest and his work.

The following morning, August 21, the priest reported he had arranged for a party of natives to take the crew to Te Chang. As they were getting ready to leave, three B-29s and three C-46s, flying quite low, passed overhead. One B-29 circled, then rejoined its flight.

Ten bearers, two guides, two armed guards, three burros and one small horse had been provided by the priest. Also, a note which, he explained, would act as a passport. The crew tried to reward the priest and the natives for their help; it was with reluctance that the priest finally accepted a contribution to the mission from Colonel Sullivan.

After breakfast, the party set out on the trip to Te Chang. The route was circuitous; when they finally arrived at the Ya

Lungchang River the boatman refused to ferry them across until Colonel Sullivan produced the passport. The balance of the day was spent traveling over rough terrain; at one point their route lay over an 11,000-foot pass. In the early evening, the group arrived at the hut of a Lolo chieftain. At first, he was uncooperative, but after studying Colonel Sullivan's passport, which he probably could not read, immediately ordered hot food for the party, then made a place for them to spend the night.

Early the following morning, the group headed for Te Chang, arriving without incident later that afternoon. The Chinese then took them to Hsichang, where they were able to contact their base. By August 25, just six days after the take-off, the men were back at their base, ready for a new plane and a new adventure.

Just as the flights over the Hump created heroes who had walked out, the combat missions flown by the 20th Bomber Command created heroes who brought battle-damaged planes back across miles of water and enemy-held territory.

One of these was Captain Charles "Doc" Joyce, pilot of the "Raidin' Maiden" out of Salua Field. Salua Field, located a few miles from command headquarters at Kharagpur, was usually crowded with spectators when the Superforts returned from an important mission. They were there in force that day in November, sweating out the first of the raids on Singapore, when word reached the tower that Doc Joyce's plane was in trouble.

Immediately, staff officers began pouring from the shady, latticed verandas, streaming out onto the hot dusty road to scan the Bengal sky. For Doc Joyce was not just another pilot in bad luck. A short, slightly built chap with a vague, unruffled air, he had already participated in one of the most hair-raising landings in the 20th's hair-raising history.

It had happened when his Raidin' Maiden was returning from Formosa. With two engines out and the gasoline indicator crowding the zero mark, he was faced with the task of making an emergency landing on an unfamiliar fighter strip that was trapped by a network of mountains uncharted on his aerial map.

Circling three times over the tiny narrow field, scarcely able to see beyond his wingtips, with clouds intermittently obliterating his vision of the ground, Doc finally managed to ease his plane down on the rain-soaked runway, coming in blind at 500 feet with, as he learned a moment later, an 11,000-foot mountain waiting on one side and a 3,000-footer on the other.

As if that ordeal were not enough, on takeoff from Salua Field he had blown an engine, circled the area in a hectic, dizzying arc, brushing trees, skimming native huts, driving onlookers in a pell-mell dash for safety, until at last, when everyone had written him off, he had brought the great plane down for a perfect landing.

Now once again fate seemed to be closing in on Doc Joyce. His trouble began over the Singapore naval yards. Finding opposition weak as he made his approach, he had coolly taken a full eight minutes, hoping with his slow and accurate run to place his bombs squarely on the target.

But enemy flak had suddenly bracketed him, catching him with a terrific barrage, severely damaging his right wing and left flap. For more than 1,500 miles, first over the hostile Straits of Malacca, then over the shark-infested waters of the Andaman Sea and the Bay of Bengal, his Raidin' Maiden limped its way toward home. Alone up there in the sterile wastes of space, dodging tropical thunderheads, their fate a series of nickering symbols on an instrument panel, the crew stuck it out, until finally, when they were only 25 miles from home, No. 1 engine began to sputter.

"How much gas left, Charley?" Joyce asked over the interphone.

Tensely the crew listened, their hands already playing over the ripcord handles of their parachutes.

Flight Officer Charles Passieu bent over his gasoline gauge. At last came his sardonic reply: "Enough to fill your lighter, Doc."

They were at 10,000 feet, still with "money in the bank," as the Air Corps phrase went. Over the intercom came Joyce's calm voice ordering them to stand by. The rear exit and emergency door in the tail had been opened and the front wheel was being lowered, making available for escape the well in front of the plane. They were sitting there now, feeling No. 1 drying up on them, when all of a sudden No. 3 went out. For a moment, the pilot stiffened, an unlit cigar incongruous in his youthful face. Then he began contacting the control tower,

"Two-Six-Five to Tower, Two-Six-Five to Tower," he said casually. "No gas left. Crew bailing out. Coming in on straight approach landing from north..."

Immediately, Joyce called for front cabin crew members to begin bailing out, simultaneously ringing the alarm bell for those in the rear of the plane. Silently, their faces grim and expressionless, the men began dropping through the nose wheel well; first the navigator; then the radioman; the bombardier, and the copilot. Only Charley Passieu remained. Observing that all the chutes had opened without mishap, he stepped over to Joyce and said, "You aren't going to ride it down, are you, Doc?"

"Oh, hell yes."

"What if the other engines go too? The gas indicator says absolutely zero."

"We can make it."

For a moment, Passieu hesitated, knowing what it would mean if they had to try a dead-stick landing. Months of spare time speculation had gone into consideration of such a situation. There was not a technical expert in the country who would advise trying it. For this B-29, with its great weight of 120,000 pounds, its 11 miles of wiring winding through its framework, its 50,000 pounds of aluminum, its 152 electric motors, its tunnels, bomb bays, pressurized cabins, and the myriad other features of its complicated existence; this wasn't an airplane, it was a monster creation of sheer power. Once those four great engines ceased their attack, once that giant wingspan of 141 feet began to feel its life-flow waver; then the odds against setting the plane down safely suddenly increased a thousand-fold!

While Passieu hesitated, trying to decide whether to bow out in his parachute or ride the plane down, the last two engines sputtered out, leaving Joyce with a dead stick in his hands. To add to Doc's troubles, No. 3 prop was refusing to feather, its windmilling cutting down airspeed, threatening to throw the plane into an immediate stall. Looking at Joyce, realizing once again his skill and courage, Passieu quickly climbed into the copilot's position.

Salua Field was now in view, crowded with frenzied, running people, but Doc Joyce seemed completely unaware of the spectacle he was providing. He sat there bent toward the windshield, alert to every quiver of the gliding, engineless machine, keeping its nose pointed downward in a straining quest for speed. He wavered when he realized he was going to fall short of the runway. He still had the plane under his control and the temptation to bring the nose up slightly and stretch the glide began to haunt him. Like an evil dream it fell upon his senses, drugging him with the desire to trade a portion of his speed for a few more yards of distance; those few yards which would carry his plane to the runway. Against all the animal logic of life he fought, clinging tenaciously to the velocity of his steep descent, fighting with the hard knowledge of his airman's training the ever-increasing threat of stalling out—that fatal instant when the wing goes suddenly numb and the plane begins to fall in a tortuous turn to earth...

From the ground, the crowd could see the two men in the cockpit. They saw Passieu bobbing in his seat as he read altitude to Joyce, and behind them, back there in the sky, were the blossomed parachutes of the other crewmen. By now it was apparent to everyone that the plane was falling short of the field. There was a sudden pause in the surge of the crowd as the plane hit the ground. It came in "hot," at a terrifically fast landing speed, tearing at the Bengal soil, obscuring itself momentarily in a great cloud of dust and flying rocks. Then out of the dust emerged the long silvery nose of the Raidin' Maiden.

For a moment, there was silence, then a spontaneous cry rose from the crowd. The plane rolled straight onto the runway, rolling with all the ease and assurance of its own aerodynamic perfection, rolling until it came to a graceful, glistening, silent halt.

As Doc Joyce and his flight engineer emerged from the pilot's cabin they were greeted by a rush of excited people. The Raidin' Maiden was towed off to clear the runway for other B-29s, and within a moment the area was crowded with well-wishers shouting questions.

"Quite a hot landing, eh?" grinned Joyce.

At that moment he saw some of his crew dropping from the rear of the plane. "What the hell?" he cried in amazement. "I thought you'd jumped way back with the others!"

"We were waiting for the bail-out alarm," the men said.

"It must have been knocked out of order. Why didn't you jump anyway?"

"We were waiting for your signal," they repeated.

For a moment, Joyce stood there in silence, touched by their simple devotion to duty. Then a broad grin broke across his youthful, dirt-streaked face. "Hell, I'd never have dared it if I knew you lugs were back there."

Then there was the "Heavenly Body."

It had happened near Nagasaki, on October 25. They had just bombed Omura and were on their way home at 20,000 feet. Still tense, they watched the great plane chew up space as it approached the East China Sea. In the front cabin, someone, striving for humor, inquired whether it was time for 'eats.' A moment later, the intercom came suddenly to life.

"Fighter coming in from two o'clock high," snapped the top gunner.

As Captain Jack Ledford, pilot of the Heavenly Body, turned for a quick appraisal of the situation, other Nips were reported over the interphone. He sat there in momentary helplessness, feeling his plane tremble as its guns strove to fend off the attack. There was an awesome pause, then crashing confusion as a 20-mm. shell burst into the cabin, shattering instrument panels, snapping wires, damaging electrical equipment upon which depended their return to safety.

Ledford felt as though his side had been slammed with a sledgehammer. Dazed, his hip bone fractured, his kidney raw and exposed, he felt his plane slowly sliding under the formation, falling back where it would become easy prey for the enemy fighters already beginning to close in.

"Take the controls," he shouted to his copilot, Lieutenant James DeCaster. "I'm going to contact the formation leader! We're going to need help, and fast!"

After the formation leader had been contacted, and other B-29s were dropping down for protection, Captain Ledford discovered that his flight engineer had been seriously wounded. A fragment of the shell had hit Master Sergeant Harry C. Miller in the head, piercing his flak helmet; he lay inert over the debris of wires and gadgets. Mist began to cloud the cabin. The shell had caused complete loss of pressure within the aircraft, necessitating the immediate use of oxygen.

"Take care of Harry," said Ledford to Lieutenant William L. Gardner, the bombardier, who was already passing out the oxygen masks. "I'll take his place. We've got to keep this damned thing airborne."

"You're all cut up, Jack!"

"I'm all right."

Ledford dragged himself over to the flight engineer's controls and began to grapple with the problem of keeping the bomber aloft. The ship was in bad shape and still hundreds of miles from friendly territory. There was a huge shell hole in the fuselage. No. 3 engine was shot up, No. 1 engine was threatening to quit because of lack of fuel, and the plane was still losing altitude.

With blood seeping from his wounds and mist clouding his vision, Ledford began transferring gas into No. 1 engine. Ignoring pain, retaining consciousness only through sheer courage and determination, he crawled into the bomb bay to make the necessary adjustments. For nearly an hour he worked, watching the performance of the engines with a deadly calm, nursing the plane along in its shaky flight over the East China Sea, until at last, so weakened by loss of blood that he could scarcely move, he turned over the engineer's controls to the tail gunner. Only then did he allow himself to be dragged back to the pilot's position, where Sergeant Gilbert Rodeneal could dress his wounds.

"Is it bothering you much, Captain?" asked Rodeneal. "I can give you an opiate. That'll deaden the pain."

"No, I'm okay," said Ledford, preferring to keep his head clear for the trouble that lay ahead. "How's Harry?"

"In bad shape, sir."

"Is he breathing all right? We can drop lower if he's having trouble with his oxygen mask."

"He's breathing okay now," said the sergeant.

They all knew how fond the captain was of his crew, especially of Harry Miller, who had given up a chance at OCS to fly B-29s.

Ledford headed for Liangshan, 500 miles north of Chungking, where the weather was reported clear. But all the way across the China Sea and on into the interior they encountered terrific headwinds which slowed the plane and drained the fuel reserve. To complicate their task, the radio operator began picking up a series of mysterious messages from an unidentified radio station; navigation instructions which would have led them, they learned later, directly to a Jap fighter field.

It was soon apparent that the Heavenly Body would never reach Liangshan, and Ledford asked his navigator Lieutenant Howard Oblender for an emergency field.

"We ought to be nearing Laohokow pretty soon," announced Lieutenant Oblender.

"Hell, that should be free of Japs. Jack Grewbaugh bailed out there only a month ago."

As the Heavenly Body moved toward Laohokow, the 12,000-foot peaks of the brown, barren mountains of central China suddenly loomed before them. With barely 50 gallons of gas remaining in each tank, Ledford knew that they would never cross them with their present load. Yet if Harry Miller was to be saved it was imperative that the ship be crash-landed on the fighter strip behind those peaks. Without hesitation Ledford gave the order for the rear gunners to jump, hoping thus to gain sufficient altitude to clear the mountains and reach the fighter strip on the other side. The three gunners dropped from the plane and disappeared immediately into the undercast. Lightened somewhat, the great plane began straining and throbbing for altitude.

The men were eyeing the brown, somber mountains ahead, when suddenly one engine went dead and a second began to sputter. Desperately they looked at Ledford, wondering whether he would give them the order to bail out, too. Their hope flared up when a break developed in the undercast. They caught a fleeting glimpse of the land beneath them, but it was too rugged to crash-land the plane. If they were forced to jump now, it would mean abandoning Harry Miller to certain death. No one said a word.

It was at this moment that Sergeant Rodeneal had an idea. "Why don't we use the captain's damaged chute on Harry and tie it to something in the plane? We've got an extra chute along, and maybe Harry will pull through all right."

Ledford nodded. Immediately they ripped open the chute, cut off the shroud lines, attached one end of the lines to the navigator's table and the other to the ripcord ring of the unconscious engineer. As they dragged Miller into position, Ledford said quietly, "I'm going along with Harry. I want to be near him when he lands. He's in bad shape."

With the help of Sergeant McCullough, Ledford dragged Miller into position and, making certain the lines were securely fastened, let him slip out the well of the nosewheel. Tensely they all waited. The shroud lines snapped, and the chute abruptly blossomed out. A moment later, Ledford followed his friend through the hatch.

At first, Ledford had no sensation of falling. The rush of wind had taken his breath away and he lay on his back in a tearing curtain of space. Then suddenly his body began to spin like a pinwheel. It turned so violently that he feared he might lose the presence of mind to pull the ripcord. Having read that a British officer stopped this rotation by sticking out his arm, Ledford stuck out his arm. Gradually the turning ceased. Finally, after dropping almost 5,000 feet, he jerked his ripcord and was rewarded with the jolt that told him his parachute had opened.

Floating earthward, feeling almost as though he would never get there, he turned in his harness and caught sight of the other chutes. But when he finally located Harry Miller, dangling limp and unconscious, he realized that air currents were separating them, and Miller would fall behind a hill and beyond his help. A moment later, he landed in a wet rice paddy, in the midst of a bewildered group of Chinese peasants.

Dazed and shaken, Ledford beckoned to the Chinese, crying, "Ding Hao! American flyer! Ding Hao!" He was covered with mud, groggy and almost inarticulate, a frightening spectacle as he staggered toward them.

The Chinese peasants gathered around, staring, pointing their fingers, grinning sympathetically but making no effort to help him. "American flyer," Ledford kept saying, pointing to himself, "American flyer in airplane crash!"

It was not until two local soldiers arrived on the scene that he was assisted to the village. Ancient Frenchien, deep in the mountainous interior of China, had never seen an American before and the town went wild with excitement. In an instant the market was deserted, and hundreds of people were milling around Ledford. Vainly he tried to find one person who spoke English, hoping to organize a search party for Harry Miller.

In the midst of the confusion, he saw a small, bespectacled man hurrying toward him, pushing his way through the crowd.

"Mr. Yung, village postmaster," cried the man excitedly. "Study long time with Christian missionaries; speak good English."

"Where am I?" Ledford asked helplessly.

"Seventy miles from Laohokow," chirped Mr. Yung. "Five hundred miles from Chungking... eighty miles Japs close by."

"Are the others all right; the wounded one, too?"

Mr. Yung, his eyes suddenly serious, replied, "Wounded one in hospital. Others on way over here."

For the first time in hours, Jack Ledford began to feel a little better.

Presently a local doctor arrived, a Chinese who had received his medical instruction from the Japanese. Ledford was stretched out and his wounds attended. It was the doctor's opinion that Ledford was in a serious condition and in need of an immediate operation. By this time Oblender, DeCaster and McCullough had joined him, and together they discussed the possibilities of getting an American surgeon flown in for Harry Miller. At first, Ledford opposed having the Chinese doctor do any serious work on them. But then when he thought of Miller's critical condition, and how small the chance was of getting an American doctor to this remote spot in time, an excellent test of the local doctor's skill occurred to him.

"If he handles me all right," Ledford laughed, "we'll let him work on Harry later on."

It was not until the next day, when they were getting ready to depart, that Ledford learned Harry Miller was already dead; had in fact died a few minutes after landing. Mr. Yung, not wishing to upset the injured pilot, had withheld the information.

And there was the "Windy City."

"How are we doing on fuel?" said Lieutenant Gordon Teach to the flight engineer.

"We have a chance if we get a break on the weather," replied Lieutenant J. W. Ward. "We're good until 2231, if my figures are right."

Major Gus Askounis, who had listened in over the interphone, bit at his cigar, contemplating the thunderheads that lay in his plane's flight line. The Windy City was returning from a daylight raid on Yawata. It had been badly mauled by Jap flak, with possible damage to the landing gear, and in turn it had shot down one enemy fighter and damaged another. But what worried Pilot Askounis was the dwindling fuel supply. Rough weather and the long formation flight had taxed the closely calculated gasoline reserve; their home base in Chengtu lay many hours away.

"Give me an ETA, Jack," said Askounis to his navigator, Lieutenant Jack Diamond.

"My Estimated Time of Arrival is 2231," said Diamond. "Ground speed and wind currents have changed."

With a start the pilot realized that their fuel supply and ETA were in perfect accord: there was absolutely no margin for error. The coincidence was just too much for Askounis. Shifting the cigar to the other side of his mouth, he said, "You sure of that, Jack? Better check those figures again."

Diamond checked. "Still 2231," he said.

As darkness settled over the rolling ridges and sharp peaks of the Chinese countryside, the pilot, copilot, engineer and navigator held a hasty conference. Their predicament was grim, for while they seemed to have enough fuel to reach home flying a straight line, they did not have enough to detour the thunderstorms.

"We might squeeze into some other field on the way," said Lieutenant Teach.

"Too risky at night with our shot-up landing gear," said Askounis.

While Diamond and Ward were working out the most economical letdown from their high altitude, the radio operator, Sergeant William Mann, began calling for a position pickup. He was unable to contact the home field, but oddly enough a field on the India side of the Hump was coming in clear as a bell.

"Sugar Fox, Sugar Fox from Two-Five-Three, Two-Five-Three," Sergeant Mann called. "Give us a QDM. Over..."

Then more urgently: "Sugar Fox from Two-Five-Three! If you don't give us that QDM in ten minutes we're bailing out!"

Major Askounis spoke calmly into the interphone to the men in the rear of the plane. "We're running out of gas, fellows," he said. "Be ready to jump if I give the signal. You've been briefed on bail-out procedure. Follow that plan and you'll be okay."

They were down to 6,000 feet, approximately 40 miles north of their field, if their navigational figures were correct, when Sergeant Mann received the radio message that gave them their heading. Major Askounis began to turn the plane on course.

"There it is! The field beacon!" someone shouted excitedly.

At that very moment the fuel pressure on No. 4 engine began to drop rapidly. It was apparent they were going to lose it.

"Okay," said Askounis. "One down, three to go!"

Dropping down several hundred feet a minute, the plane began to nose toward the field. They were now about four miles away, but Mann was still unable to contact the tower. With other ships most likely preparing for landing, it would be folly to endanger the traffic pattern. Grimly Major Askounis faced the cold fact that a normal landing would be impossible.

"Bail 'em out," he said to Lieutenant Teach on the intercom.

They were down to 2,500 feet now, with Askounis banking the plane to the left so that the men in the rear, who were to jump from the right side, could clear the stabilizer.

Staff Sergeant Fred Brownwell, the senior gunner, was the first to jump. He fought his way out of the slipstream, tugged several times at his ripcord, then rode the blossoming parachute down to a rice paddy. Staff Sergeant Herman Sigrist followed a moment later, crashing into a tree in the center of a Chinese courtyard.

"No. 1 engine is out," said the flight engineer to the pilot. Desperately Askounis tried to lower the nose wheel so that the men in the front cabin could drop through the wheel well. But the power system was damaged, and the wheel wouldn't budge. The bombardier jumped up and down on the wheel, trying in vain to dislodge it. Askounis turned the controls over to the copilot and began to wrestle with the emergency landing gear release. Their situation was growing more impossible with each passing second. And then, No. 2 engine began to sputter. In another moment the giant plane was running on only one engine!

Meanwhile, in the rear, Staff Sergeant Therman Hassinger was rolling out of the plane. His parachute opened dangerously close to the ground, and he began calling out in the darkness, trying to locate the others. Then he crashed through the thin tile roof of a Chinese house, into a bed already occupied by several people. To the screams of an infant and the indignant outcries of its parents, he fought free of the tiles, snapped on his flashlight, and found himself confronting a naked Chinese woman.

With a screech, she grabbed her dress and fled. The husband began waving his hands, talking excitedly in Chinese, pointing to the hole in the roof and the tiles and dirt about the room. Hassinger finally managed to show him that he was an airman, and amid yelling and arm-waving, with the wife peeking from around the corner, he was led out of the house to the local authorities.

The Windy City was still fighting its way along, hovering close to stalling speed. Lieutenant Teach put the plane in an almost vertical dive to regain airspeed. Major Askounis was still struggling to lower the nose wheel so that the men up front could jump.

"We're too low to jump now!" Teach shouted.

Askounis gave up. They were trapped in the giant plane and would have to ride it down to a crash-landing—with only one engine functioning!

With the plane dropping nearly 500 feet a minute, and No. 3 engine running on half power, they began to take their positions. Sergeant Mann stayed in his seat, continuing to signal the tower. The bombardier stretched out on the cabin floor on his back and braced his feet on the bombsight stanchion. The navigator placed a padded parachute seat on his desk and put his head down, cushioned in his folded arms for protection. Teach called out the airspeed as the plane dropped. The landing lights were lowered and working.

Suddenly Major Askounis caught sight of the operations building and the runway. He could guess at the location of the belly-landing strip!

"Airspeed one-forty... one-thirty... one-twenty," Teach intoned.

Like a great wounded bird, the giant plane came in, skimming over the buildings, touching ground with a sudden shower of dirt and rocks. Propellers tore into the turf and bent under the strain. The twin nose wheels spun crazily. Out of the dust the plane gradually stopped skidding, until at last it lay there exhausted and motionless, with only the steady snarl of the putt-putt in the rear to disturb its silence.

Fearing fire, Major Askounis and his remaining crew quickly jumped out of the plane. But no fire developed. The last engine had run out of gas at the last moment. The Windy City had made a dead-stick landing.

TO THE MARIANAS

BEFORE DUSK ON JUNE 15, 1944, B-29s were roaring down their runways in China on their way to their first strike at Japan, Yawata. And 1,350 miles to the southeast, mighty American naval forces were sending barrage after barrage into Saipan even as the first assault forces moved toward the beaches and the strongly entrenched enemy.

And back in Washington eyes were focused on both operations. Eagerly awaiting the first reports of the action in the Mariana Islands was 41-year-old Brigadier General Haywood S. "Possum" Hansell, Chief of Staff of the Twentieth Air Force. For it had been Hansell who had first recommended the seizure of the Marianas as a B-29 base; a recommendation that higher authorities had accepted and were now, after months of work, acting on. In his drawer marked "top secret" were orders appointing him commander of the 21st Bomber Command, with headquarters in the Mariana Islands.

Hansell, like LeMay, had served in the European Theater as a wing commander. A brilliant leader, with a mind that worked like a fine watch, Hansell had been brought to Washington by General Arnold to become Air Planner for the Joint and Combined Chiefs of Staff, then Deputy Chief of Staff for the AAF. Later, General Arnold had named him Chief of Staff of the Twentieth Air Force; now "Possum" was again on his way to combat; a combat so new and daring that its very nature was top secret even to the handpicked crews who would participate.

The reasoning behind this secretiveness was simple. The operational problems of the long-range bomber program in the Marianas were believed insuperable by many important military men. Even the most confident and daring were awed by the thought of flying 1,500 miles over water (most of which was Jap-controlled) to reach a target, then returning over the same route to land on pinpoint islands in the middle of the vast Pacific. There was no other place to set down except on those few islands, so that a plane running into trouble over the target, or developing engine failure during any part of the flight, or running out of fuel, was almost certain to wind up in a watery grave. Should crews manage to survive the crash landings in the ocean, their chances of being picked up by friendly air-sea rescue units were remote.

Hansell knew the attitude of many flyers toward the still relatively new and untried B-29; India-China operations had shown the plane to be far from perfect mechanically. He was also aware of the low morale of the B-29 crews then flying the Hump; he knew that the long, overwater hops would be infinitely more dangerous, and that the planes which returned to their little island would have to land in patterns of air traffic that would never be allowed at commercial fields back in the States.

Early in 1944, when the decision had been reached to operate the long-range bomber program from the Marianas, the Army Air Forces was advised by Lieutenant General Robert C. Richardson, Jr., commander of the U.S. Forces in the Pacific Area, that the Marianas could be taken in a summer campaign. The General based his estimates on information gained in the Marshalls campaign; information which clearly pointed out the weak Jap defenses in that area.

However, little was known of the Marianas, despite the fact that Guam had been under the Navy's direction for four decades. Geographically the islands were a complete blank; checking and rechecking failed to turn up even an accurate contour map. Guam was known to be a typical tropical island, rising sharply from the sea; its southern half mountainous, the northern half topped by a thickly wooded plateau. It was in the northern half that the AAF hoped to be able to build a series of airfields. Tinian, located some 150 miles to the north, and Saipan, which sat just a few miles beyond Tinian, separated by a narrow channel, had been under Japanese control since World War I. Both islands were complete mysteries to the United States, but it was thought they could be converted into airfields. Several months before D-Day, the Navy obtained approximately one dozen aerial photos of the three islands. The photos were immediately rushed to Washington, and, with a sigh of relief, General Arnold and his planners saw that very long-range fields could be built. The pictures of Guam revealed the high, steep bluffs and the heavily wooded plateau. The engineers knew that underneath the wooded area would be a firm base upon which runways could be constructed. In Tinian the AAF would gain a real prize, for the island was quite flat and covered with cane fields.

The capture of Eniwetok in the Marshalls allowed B-24s to photograph all three islands almost daily, and from these photos engineers constructed scale models. Then, after elaborate calculations, the engineers expanded the models to include airfield sites and maintenance headquarters. To the Navy went the task of taking the islands, and at their request, of building the bases. The timetable was a rough one. Saipan fields were to be ready for operation in October, Guam in December and Tinian in February or March. Despite one of the bloodiest campaigns in the war, the fields were ready on schedule.

Marines and Army infantrymen landed on Saipan June 15, and a few hours later barges carried engineers to the bloody beachhead. The Japanese proved to be a tough foe, and it wasn't until July 10 that the "all secure" order was issued. By that time everyone in the Marianas—the Marines and the doughfeet as well as the engineers and the Seabees[26]—knew the B-29s were coming. Speed was the watchword as engineers worked day and night under enemy fire to build the giant runways for the Superforts.

While crews of the new 21st Bomber Command were training in Kansas in August, ground units, brought to Saipan by boat, were settling themselves in, rolling up their sleeves and starting to build the supply dumps and maintenance faculties for the B-29s to come. Headquarters personnel for the 73rd Bombardment Wing, which was to have the responsibility for combat operations from Saipan as well as the servicing of the B-29s on the island, landed on September 7; and on October 20 Brigadier General Emmett "Rosey" O'Donnell, Wing Commander, arrived. O'Donnell was another handpicked general assigned to the long-range bomber program. Just 36 years old, he was a brilliant airman who could work well in harness with his 41-year-old boss, "Possum" Hansell.

On October 12, 1944, eager Americans lined the runways of the Saipan airfield, alert as always to the dangers of Japanese snipers who were still active despite the "all secure" order. They spotted a small speck far in the distance. In a matter of minutes, the "Joltin' Josie" was circling the island, then came in for a perfect landing. And from the plane stepped General Hansell. The first B-29 had arrived! By October 26, 46 B-29s were parked at

---

[26] The Navy's Construction Battalions, or C.B.'s (hence, 'Seabees.').

Isley Field, and more were due at the rate of five per day until the full strength of 180 planes scheduled for the 73rd Wing was reached.

"Rosey" O'Donnell's wing arrived on Saipan in the middle of the rainy season. There were no tents, no mess halls, no latrines but plenty of mosquitoes and, shortly thereafter, Jap bombers. DDT licked the insects, and the bombing of Jap runways at Iwo Jima sometime later stopped the bombings.

Each of the groups in the 73rd Wing became its own construction battalion. General O'Donnell and his staff picked the site for wing headquarters, and the commanders of the 499th, 497th, 498th and 500th Groups, plus the three service groups—the 330th, 63rd and 91st—all spotted, cleared and built their camps. Staff officers, command pilots, medical officers, as well as cooks and bakers and tail gunners, worked as carpenters, road builders and ditch diggers in addition to their other duties.

Between October 28 and November 11, six training missions were flown at three-day intervals, against varied targets. Four missions hit at Dublon Island, in the Truk Atoll, where the Japanese had a submarine station, and two more were flown against the Japanese airfields on Iwo Jima. These raids were primarily training raids—to give crews experience in navigation, radar approach, cruise control, and night landings.

No planes were lost on these missions due to enemy action; but some were lost at sea, and generally the missions were unsuccessful. Bombing results were poor, formations were ragged, radar approach through bad weather was inaccurate. Yet the fault did not lie with the fliers themselves; it simply reflected their inadequate training. The 73rd Wing had been in existence less than eight months; the vast majority of its crew members were green and inexperienced, yet their job was to fly the largest, most complex aircraft in the world—and to pioneer new bombing techniques. The 58th Wing, which had been in operation in China and India since April, had learned many lessons through bitter experience, but these men were slow in arriving to help out the 73rd Wing; and when they did arrive, their technique was too often inapplicable because the two theaters raised entirely different problems.

The shakedown missions were only part of the preparation for bombing the Japan homeland from the island bases. At daybreak on November 1, the Superfortress "Tokyo Rose" (named after the Nipponese radio propagandist, whose stock in trade was a sexy voice and highly inflated reports of American losses) took off to snap the first reconnaissance photos of the Japanese capital. It was the second time during the war, and the first time since Jimmy Doolittle's carrier-based attack in April 1942, that an American plane had flown over Tokyo.

Captain Ralph Streakley kept his stripped-down B-29 over Tokyo for 35 minutes, filming an area which included the major industrial sites and the Emperor's palace, which was to be out of bounds when the bombs fell later. Jap fighters and antiaircraft fire menaced Streakley's ship but inflicted no damage.

The captain brought the Tokyo Rose home with only 30 minutes' flying time left in the fuel tanks and received the Distinguished Flying Cross for his hazardous mission. Streakley and his colleagues of the 3rd Photo Reconnaissance Squadron went out several times to photograph Tokyo. The film they brought back meant the combat crews would know what they were aiming at. They weren't sure they could hit it, but they at least knew it was there.

The flight of the Tokyo Rose over Tokyo brought a flurry of information from Japanese radio propagandists, including the plane's namesake. Calmness, coordination and faith in the emperor were emphasized, along with the erroneous report that several planes had appeared simultaneously, one of which had been shot down. Work on air-raid shelters increased rapidly.

Meanwhile the 73rd Wing was suffering from Japanese raids. Iwo Jima was only 750 miles away. Easy bombing range. And the enemy knew that the use of Saipan by B-29s was a pistol at the very head of the Japanese Empire: Tokyo. Consequently, their pilots braved every kind of opposition in fighter planes and antiaircraft fire to bomb the B-29s on Saipan. Many times, the raids were turned into slaughter by the fierce fire from air and ground alike. But too often the planes got through.

On some occasions, they would come sweeping down into Saipan's Isley Field at altitudes so low that radar was unable to detect them and give warning. Between October and January, the 73rd was bombed and strafed every moonlight night by Iwo-based enemy bombers, and in addition suffered from devastating low-altitude daylight raids. And these Japanese raids against the

Superforts were far more injurious to us than our raids were to them. Seventeen B-29s were lost or rendered unfit for combat. These planes were being produced at the rate of just two a day; they cost close to a million dollars and thousands of precious man hours and had been flown 10,000 miles to be in a position to hit against the enemy's homeland. And they were now useless burned-out hulks or relegated to mere cargo work.

With nothing determined in the way of tactics, with little known in the way of long-distance cruise control, and with practically nothing reliable in the way of weather information, the 73rd Wing had to be an experimenter and a pioneer. During November and December, it did pioneer, and learn, but at a high cost.

A major mission was flown against the Musashino Engine Factory, part of the Nakajima Aircraft Company, located a little north of the outskirts of Tokyo proper. For this mission on November 24, 111 planes were airborne; only 24 of them bombed the primary target, a performance record that had been repeated over and over again in the 20th Bomber Command, but new to the 73rd Wing General O'Donnell led the raid; "Possum" Hansell having been grounded by a new regulation forbidding commanding generals from flying over enemy territory.

During seven missions against important Japanese aircraft plants a total of 1,550 tons of bombs were carried by the Superforts of the 73rd Wing. Only 1.8 percent of these bombs hit within a 1,000-foot radius of the target; during 350 sorties on the Musashino Engine Plant in Tokyo there were just 34 effective bomb bursts within the plant itself.

Mechanical defects prevented 51 percent of the planes from bombing the primary target and caused 76 percent of the aborts, while personnel failures accounted for 22 percent of the planes missing the primary target. Most of these mechanical defects were in the Wright R-3350 engine which powered the B-29. The principal troubles were blown cylinders, defective valve push rods, broken valve springs, defective fuel pumps, and faulty fuel transfer systems. Not all the blame could be laid on the builder of the engine. It was still a very new engine: the mechanics, the pilots, and engineers were not yet accustomed to it and they were too often ignorant of how it should be handled for maximum performance. And the engine was being subjected to terrific strains.

It was pulling 70 tons through the air at over 200 miles an hour, for as much as 18 hours on end. It had to function at sea level and in the cold, rarefied air six miles up.

There were also assorted mechanical troubles with propellers, turbo-superchargers, bomb-bay doors, bomb racks, and bomb releases. The personnel failures resulted primarily from insufficient training. Navigators were not well orientated: checkpoints were almost unavailable; one piece of ocean looked just like another; islands had to be avoided for they were in Japanese hands; in the tropics the stars, by which so much navigation must be done, look a little different; errors meant using too much gasoline, so lost aircraft could not reach the primary target. The bombardiers and radar operators, undertrained back in the States, were unable to recognize the target through their scopes. Nothing but continuous practice and knowledge of the territory could correct this. The pilots and the flight engineers did not know the ins and outs of cruise control, which led to a waste of gasoline, and high-power settings, which tore up the engines.

But above and beyond these, a big factor in the poor bombing record was weather. In a December 3 raid against the Musashino plant, gales were raging over the target area at the unbelievable force of 230 miles per hour; nothing comparable to these gales had been encountered anywhere else in the world, and the crews were entirely unprepared for them. Planes flying downwind reached a ground speed of 500 miles per hour and more, which meant that green bombardiers and radar operators never had a chance even to focus the target Planes flying upwind were practically standing still. Bombing tables were useless; the bombs usually fell wide; or in the ocean.

In a report to General Harmon, Deputy Commander of the 20th Air Force, General Hansell wrote:

"Experience indicates that the most vital factor influencing every operational decision and the performance of every operational mission is the WEATHER."

Pilots and aircrews cursed "that damned bloody soup." For Japan, the weather, more than any of her man-made defenses, saved her from earlier, easier destruction.

Early in December, General Hansell ordered that three ships fly over Japan every night on weather observations. The 73rd

Wing supplied the planes and crews, and a volunteer weather observer went along. The planes were in no way equipped as special weather observations ships: they lacked many of the instruments that might have been valuable but carried a few bombs. There was a difference of opinion as to whether the principal mission of these ships was bombing and harassing or gathering full weather data.

If the morale of the men in India and China was low, the morale of the men of the 73rd Wing, only recently arrived from the training fields of Kansas and Colorado, was lower. They had no way of knowing the over-all picture. Their vision was limited to themselves, to their squadron, and to their group. In its first two months of operation, the 73rd Wing lost 51 crews. Every combat crew had seen friends go spinning down. In every Quonset hut, bunks were empty. Every supply sergeant had received blankets and pillows for reissue to new men. Every mail orderly was used to writing "Deceased, return to sender" on envelopes. That was the way it went in every theater, in every branch, but here it was the uselessness of their losses that broke the spirit of the men. They knew they were doing little damage to the enemy. They had seldom been able to see Japan, to look down and see plants blazing and smashed. They saw clouds, flak, fighters, foul weather, and an endless ocean that seemed to be hungry to swallow more and more B-29s and more and more men.

There was little or no relief on Saipan. Promotions had been delayed, then delayed some more. No rotation system had been set up, although it was rumored that crews would be sent home after completing 35 missions. At night, men gathered in small groups; their talk wandering aimlessly around the subject of home and rotation. Pencil stubs would appear, and each man would calculate for himself the chances of getting home. At the rate they were losing crews, not one of them would survive 35 missions. For the men stationed on Saipan at Christmas time, 1944, the air raids were about over. The Japanese runways at Iwo Jima had been destroyed; the angry Jap raid that struck Saipan on Christmas night was the last The Japanese could not fly from their home islands to Saipan and return. The B-29 could.

On that Christmas night, after thee all-clear sounded, one crew, interrupted in its festive get-together, drank a toast "To Tomorrow." But for the twelve, tomorrow never came.

On December 27, 1944, they took off from Saipan in their Superfortress, "Uncle Tom's Cabin." Piloted by Major John E. Krause, a rosy-cheeked youth from the Wisconsin dairy land, Uncle Tom's Cabin was the lead plane of the lower element of that day's formation and was beginning its bomb run on the Musashino Aircraft Company on the outskirts of Tokyo when the action opened.

A Jap single-engined fighter, one of thirty or more, dived on them at an estimated ground speed of 700 miles an hour. It missed the lead plane of the upper element by 100 feet. It missed another plane and rocketed into Krause's, its left-wing ramming into the right side of the Superfort Horrified, men in nearby bombers expected the giant to drop, but Krause brought it quickly back into control.

From the Superfort's cabin, broken open by the huge gash, padding and equipment went streaming out into the sky. A sheet of yellow flame spurted from the plane. As the wounded bomber poured out its return fire, Jap planes were falling and exploding, but whenever one fell, another roared in to take its place.

Jap machine-gun fire bit into the Superfort's No. 4 engine. Black oil and gray magnesium smoke began streaming from it. Still losing altitude and still knocking down enemy fighters, the bomber fought its way back to the right side, under the other Superforts on the bomb run. Then another Jap Tony crashed into the crippled plane. The enemy exploded and with him went the No. 3 engine, torn from its nacelle. The bomber staggered and shuddered, but Krause again gained control and brought it back on its bomb course.

Then came the third ramming; a Tony firing away at the Cabin's underside failed to pull away in time and drove straight into the plane's belly. The bomber broke into a spin, fighters following it down. At 500 feet Krause again got control, and his gunners made their ninth kill.

But the Cabin had flown its last. Still firing defiantly, it flew level for a moment; then its nose dipped, and it dived straight down into Tokyo Bay.

A New Year, An Old Story

While runways and buildings were being constructed in the Marianas, and the B-29s of the 73rd Bombardment Wing were arriving at Isley Field to take part in training missions and begin their attack on Japan, the 20th Bomber Command in India was still in business. Under the direction of General Curtis LeMay since August 29, 1944, the 20th continued to strike at the enemy from its bases in China and India.

General LeMay had arrived in India with plans for changes in both tactics and training. In Europe, he had used a twelve-plane bomber formation which he thought would work equally well in B-29 operations. He also wanted to place more emphasis on daylight precision bombing with both bombardier and radar operator working the bomb run; visibility over the target would determine who would do the bombing.

Precision bombing required more training than the crews of the Command had received. Lead crews were selected for intensive training, and all crews were given practice sessions which increased in frequency as the Superforts were gradually freed from the job of transporting supplies over the Hump.

It had been recognized from the beginning that supplying the bases in China was going to be a problem. But in 1943 when plans for the B-29 were made, China was the only base area available from which the planes could reach Japan. The hope that the 20th Bomber Command could operate as a self-sufficient unit capable of transporting all the supplies needed to support missions flown from China soon proved impossible and the Air Transport Command took over some of the Hump flying. Its share increased as time went on, and it became apparent that supply activities were cutting far too deeply into the combat effectiveness of the Superfort.

"Four missions a month—sometimes only two—were the best we could do out of Chengtu," reported LeMay shortly after he arrived in India. And this wasn't good enough for LeMay, who had earned his reputation as a tactical genius the hard way.

In the fall of 1942, he had led the 305th Bombardment Group to England, and with it proved the value of strategic precision bombing in daylight from high altitude. Rough as a cob, "Old Iron Pants" LeMay worked his crews as relentlessly as he worked himself. Day and night, they had been drilled in take-off and landing procedure, in formation flying, in pattern bombing, in navigation, in gunnery, in cruise control (fuel management). Even on the dullest training mission, not one crew member had been allowed to relax or to leave his assigned position. In combat this training paid off.

In September 1943, at the age of 36, LeMay was named Brigadier General, commanding the 3rd Bombardment Division, which became the most renowned in the Eighth Air Force. In March 1944, he became the youngest major general in the United States Army.

The waste of strategic air power involved in ferrying fuel for a mission was not the only problem confronting LeMay in India. Time after time strike photos showed that little damage had been done to the enemy. As the Japanese radio reported, "The Superforts are not able to achieve much of anything... An insignificant number of bombs and incendiary bombs unloaded on the capital fell mostly on the grounds of schools, homes, and hospitals."

This problem LeMay finally solved not with the planes and men of the 20th Bomber Command, but with his 21st Bomber Command. Flying from the more favorable base area of the Marianas, the 21st finally brought the war home to the Japanese in an unmistakable manner.

Although the 20th Bomber Command did not bring great destruction to Japan before the end of its operations from India in March of 1944, it did provide a most important combat test for the B-29. Developed and produced in record time as it was, the Superfort arrived in India with many weaknesses still to be corrected. The rugged flying conditions in the CBI provided the shakedown that was needed to make the complex bomber a smooth mechanism. Corrections and improvements worked out in India were put to good use in the Marianas.

The 21st Bomber Command profited from the 20th Bomber Command's experience with the Superfort in still another way. In flying from India and China, crews learned to appreciate the outstanding qualities of the B-29. They ceased to compare it unfavorably with the B-17 or the B-24 as time after time the Superforts made it back after a mission with battle damage that would have downed another plane. A feeling of confidence and affection gradually replaced the dislike and distrust of the early days in India. This, too, carried over to operations in the Marianas.

It had always been understood that as soon as more suitable bases were available from which to strike at Japan, Superfort operations would be shifted from the CBI. The transfer of General LeMay to the 21st Bomber Command at the end of January 1945, meant that the vital missions would be flown from the Marianas. The 20th Bomber Command had served its purpose; emphasis was now on the men and planes of the 21st.

When LeMay assumed command of the 21st on January 20, it had been under the direction of General Hansell for four months. During that time there had been training missions and then strikes at aircraft factories in Japan, strikes which had been costly in men and planes without doing much damage. So now LeMay, the specialist in strategic bombing, was replacing Hansell who had earned his reputation as a planner.

LeMay found operating conditions better in the Marianas than they had been in India, but he found many of the same problems: the weather was almost always bad; too many Superforts were failing to reach the target, and when they did, bombing was apt to be inaccurate. In typical LeMay fashion, the General had flown his own ship to Guam accompanied by a copilot and five staff officers, making only one stop for fuel en route. He arrived just in time to watch General Hansell receive the Distinguished Service Medal and then head for the United States.

With the coming of LeMay to the Marianas, a new cast of characters took over the direction of B-29 activities in the Pacific. Like their chief, the staff surrounding the General was composed of young men, battle tested in other theaters of war, and trained in strategic warfare. As Chief of Staff, 39-year-old Brigadier General August Kissner was well indoctrinated with the LeMay philosophy, having learned to fly with him at Kelly Field back in 1929, and also having served with him in England. Colonel James D. Garcia, the 31-year-old intelligence officer, had been with LeMay in China; he was to hold down the A-2 job in the Marianas until August 23, when he crashed to his death in a take-off from Guam. Deputy Chief of Staff for Operations was a 33-year-old Southerner, Colonel John B. Montgomery, who had been associated with "The Cigar" back in 1938, when they flew a B-17 600 miles out to sea to meet the liner REX in an early strategic exercise. Running Supply and Maintenance for the Command was Colonel C. S. Irvine, a tireless, rugged veteran of the First World War.

The effect of LeMay on the 21st Bomber Command was dynamic. The officers and men had heard many stories of the young general; they were eager to show him their own metal.

LeMay, in his shyness, seemed almost rude. He was a big, husky, healthy, full-faced man with jet black hair who was always clutching a cigar or pipe tightly between his teeth. Even in a small room he had difficulty in making himself heard, and staff members reported he would sit through a conference without once making a comment. But he soon made it clear that for the first few months of his stay, training was to be Number 1 on the agenda of every pilot and crew member in the Marianas. The bombing of Japan was a secondary mission that took place every four or five days. The number of planes used in the combat missions was reduced, the balance turned over to the training program. Every man in the command was soon well aware that something new had been added.

In spite of the increased training, the missions to Tokyo seemed to get tougher all the time. Stories of the raids were told for days afterward by the men who participated, and one of the best was the story of "A Square 52."

Superfort "A Square 52," piloted by heavy-set Lieutenant Lloyd Avery, came wheeling in toward the coast of Japan at 2 o'clock on the afternoon of January 27.

At the briefed altitude, 29,000 feet, the air over Japan was bright and frosty. Below, a winter snow lay over Tokyo's streets.

Inside the plane the crew was warm; they were flying pressurized over the target, and their oxygen masks hung loose, ready to be slapped on fast in an emergency.

It was their eighth mission to Japan; the last, as it turned out, that they would ever fly together.

Looking out from the blisters,[27] waist gunners Clarence O. Leach and Marvin E. Meyer could see other men from their 870th Squadron flying close formation behind Lieutenant Colonel

---

[27] Gun turret.

"Pappy" Haynes, Squadron CO. It was nice, Leach thought, to look out and see other planes; it gave a man a feeling of having a few friends around. Gunner Jim McHugh and radar operator Walter B. Klimczak chewed hard on their gum.

"Japan coast straight ahead," announced the navigator, Lieutenant John Faubion.

In the blisters, in the tail, in the turrets, the gunners squinted anxiously through their Plexiglas, searching their area of sky.

"There they are ... at three o'clock high. God, about forty of 'em!"

Coming into the coast every man aboard A Square 52 could see the enemy waiting, ready to pounce.

"They're alerted for us! Those two weather ships ahead of us must have brought 'em up!"

"This ain't our, day, Lloyd!"

"I'm ready to go home right now, Mother dear!"

Over the coastline now, the fight began. Forty enemy fighters piled into this first flight of 12 B-29s—from above, from in front, from the sides, from the tail.

Gunners screamed over the interphones for turrets ...

"Eight from two o'clock above!"

"I got four barreling in here!"

The Japs came plunging like madmen through the formation.

"Seemed like they were all hopped up," said McHugh. "Some of those 40 planes blew up smack in the faces of the rest of the Japs. But the sight of wings falling off, of planes going down smoking, spinning, blowing up, and disintegrating into a million pieces didn't frighten off the rest of those mad devils. They came diving in like crazy, pumping tracers and 20-mm. at everything in sight. They must have been crazy to stand it."

Six miles up in thin, subfreezing air, the Superforts plowed through havoc toward their target—the Musashino Aircraft Engine Plant, Tokyo.

"God almighty, how much longer to the damned target?"

"Three minutes and we'll be on the bomb run."

"Roger... You ready down there with the sight, Gage?"

"Roger!"

Without a break to reform, the Japs attacked again. Six from the tail and six more from 12 o'clock peeled off and attacked from above and in front

"Give me your turret, Mac..."

"Hell, no—the whole damn Jap air force is over here. I need three more besides."

McHugh swung his upper turret, let fly with his four synchronized .50's at the attackers from 12 o'clock. One Tojo plunged through. McHugh's tracers riddled him, but still he didn't stop. At 400 miles per hour he plummeted in at the Superfort—and crash! The Tojo rammed A Square 52, smashing into the left wing, tearing great hunks of the No. 1 engine nacelle out of the flap, shearing off half the left aileron.

A Square 52's metal frame shivered through every one of her 100 feet as she recovered and headed on into her bombing run.

The Tojo spun down out of control and at 25,000 feet blew up. The collision had torn off its entire left wing.

Despite the impact of the suicide dive, despite scores of fighter attacks, bombardier C. R. Gage never budged from his sight. Way forward—hunched over his apparatus—Gage was a little man in a glass house. The roof of his compartment was glass, the wall and the floor glass. Every Jap fighter pilot in the sky could see him, hunched over his sight.

Gage touched a switch, then called out, "Bomb-bay doors open."

The giant plane settled on its run, continued into the target like a walker on a tightrope. She had to sit straight and level, on course. There could be no evasive action. This was the easiest time of all for enemy fighters and enemy ack-ack.

Bright, vicious tracers flashed past Gage's greenhouse. Ugly bursts of flak rocked 70 tons of American airplane and bombs and men.

Intent, absorbed, Gage read his sight, delicately twisted the knobs, concentrated on the crosshairs, whispered steadily into his throat mike. Deliberately his hand reached out; forefinger and thumb closed over a toggle switch.

"Bombs away! ... Bomb-bay doors closed! ... Free to turn! And for God's sake turn fast!"

The bombing was done. Twelve 500-pounders arched and tumbled on their way down to the Musashino Aircraft Engine Plant.

His bombs away, Gage jumped back to his guns, and in two quick, short bursts, blasted the canopy off an incoming Zeke, killing the pilot. Amidship, Jim McHugh threw his four .50s onto another Zeke, attacking from above, and shattered him. Another confirmed kill.

Alone and isolated in the tail, many feet away from Gage, Avery, and the others, sat tail gunner Charles D. Mulligan. He'd been having a busy time alone back there, fighting off the attackers from the vulnerable tail of A Square 52. Mulligan had chalked up three certain kills between 2 and 2:20 o'clock.

But still the Nips came diving in at Mulligan, plunging through his fire to within a few feet and then pulling wildly away. Now, right above him, flew one persistent devil. Mulligan's guns were tracking him, waiting for the moment to kill—waiting to catch the unprotected belly, loaded with gasoline. In a tight chandelle, the Jap turned in for another attack... at 30 yards Mulligan let fly with everything he had. The Jap never stopped. He tore smack into the tail, smashing his plane to pieces on the giant fin, then plunged on down to death.

And he almost took A Square 52 with him. His suicide dive tore off the left stabilizer and the whole left side of the tail.

"There was a terrific crash," Pilot Avery wrote in his diary. "The nose dropped down violently and we went into a sudden dive. I pulled back hard on the control column and kicked the rudders. All the control cables seemed to be broken, because I could get no effect—the plane persisted in her nosedive. I called to Gage, the bombardier, to open the bomb-bay doors so that we could bail out, and started to check my parachute. I found I wasn't wearing one. Back during the formation climb, I had forgotten to strap it on. Fox, my copilot, was on the controls with me. He thought he was just helping me out with his extra strength. But as it turned out he was actually flying the plane alone.

"When Bob Watson, our engineer, went back later on to examine the damage he found that every control cable except one had been destroyed. We had just one thin strand of cable left, to the elevators—and that belonged to Fox. The impact had destroyed the entire left stabilizer, and ripped open the entire left side of the tail section.

"We dived, out of control, 9,000 feet. Nobody expected to get out of it alive. But Fox, using every ounce of his strength, managed to level the ship out at around 20,000 feet. It is a miracle that our meager control cable didn't snap. If it had, we would have died—in Japan."

Eager Jap planes closed in on the cripple, but the gunners were on the job. Sergeant Marvin E. Meyer, right blister gunner, shot down a Tony and a Tojo. Sergeant Clarence O. Leach, left blister, shot down a Tojo and an Oscar, Three of these four blew up; one went down in a flaming spin. Gunner McHugh accounted for four enemy planes; tail gunner Mulligan had shot down three, in addition to the one which rammed him; and Gage, the bombardier, had accounted for one. Their total kill: 14 enemy planes.

Off the coast, Avery let down to 17,000 feet and depressurized. Mulligan couldn't be raised over the interphone; no one knew whether he was dead, whether he had been thrown out of the wrecked tail section, or whether he was somehow alive and the interphone system was out And no one could just look back and see because the pressure door to the tail was closed.

It was thirty minutes after the second ramming before Leach and Meyer could make their way aft to Mulligan to see if he were in trouble. Mulligan was—in the worst way. Bleeding and unconscious, his head between his knees, he crouched in the wrecked tail section. Twisted metal, broken guns, smashed equipment and splintered glass were piled on top of him. Only this debris, which pinned him to the floor, had prevented him from falling out of the gaping hole.

First the heavy door had to be torn off. Using all their strength and their long jungle knives, they managed to pry the door open and climb through. Leach took off his own oxygen mask and fed Mulligan full rich oxygen from a walk-around bottle. This revived him for a moment Then, ready to pass out himself from the heavy work and his own lack of oxygen, Leach retreated. As Meyer went back to help, Leach sat down and relayed over the interphone the news of Mulligan and the terrible damage.

Working in shifts, with additional help from Gage and McHugh, Leach and Meyer took more than half an hour to rescue

Mulligan. The temperature was minus 27° C.; the gale was terrific. With the draft and slip stream of the engines pounding directly in upon them, they had to work in clumsy clothing and gloves. They cut away and threw out Mulligan's helmet, parachute, harness, flak suit, web belt, canteen and guns. Finally, they cleared enough room to pull out the body of their tail gunner.

Up front the pilots were having trouble. They had a wrecked plane on their hands and 1,500 miles of ocean ahead of them. In the tail the load was heavy; four men working and moving around threw the ship off balance; and there remained scarcely more than a strand of cable to control the plane.

In the radar compartment navigator John Faubion and radio operator Lewis Heliums were giving first aid to Klimczak, who had been shot through the leg, back and arm. He was bleeding profusely, and the small dark compartment was crowded with more wreckage. The wool-like powdered glass that acted as insulation coated their hands, faces, and tools, yet they administered gently and skillfully to their crewmate. They gave him morphine, they stripped off his clothes and sprinkled his wounds with sulfanilamide, fed him full rich oxygen, and wrapped him carefully in blankets in order to keep his body warm and prevent shock. They ripped open the emergency medical kits, and over Tokyo Bay Heliums thrust a needle deep into Klimczak's forearm and poured plasma into the wounded man's fast-collapsing veins.

With Klimczak's wounds dressed, "Doc" Heliums and the others went to work on Mulligan, whom Gage, McHugh, Leach and Meyer had scarcely been able to haul into the warmth and protection of the already crowded radar room. At first it was impossible to get at his wounds; due to the extreme cold in the exposed tail, all his clothes had frozen stiff and were covered with ice. Using their jungle knives again, they finally cut off his clothes. Because all their blankets had been used on Klimczak, the men wrapped up the tail gunner in their own clothing.

Mulligan's hand had been shot through; he was covered with deep gashes from the splintering glass and metal. These wounds they dressed. It was difficult work because the sudden warmth of the radar room had caused the formerly frozen wounds to bleed profusely.

The floor was slippery now with the mingled blood of Klimczak and Mulligan, and it was difficult to stand. Mulligan was given two units of blood plasma, and all the crew except the two pilots and the navigator went off oxygen so that the wounded men might have it continuously.

When all that could be done for the wounded had been done, Watson, the engineer, went through the plane to survey the damage. His report wasn't encouraging. No repairs would be possible in the air, he said. There was just one thin and unreliable control cable to the elevators; half the left flap and half the left aileron were gone. The entire left stabilizer was gone; the entire left-hand side of the tail compartment was gone; the No. 2 engine nacelle was damaged and in danger of catching fire; all the radio and radar equipment had been destroyed with the exception of the pilot's high frequency radio; the drift-meter was gone; the flux gate compass was gone; and finally 400 gallons of gasoline had been lost through the damage to No. 1 engine. In addition, two crew members were seriously injured. Chances of making a successful 1,500-mile over water flight in bad weather and in darkness were slim.

Each man knew that. There was nothing to do, except hope and fly.

Faubion checked his courses over and over again. Avery and Fox flew gently, carefully, knowing there was just a thin, half-broken control cable to keep them in the air. Engineer Watson nursed his engines, hoarded his small store of precious gasoline. McHugh, Gage, Leach, Meyer, and Heliums—there was nothing to do, nothing except silently pray—listened to the rough, uneven breathing of the wounded, waited for the first coughs of a failing engine.

The black night hours dragged by. The men were afraid to talk. They didn't want to think.

Avery, up front, was glad he hadn't gone lower than 17,000 feet when he left Japan. They needed every foot of that altitude. Below them weather was bad with rough rain clouds, which would throw the plane around. And he had just that one torn cable—any extra strain might snap it. Through the night they ploughed on, counting off the slow minutes and the endless miles.

Then, suddenly, somehow, they were only minutes away from Saipan. Now the letdown. It would be rough, but to bail his crew out over the island, and let the plane crash into the sea, was impossible. Aboard were two wounded crew men who couldn't bail out. A landing had to be made. Now started the "Prayer to the Tower."

Time and time again, every few moments, Avery called Saipan Tower: "Blue grass. A Square 52 calling Bluegrass. I have wounded aboard and am in distress. Request permission to make an emergency straight-in approach. Over."

Avery heard nothing but the static in his earphones. Again, and again he sent out his prayer to the tower: "Wounded aboard—am in distress—request emergency straight-in approach."

And never an answer.

A Square 52 flew on, closer and closer to Saipan. Gas was low; every gauge was registering empty. The pumps were sucking up the last quarts and pints that swished on the bottom of the vast tanks. Without permission for an emergency straight-in approach, Avery would have to make a night landing on nearby Kobler Field—on a runway new to him. With his plane in such bad shape and gas so low, the idea of attempting a crash-landing at night on a strange field frightened him more than anything else on the entire flight.

One more time before breaking off his approach, Avery called, "...wounded aboard, request emergency straight-in approach..."

At the very last moment the tower came through:

"A Square 52, this is Bluegrass. You have permission to land. You are cleared Number One for an emergency straight-in approach. Ambulances and fire trucks are waiting. You are clear to land. Over and out"

It was up to Fox. He alone had controls left. In the darkness he cut down between two other B-29s in the traffic pattern. Approaching the field, power suddenly failed him; the giant ship slouched, fell off, sank below the level of the cliffs. Fox hit the throttles full forward to maximum power, strained the last elevator cable to the breaking point, lunged back on the stick, and somehow lifted the torn ship up and over the cliff. Then he nosed down and in.

A Square 52 hit the runway with dead engines, the last ounce of gasoline drained. She hit nose wheel first at 180 miles per hour instead of the usual 100. The nose wheel folded up—crashing through the fuselage and into the cockpit. The props chewed into the coral. The ship shook and split in two. Avery was knocked cold, his head slamming into the instrument panel. Aft, Meyer, Leach, Heliums, and McHugh packed their bodies solid around the wounded men for protection. The impact of the crash-landing bruised and cut them. Fire started in No. 1 engine. McHugh and Meyer thought she would burn and grabbed Mulligan, pulling him from underneath the clothing piled about him. Still delirious, Mulligan fought furiously as they dragged him stark naked out of the plane and across the runway to safety.

Klimczak was left inside, too sick to be moved. To reach him a hole was cut through the fuselage and a stretcher passed up to first-aid men who gently loaded him onto the litter and carried him out.

From the runway, McHugh and Meyer looked back at the wreckage. A Square 52 did not burn; there was too little gasoline left in her. But she had fallen apart; her entire tail section had broken off and was lying at a 90-degree angle to the nose. How she had brought them home, God alone knew.

But once again bombing results were poor, and once again the list of the men who didn't get back was a long one. Radios in the United States reported: "Last night Marianas-based Superforts blasted again at the heart of Japan when they bombed Tokyo in force. Superfortress gunners, in one of the greatest air battles of the war, shot more than 60 enemy planes out of their own sky."

Few paid any attention to the tag line: "Eight of our Superforts are missing ..."

Rescue at Sea

During the latter part of January and through February 1945, General LeMay continued his policy of training, training, and then training some more, with combat missions still the secondary objective.

"That guy's a pistol," said one young pilot after a long overwater training session. "He keeps us out day and night learning to fly these damn airplanes, then we go up to Japan, and we're lucky if we get back, practice or no."

The B-29 force in the Pacific was still woefully weak. Plans had called for a force of more than one thousand Superforts in the Marianas alone, but by the end of February there were exactly 360 planes in operation. And this number was constantly in danger. It took some 7,650 gallons of gas for one of the planes to make the 15-hour round trip to Japan, and unless the crew paid absolute attention to the power settings ordered by the operations officer, they were more than likely to wind up "somewhere in the Pacific."

Ditching was the fear of every combat crewman. An air-sea rescue operation begun in time was often successful in picking up crews forced down at sea; but more than a hundred million dollars' worth of airplanes, and hundreds of airmen lie scattered along the bottom of the ocean between Saipan and the coast of Japan; men and planes of the 21st Bomber Command who ditched and were never heard from again.

"The mission of the 21st Bomber Command involves distances hitherto unencountered in combat aviation," said General LeMay in discussing this problem. "From bases in the Marianas, B-29s of this command traverse 3,000 miles of ocean to attack targets on Honshu. Under the circumstances, it is inevitable that some planes are lost at sea. The objective of air sea rescue is to assure that as many men from these planes get back as is humanly possible..."

Through the chain of command that ran from the spacious Washington offices of the Twentieth Air Force to the tiny, kerosene-lighted tent of Harold Brownlee, Corporal, Air-Sea Rescue, Pacific Ocean area, human life was regarded as the most precious commodity in the Army Air Forces. No expense of manpower, of planes, of gasoline was spared in the attempt to bring back the crews who went down at sea.

An Air-Sea Rescue Task Group was established and equipped with Air Force bombers. Navy patrol planes, submarines, and destroyers, known as superdumbos, air dumbos, lifeguards and sea dumbos. Before every mission this agency was notified, and along the route to Japan, even into Tokyo Bay, were posted planes, destroyers and submarines.

Why, despite these precautions, was the Pacific Ocean strewn with the corpses of ditched Superforts and their crews?

Principally because the search area for a ditched plane might cover 150,000 square miles; and a B-29 was just 99.9 feet long and 141.3 feet wide in wing spread, and a life raft was 8 feet long, 3 feet wide.

Theoretically, if a B-29 was able to give an accurate report on its position before ditching, the crew could have been rescued in a matter of hours. Actually, when for any one of many reasons the position of a downed ship did not reach home base, the invariable result was a terse announcement: "Down at sea. Crew presumed dead." However, air-sea rescue facilities did save 596 air crewmen from 83 B-29s that crashed or were ditched during nine months of combat.

One of the most successful of these operations took place after the rough February 10th mission against Ota. The "Deacon's Delight," piloted by Lieutenant John J. Halloran, was coming home on two engines. With No. 1 and No. 3 engines shot out over the target by enemy fighters, with a fire in the radar room, the crew knew they would have to ditch. As soon as they had cleared the coast of the Japanese Empire and shaken off the last fighter attack, Sergeant Sol Serkin, the radio operator, pounded out a flash message to Wing Mission Control on Tinian. "Two engines out... airspeed down to 150 mph ... position on routine course home, 50 miles south of Japan."

Master Sergeant Samuel L. Burch, the flight engineer, had a frantic time transferring fuel from the No. 1 and 3 tanks back into the center tanks and out again to the wing tanks.

Navigator Paul M. Shuford was up against the toughest problem he had ever faced. He had no Loran set, no radio compass, no radar. Every mechanical aid to navigation had been destroyed;

only Shuford's brain, judgment and pencil could get them home. Five hours after they had started back, he felt sure they were still on course.

At 10:45 P.M., Pilot Halloran switched on his emergency signaling equipment. For half an hour every gas gauge in the plane had been registering empty. At his fuel pumps, Sam Burch sucked-up the last pints of high octane and fed them to his dying engines.

Then out of the night, shining vertically up from the black ocean, came a powerful beam of light—just two miles west of the floundering Deacon's Delight. His heart pounding with hope, Halloran leaned into control surfaces and pulled the Superfort over to investigate.

Below, the radar man aboard an air-sea rescue ship had picked up the emergency signals, and the captain immediately ordered his searchlights to be beamed up into the sky. The chances that the B-29 would be close enough to see this beam were minute, but they paid off.

Halloran yelled to his crew to take ditching positions, braced himself, shoved his flaps down, and eased the Deacon into the ocean at 90 miles per hour, just 100 yards off the starboard bow of the rescue ship, the Bering Sea.

Within five minutes his entire crew had been hauled aboard. Still the Deacon floated, her back unbroken. To save other planes from investigating her, the Superfort had to be sunk. The gunners aboard the Bering Sea pumped 400 rounds of 20mm. and 40-mm. into her, but still the Deacon refused to die. Twice the Bering Sea rammed the Superfort before she went down.

Halloran called Air-Sea Rescue "the finest taxi service in the world. Just waiting at the station when you want them..."

Eight crewmen from another B-29 had to wait three days to be rescued, three days of pitching and tossing in a yellow life raft.

Their Superfort had left Saipan early in the morning on February 27 for a routine daylight flight over an island south of Japan. They were supposed to take some pictures, drop their bombs, mosey up toward Japan to see what was cooking, and then head back home.

It was the 18th mission for Captain Edward A. Everts, a weather officer with the 21st Bomber Command; it was also supposed to be his last one. Although he didn't know it, orders were already en route from Oahu for him to report back to the States to attend Command and General Staff School at Fort Leavenworth.

"Everything started off that day in good shape," Captain Everts said. "We made the trip in scheduled time and arrived over the target at noon. We got our pictures and bombed from about 30,000 feet. No interference, no flak, everything fine. But just then the No. 3 engine began throwing oil. We canceled the rest of the trip and headed back for base. The engine kept getting worse, so our pilot, Lieutenant Charles D. Brodie, decided to feather the prop. Well, the damned thing wouldn't feather. It started to windmill instead and was soon turning at a terrific rate. It was only a question of time until the prop would melt off. Then the No. 2 engine also started throwing oil. We succeeded in feathering that, and then we started to sweat it out.

"We were down to 5, 500 feet still plugging along some 350 miles from base when everything went haywire at once. The No. 3 prop finally let go with terrific force, the shattered blade slicing back and laying open the whole right side of the plane. At the same time, the blade cut all the right control cables which caused the bomb-bay doors to open. Lieutenant Brodie had no control whatever. The copilot, Lieutenant Francis J. Marshall, who held down the right seat up front, fought the big plane for a few seconds and found he had very limited control. He gave her full left rudder and she still yawed to the right, so he cut out the No. 1 engine to even out the pull... We were going down like a barrel of stove bolts, but we were on even keel thanks to that No. 4 engine. Of course, the bomb-bay doors were open which complicated things. To my knowledge, ours was the first B-29 ever to ditch successfully with the bomb-bay doors open.

"There was no time to get set for ditching. The navigator, Lieutenant R. F. Nielsen, dashed by me and smashed out the astrodome, then stopped to pick up two extra clips of cartridges for his .45. That slowed us up a little on our way to our ditching stations. I was not even braced for the shock... I was standing behind the turret when we hit, and the impact bounced my head against it a couple of times like a bell clapper, breaking my glasses. That left me half-blinded and dazed all at once. It was a beautiful ditch job considering the shape we were in, and the crash wasn't half as bad as I dreaded.

"The plane broke into three pieces with the impact. The nose snapped off just aft of the pilot's compartment, dove 20 feet under the sea and then bobbed up again just long enough to let them out. The aft section broke behind the wings, floated for a few minutes and then sank. The center section and wings stayed afloat for a couple of hours, which probably saved our lives.

"We ditched according to procedure for our section of the plane. The navigator, Lieutenant Nielsen, went out the astrodome first. Right on his heels was Major Hugh Mahoney, group navigator, who had come along for the ride. Then myself and finally the radio operator, Sergeant Niemann. The two seven-man rafts worked automatically when we hit. One of them inflated right away. Major Mahoney climbed aboard while we struggled with the second raft which was only a quarter inflated. We were fouling up the good raft, so the Major cut the line to give us room to work, but that was a mistake. The raft took off like a goosed antelope with Major Mahoney aboard all by his lonesome. He and the rest of us hollered and waved our arms, but the current and the waves were too much, and in five minutes he was out of sight leaving the rest of us battling with the remaining raft.

"With the breakup, the aft section of the plane hadn't drifted as fast as the wing section. The four men back there all got out after the crash, I think, but the current was taking us too fast and they couldn't catch up. They drowned trying to reach the raft. It was all confused. We were banged up and dazed and fighting the water and didn't know what was going on. The automatic inflation valve had fouled up. We finally got the hand pump going but didn't make any progress until we thought of dragging the raft up on the plane to inflate it. That worked, but it also tore a rip in the bottom and punctured two small holes in the side. We had to pump her up every hour from then on."

Aboard the seven-man raft, the eight survivors took stock. They had hit the water at 5:15, still more than 300 miles from home. It was now dusk. Sergeant Billie Aycock, who had gotten a bad crack on the head when the Superfort hit the water, was only half conscious. The bombardier had a ragged gash on the side of his face which wasn't pretty, and most of the rest were banged up somewhat, although none suffered serious injuries. The raft had standard equipment, but it carried no shark repellent,[28] nor did it have a Gibson girl radio.[29] They had been in constant touch with the base on the trip back, however, so their position was known; the planes would be out looking for them as soon as it was fight. They had rations for 15 days, but they decided not to eat or drink for at least 36 hours anyway, just in case.

With the coming of darkness, the sharks appeared. Two of them. And from then on there were always sharks following them, sometimes as many as five. The men set up watches to prevent the raft from capsizing during the night, but no one really slept. When they managed to doze off, they would waken as they slid beneath the water that half-filled the raft. As they huddled together, they made bitter jokes about the procurement officer who had managed to pile seven midgets on each other's shoulders in a raft in some Wright Field swimming pool and then announced: "See! It holds seven men! We'll call it a seven-man raft." This one was holding eight full-size men in a space not much bigger than a double bed.

Captain Everts continued the story: "At dawn, we tried to get set for a long haul. We had one sea anchor out and put out a small pilot chute to balance it. The sharks moved in slowly, looked it over, and then slashed it to bits. That was when we decided not to bother trying to catch any fish. We figured we were heading southwest toward the Philippines, but it turned out we were in the equatorial current that sweeps northeast past the Philippines, joins the Japanese Current off Formosa, swings up past Japan and toward the Aleutians.

"Quite a current, too. We were averaging five knots an hour with the sea anchor out and a half-filled boat to slow us down. If we had known where we were heading, we'd really have done

---

[28] World War 2 saw the first use of shark repellant, a necessity borne from the phenomenon of carrier-to-carrier based aerial combat, and the resultant need to protect downed aviators afloat in the Pacific. Scientists discovered that the odor of a dead shark worked best to deter predators, and created a repellant based on the active chemicals found in a dead shark's body. Today, a more sophisticated formula functions as an irritant to the shark's gills.

[29] A survival radio; nicknamed a 'Gibson Girl' for its hourglass shape. Early 20th Century artist Charles Dana Gibson created sketches of modern, buxom American women for *Life* magazine and other publications.

some sweating. As we reconstructed it afterwards, we were barreling along straight to Formosa and would have hit it in five more days. Apparently, we did pass close to Parece Vela,[30] a tiny Jap-held rock all by itself.

"It was about 9 o'clock that first morning that we saw a plane—a B-29 heading into Saipan. We didn't have our rockets out or our sea dye handy, so she went by without noticing us. But we certainly got everything in shape for the next one to come by. But none did until the following morning at 9 A.M., when we saw a Navy dumbo cruising in patterns. It was a PB4Y1. It had been 36 hours since we ditched and we were having our first nourishment, some Charms candy and a gulp of water, when he showed up. The dumbo circled us for 45 minutes, dropping flares and sea markers to aid other search ships and then took off on her regular search sector. The sea was running in 15-20-foot swells then, and it was out of the question for the dumbo to try a landing. She couldn't have handled eight more men anyway.

"We loved that ship. That is our favorite airplane. We swore to look up those guys and beg, borrow or steal some liquor to give them. We still owe them all the drinks they can handle anytime they want to collect. We knew they had sent our position and figured a destroyer was probably on the way to pick us up, so we started to work our arithmetic overtime, trying to estimate how long it would take a ship to reach us from the Marianas. We didn't realize that all the shipping in the neighborhood was busy just then in support of the Iwo invasion, and that they would have to send one down from the Palaus. So, every time the appointed hour passed without a ship appearing, we'd start refiguring, trying to give plenty of leeway, and that hour would come—and no ship—and we would figure it over again.

"We'd been worrying over Mahoney and trying to figure out where he was. If we could reach him and transfer some of us into his raft, there'd be more room. We figured he must be 30 to 50 miles ahead of us on the same track, so on the second day we hoisted a sail to try to catch up. The sail was hard to handle, though, so we gave up after an hour or so. We never did see him,

---

[30] Okinotorishima, a coral atoll, was given the name Parece Vela by the Spanish. The name means 'resembling a sail,' in reference to the geological shape of the islet.

but that second night we saw a plane circling far ahead of us, dropping flares, and we figured that must be Mahoney they'd found. Anyway, we had several planes over us by then. Late the second day, we had three B-29s and two Navy dumbos overhead at once. They dropped extra boats and rations, but they were downwind, and we missed them. Then they dropped one upwind and we latched onto it, finally transferring four of us into the extra boat. We celebrated by eating D-rations and more candy.

"The third day, March 2, was an empty one until noon when a B-29 and a dumbo showed up to circle the rafts for hours. Finally, at five o'clock, a destroyer swirled into view, just 72 hours after the ditching. Sailors swarmed down rope ladders and helped us climb aboard.

"We stood on the deck dripping, hardly able to believe we were safe. They asked us what we wanted. We thought it over—a shot of whiskey, coffee, water or steaks—and simultaneously came out with the same desire—hot soup. It tasted like a twelve-course dinner. Then they bathed us, dressed our immersion sores with some salve, and gave us all injections of plasma to counteract shock. Those bunks felt wonderful, dry and clean, and long enough to stretch out.

"The Doc sewed up Hoyt's face gash and also treated Aycock, who was given 1,500 cc. of plasma in all before he was through. The whole crew treated us like kings. When they told us we were about 700 miles from our base, we nearly fainted. We had drifted 350 miles in three days. They also told us of the magnitude of the search which had involved more than a dozen Army and Navy planes including carrier planes and a number of ships. They were really all out to find us."

The survivors spent seven days on a hospital ship recovering, and then they were flown back to the Marianas. They arrived too late to see Major Mahoney, who had spent five long days in his raft before being rescued. That raft had drifted well within fighter range of Formosa before a Navy Martin patrol bomber spotted him, landed in heavy seas, and flew Mahoney back to the Marianas.

Another B-29 crewman, Technical Sergeant Jack B. Cannon, a central fire-control operator, was successfully pulled from the sea after he had drifted even closer to enemy territory. For six hours he had sat helplessly in his life raft within sight of the

Japanese mainland, the object of a pitched battle between a Navy submarine and two Superdumbos on one side and seven Japanese fighter planes and eight of their surface vessels on the other.

The Americans won. Four of the Japanese boats were sunk, and two others were damaged; one of the Japanese planes was shot down, two more were damaged, and the rest were driven away. Cannon was rescued, and so were six other B-29 crewmen whose plane had gone down nearby.

Cannon's adventure began when his B-29, the "Salvo Sally," took off to bomb Miyazaki airfield near the southern tip of Kyushu. Miyazaki was one of the main Japanese airbases sending planes against the fleet off Okinawa.

According to Cannon, "It was our 22nd mission and everything went fine as we swung into the bomb run. A few bursts of flak were visible about four miles away and everything was quiet. We dumped our load and closed our bomb-bay doors and then it happened. I thought I'd never see St. Joe, Missouri, again. We got a direct flak hit somewhere in the back, severing some control cables. Another direct hit tore through the front compartment, making a huge hole. Then a burst hit us between No. 3 and No. 4 engines. No. 3 caught fire and began windmilling like crazy, and No. 4 was feathered right away.

"We fell away from the formation and started down like an anvil, but the pilot finally got control. He sounded calm on the interphone. We asked if we should bail out and he said, 'Hell, no, everything's going to be all right. Ride her down and prepare to ditch.' He headed her for the coast. I sat tight until the flames swept back and my blister began to melt. Then I went to the waist. One of the men was hanging out the hatch by his hands, pleading for permission to jump. We pulled him back in and again asked the pilot whether we should bail out. He said to stick with the ship, so I went back to get some rations and water and other gear stowed there. When I got back, the men were bailing; the pilot gave them the okay when he started to lose control.

I hung on for a couple of minutes while we went lower and lower, and I could see fleets of sampans flashing past underneath as we cleared the coast. Then I went out, the last one to jump. We were about 500 feet up then. I pulled the ripcord, and nothing happened. The tail of the plane passed overhead, and I pulled again, and this time, it opened. Almost at the same second, it seemed, I hit the water."

In the shock of hitting the water, Cannon lost his gun, his signal mirror, canteen of water and the rations he had crammed in his jacket before he jumped. All he had was his Mae West and a one-man dinghy. After some trouble, he inflated the dinghy and climbed aboard. He bailed most of the water from the craft and settled down to wait after a few fruitless shouts to see if any other crew members were nearby. It was mid-morning when he hit. He passed the afternoon trying to dry out in the sun. At dusk, he began to doze in fitful snatches. At dawn, he saw the mountains of Japan.

Cannon explained, "I must have landed just inside the main Japanese Current that sweeps north up the coast. That saved me. If I had hit any nearer land, I'd have been in the onshore current and would have drifted right into the beach. I think that's what may have happened to some of the other men who bailed before I did but weren't seen again. As it was, I was heading inshore gradually anyway, and soon was only a few miles away.

"I began to paddle as hard as I could trying to quarter across the current and get away from land, but I barely held my own. Then at 9 A.M., I saw a big Superfort circling nearby. I waved my life jacket frantically, and he swooped in to drop me a lot of rations, some sea-marker dye and mirrors. Then all of a sudden, he headed off like a bat out of hell. Shortly afterward, I saw a single fighter, very high, and I crouched down in the raft. Then I heard a lot of gunfire and some bombs, and I figured a battle was on. I also thought the Japs were strafing the other guys' life rafts. I was plenty scared."

What had happened was that the crew of the Superdumbo spotted eight Japanese sailing vessels almost as soon as they had made the tell-tale drop to Sergeant Cannon. His position had been radioed to a Navy sub, but it seemed inevitable that the Japs would find him first. So, the Superdumbo went after the boats, strafing them at mast height until four were sunk and the other four headed back toward land. It then flew off to search for survivors from another B-29 that had ditched somewhere nearby.

A second Superdumbo was circling the Navy sub approaching the scene. Behind the big plane, invisible in the sun, came a Paul, a single-engine floatplane, which flashed across the deck of the sub to drop two bombs, both misses. The Superfort turned on the fighter and at first overshot the slower plane; then it turned and closed until the planes almost collided. A burst from the Fort's right gun sent the Jap down in flames. The B-29 hurried back to the sub in time to drive away a second Paul. Then five fighters attacked in succession but were driven away. The sub plowed on toward Cannon's raft.

To Cannon the approaching sub looked like a Japanese patrol boat. He was sure no U.S. ship would dare come that close to the mainland of Japan, so he took the blue blanket from the emergency kit and tried to cover the life raft so that it couldn't be seen.

Cannon later said, "I almost succeeded in not being rescued. My camouflage job fooled them for a while and they made a couple of wrong turns, but then they spotted me and came charging down on me. Just about that point I could see their uniforms and faces and realized they were Americans. I jumped up and when they came alongside, I was aboard in one, big leap. They scuttled the raft and we were off to sea again at top speed."

The sub headed away from land until dark, then turned around and headed back again. Shortly after dawn the crew saw a flash from the water which led them to two men aboard a one-man life raft. They and the rest of their B-29 crew had parachuted into the ocean the day before during a strike at the Miyakonojo airfield Four others were picked up in the next hour.

The search continued for some time to make sure that all survivors had been picked up before the sub put back into port. Only when there was no hope left was the rescue mission terminated.

The stories of the men who were rescued in the Pacific were told all over the Marianas. While there were many who ditched and were never found, the fact that some did make it back provided a ray of hope to the airmen who faced that long trip to Jaoan and back.

Iwo or Ditch

AT THE HALFWAY POINT on the route from Isley Field to Tokyo was Iwo Jima, a volcanic island used by the Japanese to harass the Superfort bases and to attack formations headed for the homeland. Its presence forced the B-29s to avoid what would otherwise have been a valuable navigation aid, and in American hands it would have reduced by half the distance a crippled Fort had to travel to reach safety. Its capture from the enemy would also provide an ideally located base for air-sea rescue operations, improve the air defense of the Marianas, and allow fighters to escort the B-29s on their Japan missions.

Consequently, after weeks of bombing culminating in a hard-fought ground campaign, Iwo Jima was taken from the Japanese. Work on the airfields began almost as soon as the first landings, and just two weeks later Iwo saved its first million-dollar Superfort and the eleven men who flew it.

The B-29 was from Tinian and had run into trouble over Tokyo. Its radar was out; after the bomb run its bomb-bay doors could not be closed. This slowed down the plane and greatly increased its consumption of precious gasoline. Weather on the way home was bad, as usual. A heavy undercast and no radar meant a rough haul for the 1,500 miles back to Tinian.

Sweating it out, Staff Sergeant George T. Carr, the flight engineer, kept close watch on his fuel gauges. The home flight was always a race between gallons and miles. And on this trip, with the bomb-bay doors wide open, the gallons were slipping away faster than the miles.

Carr leaned over and flicked the switches marked "Reserve Fuel Tanks." The gauges did not climb. He flicked the switch again and again. He checked all his instruments. Still no gas. He turned and passed the bad word to the pilot. Lieutenant Raymond Malo. Ditching seemed imminent. Carr then went aft to check his fuel line and found the transfer switch in the bomb bay shot out. Up front, Malo's mind turned over fast, remembering the ditching procedure; into the wind, between the waves, rafts ready, crew padded and braced, check all emergency equipment, hit once, hit twice, cut all switches.

Yesterday's briefing back in the War Room was still fresh in his mind, "No one will land at Iwo," was what the CO had said. "No one..." But these were eleven men—his crew, his million-dollar airplane. He was an airplane commander, and this was the time to exercise that command.

Malo squeezed the button on his mike and spoke to his crew. He'd let them decide.

"Pilot to crew—listen hard. Our fuel transfer switches are out. We can't get enough gas up to have a chance in hell of making Tinian. There are two things we can do—we can ditch. We can call our dumbos and ditch—and there is a good chance of us all being picked up quickly. Or else we can try to get into Iwo. Remember, Iwo isn't going to be any cinch. First, it's a good way from here, the weather stinks, and we don't have radar to guide us in. Iwo's runway is short, narrow, and under constant Jap fire. But we can try it. Iwo or ditch? You've got a couple of minutes to decide..."

The interphone buzzed again....

"Tail gunner to pilot—it's Iwo for my dough."

"Left gunner—hell's bells, make it Iwo. Always wanted to have a look at this war..."

"Iwo ... Iwo ... Iwo ... Iwo ... Iwo ..."

Malo smiled at his copilot, Ed Mochler. "Okay, fellows, Iwo it is. Cox, get on your radio and call the tower at Hotrocks. Tell 'em we're running low on gas, in trouble with no radar, and we'll have to ditch unless they let us come in. Let me know as soon as you raise 'em."

Corporal Jimmy Cox banged down his key, calling, calling. He raised the tower and told them.

"Okay, Monster, this is Hotrocks Tower. You can land. Runway 4,000 feet; under mortar fire; width 50 yards; steel craters on the left. Come on in. Good luck."

Navigator Bernard Bennison knew it was up to him to get the boys to Iwo, through the soup without radar. Once they were over the island, the tower would be able to "talk" Malo down. And finding the little Pacific pork chop was going to be a mean job.

Bennison did it. He came in like a bird dog, smelling his way through the soup.

Over the island, Malo began his "Prayer to the Tower." The answer crackled back, "Okay, Monster, this is Iwo. We have cleared the runway. You have 4,000 yards of dirt to get in on. The traffic pattern is clear. Follow your own pattern of approach. Half the invasion forces are here to watch you, so make it good!"

Malo was sweating. Around once—twice—three times, trying to get the lay of the field, trying to pick his spot. He had 60 tons of airplane to barrel in at 110 miles an hour and had to get it stopped in 4,000 feet. Those wonderful 8,500-foot runways back on Tinian didn't teach a man anything about this kind of landing. The brakes had to hold. What if they had been shot up over Tokyo, too?

"Flaps, full flaps—wheels down—135—130—125. Pull her up now, pull her nose up—not too fast. Stall her in this time..."

Aft, the crew lay on the floor bracing themselves for a crash, with parachutes around their heads and faces.

"120—115—"

Malo pulled back slowly on his control column. Over the runway now. Precious feet were flying by, unused. Jack up that nose a trifle—chop back the throttles—crash! The 120,000 pounds of plane was down with a bang!

Mochler threw all his strength onto the brakes, fighting for control with his rudders. One wing crashed into a telephone pole, rubber smoked from the tires; the giant plane slid, tearing at its brakes, groaning, burning itself out in a herculean effort to stop. Malo kicked hard left rudder, threw his controls left—and turned the monster. She slumped to a stop.

The spectators had had the thrill they hoped for; they crowded six deep around the giant.

The men who had worked on the runway asked: "How was it?" "Was she smooth enough?" "Level or bumpy?"

The men who had been killing the Japanese asked: "Did you bomb the hell out of Tokyo?" "How's the war?"

Now the shelling started in earnest, bracketing the Superfort with vicious mortar fire. Malo was anxious to get out as fast as possible, to get gas and fly out safely. It would be a sad note now to have his plane blown to bits by mortar fire on the ground.

Four hours later, 2,000 gallons of gas had been poured by hand into the thirsty tanks of the Superfort, enough to fly her safely over the 750 miles of ocean to Tinian. And Malo was faced with a new problem—take-off.

Brakes hard on—engine full power—bomb-bay doors now lashed shut. Giant clouds of volcanic ash and dust were blown for thousands of yards by the whirling props. The ship strained at her brakes to get off, 8,800 horses busting their guts—powerful hydraulic brakes pulling against them, to hold her on the ground ... "Okay. Brakes off..."

It was almost a catapult take-off. The giant Superfort was miraculously airborne in 2,500 feet. Iwo had begun to pay off.

Before the war ended some 2,400 Superforts in trouble landed at Iwo. Planes damaged while they dropped the devastating firebombs on Tokyo, Kobe, Nagoya, and Osaka were saved by that pile of volcanic ash in the middle of the Pacific. They came limping in, out of gas, with their props feathered, their engines shot up, their fuel lines gone, and with wounded aboard. It was as far as they could go until men and planes were patched up.

At first the patching up was done under enemy fire by a handful of skillful, untiring mechanics who worked under the worst possible field conditions: dirt, dust, lack of food, lack of water, little sleep, and a few tools. With an engine hoist and a putt-putt motor to supply power for floodlights, they worked night and day getting the Superforts into the air and on their way back to the Marianas. Gradually their number increased until an entire Service Group was waiting at Iwo to help the planes that landed there.

The Giant Pays Its Way

BUT THE ROAD TO TOKYO still seemed to be a long one. Sixteen times LeMay had sent his bombers to Japan. Fourteen times photo reconnaissance planes returned with pictures showing the targets still standing. Not one important target had been destroyed although the 21st Bomber Command had dropped over 5,000 tons of bombs on Japan. Further, losses had continued high. While there had been relatively little damage from flak, fighter interception and the long overwater flights had taken their toll. By the end of February enemy fighters had shot down 29 of the Command's Superforts, flak had downed one; fighters and flak together had accounted for nine. Mechanical difficulties had caused the loss of 21 planes; 15 were lost due to unknown causes.

The men were becoming unnerved. "Ironpants" LeMay tried almost every tactical trick in the book while his crews cursed both him and their plane.

"Hell," he answered, "I'm not here to win friends. I'm here to win a war. And the only way to do that is for my men to drop the max weight of bombs on the target." They were not doing it. LeMay sent them up at night—at high noon—in formation—singly—a hundred at a time—two hundred at a time. The reconnaissance planes returned with pictures that showed the targets undestroyed.

Then early in March LeMay decided on a bold change in tactics. The B-29 had been considered the perfect tool for daylight precision bombing, and Japan the perfect target. However, there had always been strategists who favored the use of other tactics, and their number increased as the cost of daylight missions went up and it became apparent that pinpoint bombing with high explosives was not producing the damage expected.

Because of their congestion and generally inflammable construction, Japanese cities seemed a logical place for the use of incendiary bombs. As early as March 1943, tests were underway to develop a new and more effective firebomb. At Dugway Proving Ground, Utah, a typical Japanese workers' village was built. The 'village' was complete down to the last detail, including books on shelves, furniture, fences, and sheds. Little was known about modern Japanese residential architecture, so a New York architect, Antonin Raymond, who had studied in Japan for eighteen years, was hired to design the houses and prepare.

The houses were built and furnished in accurate detail. When the exact type of grass and fiber mats used by the Japanese were unavailable in the States, the Navy imported some from Hawaii. About five blocks were laid out, complete with streets, which included 100 residences and a few small industrial buildings.

Nearby was an Army post staffed with firefighters using the same equipment believed to be available to the Japanese. In Japanese air-raid warden fashion, these men were stationed in the "village" and as fast as the firebombs were dropped, they went into action with their firefighting equipment.

Finally, in early 1944, a bomb was developed that was too much for the firefighters; they couldn't cope with the devastating fire produced. Air Force experts knew they had the answer in an improved type of petroleum or jellied gasoline bomb perfected with the aid of the Standard Oil Company, du Pont chemists and the National Research Defense Council. Now a highly efficient firebomb was available, but there still remained the problem of effective delivery.

The 314th Bombardment Wing had just arrived on Guam. It was commanded by Brigadier General Thomas S. Power, who had flown B-24s in Italy before becoming a highly successful troubleshooter in the B-29 training program of the Second Air Force. The Wing's first 25 Superforts were delivered on February 23. Almost immediately there came a request from General LeMay: Washington wanted a maximum effort against Tokyo on the 25th, one of the objectives being to knock out the city's growing home industries. They needed more planes. Could the 314th help out?

A new outfit usually had a training period to familiarize the crews with local flying conditions. His men had hardly unpacked, but General Power agreed to put up 22 of his first 25 Superforts to make an even formation. Power's observations as he led his unit on its first bombing mission were to help bring about changes in bombing tactics that greatly increased the effectiveness of B-29 raids against Japan.

The 22 shiny new bombers of the 314th Wing and the 22 green crews took off from Guam and headed out over the ocean for the assembly point 300 miles south of Japan. The weather, passable at first got worse and worse, forcing them down and down until they were flying right on the deck. Rain was pouring down faster than the windshield wipers could clear it away. As they neared the rendezvous, planes started going by in every direction. No one could see well enough to get into formation for the run on the target. The weather had ruined the carefully worked out plan for bombing Tokyo.

Realizing that he had to get his crews out before there was a collision, Tom Power gave the order to climb and led the way up through the soup. At 15,000 feet he broke out between two cloud layers and looked around. Only one of his original wingmen had managed to follow him, but there were 30 planes in all from many squadrons. They formed up and continued to climb. Finally, the clouds thinned out a bit, but by then they were flying in heavy snow. Power lined them up, and they made their bomb run at 25,000 feet without ever breaking out of the weather.

A total of 172 Superforts made it to the target that day. Using radar, they dropped their bombs on Tokyo. They were firebombs—it was the first big-scale firebomb raid on Tokyo.

Japanese newspapers reported briefly on the raid. Their stories told of 130 B-29s appearing over the capital, inflicting only slight damage. They went on to tell of an apology made by Premier General Kuniaki Koiso to Emperor Hirohito for destruction of imperial property at Omiya Palace.

The next day Tokyo radio reported two B-29s over the city. They were reconnaissance planes taking pictures of the damage done by the raid. Because of the snow covering the ground, the areas blackened by fire stood out clearly. There were some small spots where a couple of adjacent blocks had been destroyed. One big black area of over a square mile dominated the photos; it had been totally burned out.

As General Power studied the reconnaissance pictures of his Wing's first raid, he speculated on what would have happened if more planes had come in lower with a bigger bomb load: if a Superfort didn't have to climb to a high altitude, it could carry more bombs. With his operations officer, Colonel Hewitt T. Wheless, he discussed getting low-flying B-29s to Tokyo by routing them up the peninsula on the east side of Tokyo Bay on radar, then turning them toward Tokyo at a set point. Each B-29 would have an assigned heading and speed and bombing time to ensure the desired concentration of fires from the incendiaries.

In Colonel Wheless' words: "We wanted to get in below the level of the flak and above the range of the small cannon."

Word of the studies being made by the 314th reached General LeMay at 21st Bomber Command Headquarters. Late one night—it was close to 2 A.M.—he walked over to the shack which Power and Wheless shared. As he stood talking with Power on the porch, LeMay shifted his pipe to the other side of his mouth and asked, "Tom, what's all this talk about fire-bomb raids?"

Power explained the idea he and Wheless had been working on. Wheless, who was asleep, was called out to join the discussion. LeMay was interested in what they had to tell him. Very interested. He asked them to work out an over-all plan for a low-level raid and gave them 24 hours to get it ready.

Power and Wheless went to work at once. By that afternoon they had outlined their idea for a low-level incendiary raid and turned it over to the General.

LeMay studied it, checked the reconnaissance photos of the February 25th raid, and looked once more at the weather charts. The success of precision bombing depended on visual conditions over the target. Almost all his missions had been forced to rely on radar because of bad weather at high altitudes over Japan, and weather during the spring months was going to get worse, not better. That meant more bombing by radar, and radar bombing was of necessity area bombing, not precision bombing. Against Japanese cities incendiaries would work better than high explosives in area-bombing missions. Coming in at a low level would greatly increase the effectiveness of his planes. It would save gas; it would be easier on the engines, and it would probably take the Japanese completely by surprise.

The problem was to improve strike results without needlessly endangering his men and planes. Maybe low-level incendiary attacks were the answer. The firebombs were sure to do considerable damage if they were spread thickly enough. But could they get in there that close to the ground with that big plane and get out again? He might be sending his men on a mission from which most of them wouldn't return. He alone could issue the orders. The responsibility for failure would be his.

Day and night LeMay worked on plans; he studied strike results, weather forecasts, intelligence reports—everything that might affect the success of a bombing mission. He was not an ostentatious worker. Sometimes he appeared merely to be sitting at his desk, staring off into space. A staff officer remarked: "The General does less work than any man in the Army. His desk is almost always clean. We can walk in on him at almost any time of day or night and find him writing letters to the wives and children of the men in his command who have been lost in action—or just sitting there, sucking at that oversize pipe of his."

"He doesn't appear to work much," said the captain who had been LeMay's aide for three years, "but he thinks more than any man I have ever known. In England he averaged no more than four hours' sleep a night for over a year. Here, on Guam, he will be on the job all day, see his planes off at dusk, stay up all night to get their reports, and at eight in the morning he is back at his desk, prompt, energetic, fresh. It would kill most men to keep up with him."

During the first days of March LeMay made the decision—probably the greatest one-man military decision ever made.

It came late in the afternoon. An all-day drizzle had made the roads around the 21st Bomber Command Headquarters sticky with red mud. LeMay sat alone in the War Room. Hours had ticked by as he sat there, huddled and heavy in a small chair, staring at the maps through those black, overhanging eyebrows. The plan all but formed now would mean death for hundreds of thousands of Japanese.

Lieutenant Colonel "Pinky" Smith walked into the War Room and stopped short, muttering an apology as he recognized the huddled shape. The briar pipe waved at him. "No, Pinky, don't go away. I want to talk to you. There is something I've been thinking about—a new way of hitting them up there in the Empire. And I want you to draw me up a field order and a plan. Listen..."

Pinky listened to the quiet, slow words of his General. What he heard dumbfounded him, made his flesh creep.

Smith had felt like that when he first worked with LeMay back in India. Once, out there, he had heard men speak of Le May as a "butcher" when they heard one of his plans. Once they had thought of him as a "bomb-crazy madman." But both times LeMay's plans had worked. They always seemed to work. Before he spoke to anyone about them, LeMay knew—he had taken every factor into consideration; his plan had to work.

"After working with that man," Smith noted, "he seems almost like a machine—or a god. Fire a thousand questions at him in an hour. If he'll answer you, you can bet that 99 percent of the answers will be right. He doesn't open his mouth often, but when he does you better damn well listen—and act. He means every single syllable. But this time the plan was almost unbelievable."

LeMay stopped, his whole plan laid out.

There was a moment's silence, then Smith said, "Later, General, when we get down to details, I will need some more information."

"Right. Call me when you need me. One more thing, Pinky. I don't want anyone—anyone at all, mind you, who is not absolutely vital—in on this. I want it kept quiet as possible."

Smith relayed the General's words to members of the staff who were essential to the planning. With Pinky Smith talking they were free to comment:

"We'll get the holy hell shot out of us."

"It's nothing but a suicide mission."

"If we tried this over Germany, we'd lose 80 percent of our planes."

The new men—new to LeMay—said again:

"He's crazy."

"He's a butcher."

"It's impossible."

Day and night, the men worked: intelligence, operations, ordnance, weather, target information, photo interpretation, maintenance, supply. Few of them knew the plan. They knew only that such-and-such information was wanted, and fast. It was their job to get it. A mission and men depended on its being right.

The plan took on shape and detail: Wind velocities, bomb loads, gas loads, ammunition loads, man loads; airspeeds, magneto settings, oil pressures; star fixes, courses, Japanese landmarks, ocean landmarks, islands; radio frequencies, distress frequencies, code words, flash signals; number of planes, number of men, number of bombs, number of ambulances, number of doctors; initial points, aiming points, target areas, assembly points; start-engine time, taxi time, take-off time, Japan time, Washington time, sunrise, sunset; enemy flak, enemy searchlights, enemy submarines, enemy interception, enemy espionage; enemy factories, enemy power plants, enemy canals, enemy docks... the Imperial Palace of the Emperor of Japan.

At last the plan was ready.

"Our bombers will attack in maximum strength and destroy the urban area of Tokyo on the night of March 9."

It was now the job of the wing commanders to go back to their units and tell the men who would fly to Tokyo,

Rosey O'Donnell returned to Saipan, Jim Davies to Tinian, and Tom Power to the 314th to give orders for—The LeMay Plan.

In the War Room of the 500th Group on Saipan, every crew bench was packed. Each crew spread over two of the hard, wooden benches, the men up front in the ship—pilots, navigator, bombardier, engineer—sitting on the front bench; left blister, right blister, central fire control, radio, radar and gunner sitting on the bench behind. Over each crew hung a sign with the airplane commander's name on it. Some of the names looked fresh; the replacements for the dead and missing crews.

The walls of the high double Quonset hut were covered with maps, charts, and photographs of Japan, of the various targets, cities, and factories; of a few of the islands on the way up and back, and news maps of the Italian, French, German and Philippine theaters to enable the men to keep up with the war on other fronts.

At the far end of the Quonset was a big wooden stage from which the briefing officers spoke; back of it were more maps, more charts, and the cold, fatal blackboards covered with sheets of blank brown paper. Underneath those sheets of paper was the LeMay Plan: the "bad news for tonight."

The War Room was so tightly packed the men standing could barely reach into their pockets for a smoke. Five hundred men, scarcely one of them 30 years old, were sitting in their shorts and open shirts waiting.

As yet they knew no details. But they had seen the guards at every entrance, the brown paper concealing the blackboards, and they saw the War Room was more crowded than ever before.

"It's a big one tonight, Mac."

"Yeah, every guy and his brother is going out."

"What the hell... these guards, the old wrapping paper and all."

"Maybe we're going home."

"Going home! We're going to sink Japan!"

"Can it! Here's the Old Man."

On stage, center, leaning on the lectern, sandy-haired, blue-eyed Group Commander Dougherty began to talk:

"Gentlemen, for tonight we have a new plan. When you hear it, you won't like it. But after you think about it a while it makes sense. It should work. The best brains and the best information have been put into it. And if it does work, tonight can do more than any one raid ever did to bring the end of the war closer. Here it is! Three hundred and thirty-nine aircraft from the 21st Bomber Command are scheduled to go to Japan tonight—the largest force of B-29s ever to take off from anywhere."

Every man in the room whistled, poked his neighbor and grinned.

"The 73rd Wing will furnish 162 aircraft; the 313th Wing 121, the 314th, 56. Our bomb load will be all incendiaries."

The men shouted again: A fire raid sounded good to them.

One after another the briefing officers spoke.

Group Commander: "Your target is Tokyo..."

Intelligence: "Target information, size of force, tactics..."

Weather: "Tonight there will be a front at last. Over the target there'll be 2/10th cloud cover..."

Bombardier: "Your bomb load will be 12,000 pounds..."

Navigator: "This will be a navigator's mission."

Engineer: "No auxiliary tanks will be carried tonight..."

Radar Intelligence: "Your radar scope pictures will be set at..."

Communications: "Distress frequencies and code words..."

Thus, the LeMay Plan was explained to the men who would fly it.

Tonight they would go into Tokyo between 5,000 and 7,500 feet. Every other mission had been flown between 25,000 and 30,000. The altitude had been dropped five miles!

Tonight they would go into the heart of Japan singly. Every other mission had gone over the target in formation. It was formation, interlocking fire, that protected bombers from being slashed by enemy fighters.

Tonight they would go into Tokyo in darkness... For the last 10 missions, even during the day, they had been unable to see the target.

Tonight they would fly to Japan, and back—3,000 miles and more—without any bomb-bay tanks of gasoline. On almost every mission to date, planes had dropped into the swallowing Pacific because they were out of gas. And all those planes had carried bomb-bay tanks.

Tonight they would carry nothing but fire... The bomb bay of every aircraft would be loaded with tons of firebombs.

The men were dumfounded ... frightened.

LeMay, the famed high altitude, formation-flying, precision-bombing strategist, had tossed aside every rule in the airman's bible...

The men exclaimed to each other: Will any of us ever get back? No gas in the bomb bays! Five thousand feet! Didn't they shoot the hell out of us at 25,000 feet?

The factual briefing was over. Group Commander Dougherty walked back to the lectern.

"Tonight there is no other target except Tokyo. Tokyo is our primary target, our secondary target, our target of opportunity, our target of last resort. Every single bomb will be dropped inside Tokyo.

"There will be no evasion tactics over the target. Enemy flak may be thick and heavy, but still there will be no evasion tactics because of the danger of collision. Tonight we shall have over 300 airplanes up there, so keep your eyes open."

"One more thing." The airmen held their breaths. "No guns and no ammunition will be carried. Get that. No guns. No ammunition. First of all, if we carried guns, it is likely we'd open fire on each other. Secondly, we will carry all our weight in bombs and gas. Thirdly, intelligence reports indicate there will be no night fighters of any account. Therefore, no guns and no ammunition. Final poop sheets for pilots, final weather, and flimsies for radio operators may be picked up here at 5 P.M. That's all."

In tight excited knots, the airmen looked over the new incendiary bombs that they would carry for the first time that night. Gradually a feeling of optimistic excitement swept over the crews.

The first smash-in-the-eye details had flabbergasted them. Then reason and logic had taken over. Why would there be no guns, no ammunition? ...

To reduce their weight and keep them from shooting each other. How could they get there and back without bomb-bay tanks? By saving weight and flying at low altitude. Why could they get in and out at such low altitude?

Observations had shown an absence of barrage balloons, a scarcity of night fighters, a lack of automatic weapons for defense against a low-altitude night attack. And above all there was the factor of surprise. Never had a B-29 attacked below 20,000 feet.

The men felt that maybe the LeMay Plan would work. They filed away to their specialized briefings, splitting not into crews but into trades: pilots, engineers, radio, radar, navigators, bombardiers, each to their special rendezvous to learn the final information needed for their special jobs; information so technical that it was meaningless to another crew member.

Then came the final hours—the sweating hours, when the risk of the mission chilled the skin and activated the kidney. Some men played ball; some men slept; some men went to the line and helped the ground crews ready the planes. Almost everyone wrote final letters—to his mother, to his wife. Some wrote a third. They had written this letter before, then torn it up when they returned. A little shamefaced and embarrassed they handed it to a friend. "Say, Mac, just in case. Mail it for me, will you? See you tomorrow, maybe. So long."

Then the loudspeaker in the camp area crackled, announcing that combat crews could go to the mess nails. Perhaps the meal was a little better that afternoon. Take-off time for the 73rd Wing was to be between 6:15 P.M., and 7:17 P.M.

The cooks, the clerks, the friends who would be left behind, looked at the combat crews as if they were seeing them for the last time and wanted to remember their faces. The ground men knew their friends would go to Tokyo at 7,000 feet that they would have no guns or ammunition, that their job was to burn out the heart of the capital city of Japan. This would be that mission for a lot of them.

Chow over, the men picked up the flimsies from the War Rooms. Still time left. Some men took showers, changed their clothing from the skin out. It was a habit with some of them—to be especially clean when they went up to the Empire. Maybe the reason was that clean clothes and clean skin would reduce chances of infection if they were wounded. Maybe the reason was simply that taking a shower and changing domes used up time.

Then the trucks appeared, and the crews boarded them with their gear and waved to the men left behind as they bumped their way up to the flight line. They collected their flak suits, Mae Wests, parachutes, and checked over their thirty-odd pieces of personal equipment.

The light began to drain from the sky into the ocean—the dull endless ocean that swallowed up everything: light from the sky, planes from the air, crews from your own squadron.

Time: 6:05. First planes take off at 6:15 P.M. Ten more minutes to go.

The tower operators, 100 feet and more above the field, chattered together. They were having a last-minute smoke—talking about something they saw in a month-old funny paper that morning. Below them, spread over the giant field, 162 B-29s were readying for take-off. The crews were aboard—had been for an hour and more; they were checking every last piece of equipment and machinery. Out from the loudspeakers in the glass-enclosed tower came the blaring chatter of pilots asking directions, calling back information. The tower operators paid no attention. The senior operator, Sergeant Spachtaholtz, looked at Sergeant Baden's watch.

"Okay, let's go."

THE FIRST PLANES WERE READY, straining at the edge of the runway. Behind them, long lines of B-29s were formed, nose to tail, props whirling, navigation lights gleaming small and red and green and white. Giant fin after giant fin pierced the watery dusk as far as eyes could see, dwarfing the men and jeeps that crowded the side of the runway.

Spachtaholtz, ex-steel-mill worker, stretched his small, thin body as he reached into the air to pull down his signal light. He touched the trigger—the lead B-29 saw a green light.

"Take off!"

Endlessly the B-29s flashed by, heading out to the ocean, and the Empire. Squadron after squadron crept out from the hardstands, joined the nose-to-tail procession down the runway. One portside landing light hurled out a beam of yellow in front of each monster as it lumbered slowly, then faster and faster, down the 8,500-foot asphalt strip straining to lift 70 tons into the air.

Up in the tower, the brass worried, watching the boys go out. But the traffic maze—162 aircraft, 200 million worth of equipment—was handled quickly by the two quiet-voiced sergeants. They visually checked every ship for lights, bomb bays, engine fire; talked them into position; controlled their every movement; prevented disastrous traffic jams. Every 50 seconds another two planes took off from the parallel strips.

At 7:17, the 160th Superfort was on its way to Japan. Only two had failed to get off. General "Rosey" O'Donnell was pleased.

Across the bay in Tinian, another 110 ships were airborne.

In Guam, the green 314th Wing had sent off 54.

The LeMay Fire Plan was headed for Japan. Shortly after midnight Tokyo would be blazing; shortly after midnight some of these planes might be shot down; shortly after midnight many of these men might be dead.

The men left behind—the crew chiefs, tower operators, crash-truck men, ambulance drivers—felt deserted, drained of their purpose and importance now that their planes were gone.

An abort returned. Shamefaced, the crew piled out of the plane. Something had gone wrong. They couldn't make it. They felt foolish. There was nothing to do now but go back to the tents and hit the sack. The men were on their way. The climax of getting them off was over. Isley Field was empty.

In the Mission Control Room of each wing, scoreboards told the story in figures; the number of planes off, the aborts, the early returns. But no scoreboard tallied the scratched nerves, the numbed hearts, the bitten lips of the men who were on watch—the mission control officer, the air sea rescue team, the teletype operators.

On all the islands nervous radio operators were standing by to catch the first message. Telephone switchboards and teletypists were ready to flash to the wings the bad news of crashes and lost planes—the expected news of ditched aircraft—the good word of Bombs away.

At 1:21 the flash came. Bombs away... General conflagration... Flak moderate to heavy... Fighters none.

The message was dramatic but cryptic. Just as the scoreboards on the ground told the incomplete story, so the radio report left much unsaid. It omitted the horror seen and the frenzy felt.

Blink, blink, blink... Faster than their eyes could count—up and down, column after column of small green lights blinking on and off. Every one of those silently blinking green lights on the instrument panels meant another incendiary bomb had left its station, was falling, set to burst 2,000 feet above Tokyo and disintegrate into 38 separate balls of liquid, almost unquenchable fire. A major crossed himself with his left hand—his right clutched the controls—and murmured, "This blaze will haunt me forever. It's the most terrifying sight in the world, and, God forgive me, it's the best."

A crew chief cracked jokes, but he was grateful that the danger of collision over the target was eliminated by the fierce light of the fires. A colonel-pilot didn't mean to talk into his intercom: "When I first heard we were to go in below seven thousand, I didn't give the General much credit for that brainwave. It's against everything the ship is built for, but I'll fly these missions any day in the week. By God, you can see what you do. Seeing an enemy city burn to hell makes up for a lot of flak fright."

Many of these men had been attacking Japan since the previous November. In those four months more than 800 men from the 73rd Wing alone had been killed. And during those costly raids they had seldom seen their target; too often weather had ruined their formation; too often their bombs had dropped uselessly into rice paddies.

But this was the payoff!

This time every man in the Superforts was able to look out and see Tokyo blazing wildly, burning, smoking, exploding. The planes filled with the stench of smoke which sifted in through the air vents.

Tom Power had been chosen to lead the mission and to make a special report to General LeMay on how the raid went After going in on his bomb run at 5,000 feet Power went up to 10,000 then to 20,000 feet and flew back and forth across the target for almost two hours.

Some of the B-29s were carrying the largest bomb load ever taken to Japan, 18,000 pounds, twice what they could have carried if they had gone in at 30,000 feet, their usual altitude. The M-69 incendiaries which they dropped broke up and scattered as they fell, so each plane was covering an area about 2,500 feet long and 500 feet wide with burning gasoline. The great heat of the fires helped to spread them, linking the burning areas into one tremendous fire. Tokyo was a highly inflammable city; its firebreaks were unable to contain this conflagration.

Power and his crew found it difficult to judge the extent of the destruction because of the thick smoke from the spreading fires. However, they estimated the burning area to be 15 square miles; remarkably close to the actual figure of 15.8 square miles. Lieutenant Colonel Harry Besse, the 314's intelligence officer, made sketches of what he saw to give General LeMay a better idea of what had happened.

In recalling the mission, General Power said: "The 9 March firebomb raid was the greatest single disaster in military history. It was greater than the combined damage of the A-bomb drops on Hiroshima and Nagasaki. In that fire raid there were more casualties than in any other military action in the history of the world. From both a tactical and strategic point of view, it was a tremendously successful raid."

Tokyo radio reported the raid lasted from midnight to 2:40 A.M. (Japanese time), claimed 15 B-29s were shot down and 50 damaged. The Russian Tass News Agency reported that Tokyo papers failed to come out on the following day, indicating that their plants were damaged or destroyed, or that their workers had been killed or were unable to get to their jobs.

Premier Kuniaki Koiso told the Japanese Diet that "American air raids by B-29s had reached serious proportions," but that "the Government would adopt bold measures" to meet the situation; meanwhile the people of Nippon should prepare for a time when their sacred motherland would become a battleground.

The Tokyo newspaper Asahi stated that, "Three days afterwards sufferers are still wandering about at places reduced to ashes, hoping to find out whether their families were safe," and that many thousands suffered eye injuries as the result of the raging fires. There were not enough doctors to care for the injured.

Later stories indicated that even six days afterward, Tokyo had not recovered. From Tass: "The civilian population was thrown into a panic beyond the ability of the authorities to control. Thousands of refugees are still crowding the damaged railroad stations, attempting to leave Tokyo."

The German Trans-Ocean Agency reported that the Japanese government had called for "voluntary evacuation" of everyone not in essential occupations in the leading cities: Tokyo, Yokohama, Nagoya and Kobe. "In the event of an unsatisfactory response the Government will take appropriate steps," the Japanese were warned.

In the middle of a cold winter night, millions of Tokyo residents had had their homes, their clothes, their food, and their families destroyed by fire. Not only were homes, factories, power plants, the lighting system, water supply and the sewage system destroyed, but also the stockpiles of emergency food and clothing.

The war had at last been brought home to the Japanese. As the bombs tumbled, cameras clicked in the bellies of the Superforts to record the damage. Translated to New York, the 15.8 square miles destroyed would include all the industrial and half the residential section of Brooklyn, or Manhattan from the Battery up to 60th Street.

Back in the tower at Isley Field the radio flashes added up to a happy conclusion: The LeMay Plan had worked.

But the plan would be a complete success only if the crews brought themselves and their ships home.

The hours were long that day. It wasn't until early in the afternoon that the last of the planes of the 73rd Wing returned to Saipan. As each crew piled out of their plane, they were almost surprised that they were home, intact. They had been there, over Tokyo; at 7,000 feet, without guns! And now they were home safe.

Down at Interrogation, blackboards revealed their whole squadron was home, then their whole group. The entire 73rd Wing lost just one plane; one plane missing, with no word received from it. Not counting aborts, 160 planes had taken off; 159 returned. The crews were wildly enthusiastic.

For Curtis LeMay, the hours of the mission had been agonizing ones. But while his giant planes were taking off, crossing the miles of ocean, and swinging low over Tokyo, he had betrayed agitation only by constant pacing.

With Brigadier General Lauris Norstad, Chief of Staff from Twentieth Air Force Headquarters in Washington, LeMay received the special report from General Power, who landed at 10 A.M. The plan had worked. There had been antiaircraft fire and innumerable searchlights, but Japanese defenses had soon fallen apart. Damage was many times greater than that inflicted during the raid of February 25. They had proved the feasibility of low-level bombing with incendiaries.

So, at last the planes were back, the interrogations over, the reports in, the evaluations completed. Now LeMay knew. In an interview with newsmen General LeMay said:

"I believe that all those under my command on these island bases have by their participation in this single operation shortened this war. To what extent they have shortened it no one can tell, but I believe that if there has been cut from its duration only one day or one hour, my officers and men have served a high purpose. They will pursue that purpose stubbornly. They are fighting for a quicker end to this war, and will continue to fight for a quicker end to it with all the brains and strength they have."

Now through LeMay's head ran other names: Nagoya, Osaka, Kobe.

He came to his next decision fast: "Carry out the remainder of the plan; devastate Japan's major industrial cities in the next ten days and nights."

Nagoya was next!

"How soon?" the men asked. "How much time do we have?"

The answer: "Hit Nagoya as soon as possible. In one day at the most."

"One day! Hell, we can't get off the ground in one day. It'll take two days at the very least…"

They were talking into thin air. LeMay had gone; back to his War Room, back to his maps, to sit, silent, chewing on an unlighted cigar, thinking. That was it; that was an order. One day! Stretch it any way you want; double your shifts, whip everyone to a frenzy, work under floodlights during the dark Pacific night, but take no more than 24 hours.

As it turned out, only 29 hours separated the return from Tokyo from the take-off to Nagoya. In that time, small miracles were performed; the men with oil and grease on their hands did it. LeMay received constant progress reports:

"Nine engines have been changed, slow-timed and readied, sir."

LeMay puffed out a jet of smoke. "Double it."

"We've put four planes back in commission."

LeMay stared at the large wall map, highlighted in the darkened War Room.

"They never should have been out of commission in the first place."

"Thirty-three planes have been repaired, sir."

LeMay went on reading a secret report from Washington.

"It took 3,000 man-hours to do that job, sir."

LeMay never answered.

"Every plane has been given a thorough inspection—whatever it needed: 100-hour inspection, 50-hour, 25-hour."

LeMay, lighting his cigar paused long enough to nod.

If the men of the 21st Bomber Command hadn't understood, it would have been worse. Behind the impassive face and grumbled answers lay a keen understanding of his men, his planes and the difficulties of the problems to be licked. It was just another instance of Curtis LeMay's knack of understanding his men's capabilities better than the men themselves. And now the "impossible" repair work—the operations which every supply and maintenance officer believed would take a week to accomplish—had been done in 29 hours.

Proved wrong twice, 21st Bomber Command personnel began to repeat the famous Army gag: "The difficult we do immediately; the impossible takes a little longer." Only it wasn't a gag. As the plan went into full effect and the firebombs rained on Japan, the planes came back in worse shape; needing more and more work as the frightful strain of combat tolled on them.

And still the men kept up their work, following the tough schedule set by "The Cigar." Challenged by problems never confronting an air inspector, slaving cheerfully under terrific pressure, they put the planes back in the sky time after time. Mechanical ingenuity was only part of it; guts and sweat were the rest.

A grease-stained crew chief, gulping hot coffee on the flight line, said it: "We don't mind the day and night work, just as long as we can get a burned-out Jap city in return."

In the dusty ordnance dumps, GIs worked without stop, loading bombs onto trucks, carting them, unloading them at the airplanes. There, on the hardstands, groups of four ordnance men assigned to load each ship, sweated with the plane's ground crew as they crammed the giant double bomb bays with 68 M-69 incendiaries and the Pathfinder ships with 184 smaller, brighter-burning, magnesium bombs which would light up the target.

Figures tell the work done by the ordnance companies. To "bomb-up" one wing for one raid it took: 400 man-days to uncrate the incendiaries; 400 man-days to transport them from the dumps to the line; 600 man-days to load the bombs into the planes from the hardstands. In all, a total of 1,400-man-days—for one raid for just one wing! And this job of work was done through rain, heat and night, and often within 24 hours.

There were casualties among the ordnance men and ground men during the fire blitz. As many were "killed in action" on the ground in the Marianas as died in the air over Japan.

Lifting bombs hour after hour can break a man's back. Through tiredness, a bomb can slip and fall. Let it fall, and it will crush your skull. Make a mistake about a fuse, and it's the last mistake you'll ever make.

The job done by the ground crews and service groups during this ten-day battle was epic. Their work was made up of small things; changing wheels, changing engines, changing cylinder heads, repairing fuel lines, replacing instruments, correcting malfunctions in the bomb racks, in the turrets, in the radio sets, in the radar equipment, in the hydraulic lines. The list was endless because in a B-29 there were 55,000 separate parts, every one of which could go wrong, each of which was, during these hectic days, subjected to untold strain.

LeMay put it this way: "Those cities wouldn't have been burned without our ground crews; we would never have sent our planes back up so fast if it hadn't been for their magnificent work. If we'd delayed, the Japs might have been more prepared. The ground crews get as much credit as any man in the entire command."

It took the crews 29 hours instead of 24 to get ready for the second fire-bomb raid, but the afternoon of 11 March, 313 Superforts were off for Nagoya, Japan's greatest war-plane-producing center and third largest city. On this strike, General

LeMay ordered the B-29s to carry 200 rounds of ammunition in the tail turret in case the Japanese had learned that the Superforts were unarmed in the Tokyo raid.

After the bombing the Japanese issued a communique which claimed 22 Superforts were shot down and 60 damaged. Actually 285 planes had reached the target and only one was lost, a plane that ditched shortly after take-off.

But the results of the raid fell short of those achieved at Tokyo. The American airmen had become overoptimistic and spaced their bombs farther apart, hoping to destroy a larger area. Due to this greater dispersal and the warning provided by the Tokyo raid, Nagoya firefighters were better able to curb the conflagration. Only 2.05 square miles were destroyed by 1,790 tons of bombs. Clearly the way to burn down an area was to concentrate the fires, to make them so hot that nothing could put them out. The next raid was to see a successful application of the concentration technique.

Although the results of the Nagoya mission were not all that had been hoped, Admiral Nimitz wired LeMay: "Submarine stationed about 150 miles south of Nagoya reports that on the morning of 12 March the visibility was reduced to one mile by heavy wood smoke. Congratulations."

Admiral Mitscher, on the same day, wired LeMay: "Task Force 58 is proud to operate in the same area as a force which can do as much damage to the enemy as your force is constantly doing. May your targets always flame."

And General LeMay sent this word to Japan: "All the Japanese have to look forward to is the total destruction of their industries, cities, and other vital targets devoted to their war effort. But one thing I want to emphasize; we are still a long way from the attainment of our full strength. If it is necessary, we will send 1,000 planes over the target." Forty-eight hours later, on the night of March 13, 301 Superforts were airborne, of which 274 made it to Osaka. They dropped 1,732 tons of incendiaries and laid waste 8.1 square miles of the Empire's second largest city. Because of clouds over the target most of the bombs had been dropped by radar.

Perhaps the most spectacular incident on this raid was the destruction of the 150-acre Osaka arsenal. Explosion after violent explosion threw up concussions so terrific, they rocked 70-ton

Superforts a mile up in the air. One of the 313th Wing B-29s, named "Topsy-Turvy," was blown from 7,000 feet clear up to 12,000 feet, turned completely upside down, and sent into a slow roll. After falling 10,000 feet, the pilot recovered control and flew it home. Another B-29, "Jostlin' Josie" from the 73rd Wing, was hurled from 7,000 feet up to 10,000 feet, and then fell 2,000 feet before the pilot regained control. A ship commanded by Captain Jack D. Nole caught several violent blasts. The first dumped the bombardier, Lieutenant John B. Allen, into the lap of the copilot; the second pitched him into the controls; the third threw the ship on its side and hurled Captain Nole from his seat ... Something big had been blown up a mile and a half below them.

Seventy hours later, on March 16th, 334 planes were airborne; 307 reached Kobe with 2,355 tons of incendiaries for the fourth giant incendiary raid on Nipponese cities within a week. Hitting docks, shipyards, an aircraft plant, and locomotive works, the incendiaries burned out 3 square miles, 21.4 percent of the city; the fires started were visible 100 miles away.

An important factor behind the planning for the Kobe mission was the realization that visual bombing methods were largely responsible for failure to destroy greater areas in earlier raids. Therefore, all bombardiers on the Kobe mission were instructed to make a controlled radar run over the target before making visual corrections, and to apply such corrections only to their sighting on the aiming point, and not for the purpose of spreading bombs visually.

On March 19th, in the fifth massed strike by the 21st Bomber Command, the Superforts returned to Nagoya. They demolished another 3.5 square miles, winding up the stupendously successful ten-day LeMay fire blitz.

At the end of the ten days, the Superforts' record read: "Thirty-two square miles of Japan's four principal cities demolished."

Hundreds of vital war plants destroyed; hundreds of others put out of operation; gas, electricity, heat, light, water, transportation disrupted.

Countless thousands of Japanese dead.

Countless hundreds of thousands were panic-stricken; millions realized for the first time that the Empire was not winning a glorious victory.

Those were the statistics of death and destruction. In the Marianas, there were different figures.

The ground crews had put in more than 300,000 man-hours; had loaded over 2,000,000 individual bombs; had loaded more than 10,500,000 gallons of gasoline; had sent over 1,500 Superforts to Japan. The aircrews had flown 257,000 combat hours, suffered 156 casualties, and lost 21 aircraft.

The road to victory was getting shorter. The Superforts were finally coming into their own; and they were finally proving themselves to the men they carried to Japan.

Now We're in Business

ALTHOUGH THE SUCCESS OF THE incendiary strikes seemed long in coming, the weapon dedicated entirely to the destruction of Japan had first landed in India less than a year ago. And it had been only nine months since the first B-29 strike against Japan. The Twentieth Air Force itself was less than a year old. Two years and one month had passed since Eddie Allen had died in the crash of the second experimental model of the Superfort.

Since that dark day in February 1943, the B-29 program had made remarkable progress. Numerous modification and production problems had been solved; a vast training program had been set up; an entirely new military organization had come into being to control the use of the new weapon—all this had been accomplished with a speed that was amazing even when compared with the other crash programs of World War II.

And now the problem of tactics had been worked out with a boldness in keeping with the entire B-29 program. As soon as experience showed that conditions over Japanese targets seldom were right for precision bombing, area bombing with incendiaries was tried instead. The March 9 raid on Tokyo had been a gamble. Excessive losses would have seriously slowed up the aerial attack on Japan and probably finished LeMay as a commander. The gamble proved to be well worth taking because it answered that most important question: how to use the mighty Superfort to inflict the greatest damage on the enemy at the least cost in men and planes.

Japanese cities proved to be ideal targets for incendiary attack; flak and fighter opposition were surprisingly light at night; low-altitude bombing had improved the performance of the B-29, enabling bomb loads to be increased and saving wear and tear on the engines; and the use of radar had solved some of the problems created by the everlasting bad weather. The B-29 was in business at last! There were some air generals, of whom LeMay was one, who felt that continued heavy air attacks would force the Japanese to surrender.

And in the end that was what happened, but it was a type of air attack that hadn't figured as yet in B-29 planning. In the meantime, air attacks were a preparation for invasion.

The next stop on the road to Japan was Okinawa, the largest island in the Ryukyu chain. Because the chief reason for taking it was to acquire airbases closer to Japan, the Twentieth Air Force was called upon to help with photo-reconnaissance flights and strikes against airfields. The B-29s flew in support of the Okinawa invasion for the first time on March 27, and for the next several weeks the strategic mission of the Superfort was subordinate to its new role as a tactical bomber. Its job was to blast airfields on Kyushu, the southernmost of the Japanese home islands. It was hoped that this would keep the enemy from sending effective aerial interference to the Okinawa invasion area. On all fronts, however, Okinawa proved to be much more difficult than had been expected.

The Navy had considerable strength available for support—Essex-class carriers, light carriers, and their screening battleships, cruisers, and destroyers. All of these ships were modern and fast, forming a hard-hitting, mobile unit. On all other Pacific operations these forces had been able to seize and hold air superiority in the target area and, in addition, had been able to conduct diversionary raids against bases from which enemy strikes might be staged.

The Navy's control of the air over the Ryukyus, however, was disputed by the most determined aerial counterattack of the entire Pacific war. Ninety-nine percent of Japanese air activity was in the form of suicide attacks. The Kamikaze pilots would fly alone, hiding in clouds until an opening appeared, then would let loose their deadly fire. Navy air task forces were forced to remain at Okinawa to protect the fleet and the ground forces operating on the island; they conducted a continuous patrol within a radius of 20 miles of the anchored ships in Buckner Bay. On the other hand, because of the island's nearness to the homeland and Japan's apparent determination to hold it at all costs, diversionary strikes against bases from which Kamikaze raids could be launched were more important than in other Pacific operations. It was this task which fell to the B-29s. Superfort operations against the Kyushu airfields were planned to serve a threefold purpose: destroy airfield installations, draw enemy fighters from the Okinawa area, and keep them at home bases on or near Kyushu.

During the 25 days beginning April 17, the 21st Bomber Command conducted 93 attacks against airfields on Kyushu and Shikoku; a total of 2,104 sorties were flown, approximately 75 percent of the Command's total efforts during that period. Seventeen different airfields on Kyushu and Shikoku were struck by the B-29s.

During the latter part of April, Japanese aerial opposition to the Okinawa invasion was at its peak, the Command's attacks on the Kyushu fields were big ones with well over 100 planes from all operating wings participating. As Jap resistance decreased and it became possible for Ryukyus-based aircraft to be thrown into action in larger numbers, the demands on the Superforts were lessened. From April 30 to May 11, when the missions were discontinued, only one wing was committed to each day's strikes and then only in reduced strength.

When it was over B-29 crewmen claimed 134 enemy planes destroyed and 85 probably destroyed; the cost was 24 B-29s lost and 223 damaged. The B-29s had succeeded in reducing the threat of Kamikaze attack and had made it difficult for the Japanese to harass the Okinawa operation from Kyushu.

And while all this was going on, the busy Superforts took a hand in strangulation by blockade. The Navy's submarines had been cutting Japanese sea lanes and sinking ships since the beginning of the war. The gradual advance of American forces brought land-based as well as carrier-based aircraft over the sea lanes to the south. Traffic between Japan and the Asiatic mainland, and among the Japanese islands, alone remained relatively safe from attack by the beginning of 1945. Here the mines laid by the B-29s played their unique role.

The range of the Superfort left no Japanese or Asiatic harbor immune. With radar, the B-29s could operate at night and in adverse weather and could not be effectively combatted. The mines themselves were marvels of ingenuity. Pressure, magnetic, and acoustic mines could be set to defy sweeping and to explode when the damage would be greatest.

Beginning on the night of March 27, 1945, the mining campaign became a continuing operation. The 20th Bomber Command had previously run eight missions against harbors from Palembang to Shanghai; the 21st Bomber Command now extended aerial mining on a vastly greater scale to the harbors and waterways of Japan's home islands and to the Korean coast, often using as many as 100 B-29s in a single mission. The primary target area from the first was Japan's greatest shipping crossroads—the Shimonoseki Straits, the narrow waterway between Kyushu and Honshu, forming the only western exit from the vital Inland Sea. Nearly half the mines dropped by the Superforts were parachuted into these waters; after June 8 an almost continuous complete blockade of the Straits to vessels larger than 1,000 tons was in effect. Ports on the western and northern coasts of Honshu were also mined, and in July the coastal ports of Korea. In all, 8,814 tons of mines were laid during 46 missions; this was 6 percent of the tonnage dispatched from the Marianas. Only 16 aircraft were lost out of 1,528 airborne.

The results exceeded expectations. Only part of the story lay in the tonnage sunk, though over 750,000 tons of enemy shipping were lost or disabled and a further 500,000 tons damaged. The blockade of ports and waterways kept usable ships out of operation, preventing food and raw materials from reaching Japan and military supplies and personnel from departing. Traffic through the Shimonoseki Straits fell from 520,000 tons monthly at the outset of the campaign to a mere trickle of 8,000 tons monthly at its conclusion. Repair yards were soon congested beyond capacity, and many damaged ships were unable to reach repair facilities. The combination of these plagues with the constant appearance of new minefields and new mine types threw Japanese shipping into hopeless confusion and prevented effective use of remaining ships and water routes.

What this disruption of her shipping meant to Japan was summarized by Captain Tamura, head of the Japanese navy's mine-sweeping section: "The result of the mining by B-29s was so effective against shipping that it eventually starved the country. I think you probably could have shortened the war by beginning earlier."

The B-29 crewmen didn't see the results of their work, and many of them considered the mine-laying job boring. All they had to do was drop the mines at the right time and place. The navigator was the "bombardier" in aerial mining; he received exact instructions from the Navy on reference points, hydrostatic pressures, and spacing of the mines. The missions were usually flown at less than 10,000 feet with each plane carrying 12,000 pounds of mines.

The mines themselves were the result of years of experimentation. Parachutes six feet in diameter slowed their fall, then were released to allow the mines to sink to the bottom. Some of the mines were set to explode when the noise of a ship's engines or screws came within range; others were exploded by the action of the ship's steel structure.

The 313th Wing based on Tinian had been given the minelaying assignment; the results of its four and a half months of work were far better than anyone had dared hope. Half of all Japanese tonnage destroyed during that period fell victim to the 313th's mines. Although the Twentieth Air Force had been reluctant to spare its B-29s for what was considered to be a Navy job, the damage done to Japanese shipping was staggering, and it was accomplished in the midst of a full-scale bombing program for the Superforts. The plane that had raised so many doubts among the airmen who had taken the first B-29s overseas to India had become a truly versatile weapon of war.

General LeMay in the Marianas and General Arnold in Washington were eager to follow up the successful fire raids with a stepped-up strategic bombardment program in spite of the diversion of their short supply of crews and planes to other missions. Combat crews were in even shorter supply than planes because of the slow arrival of replacements for crews lost in action and those completing their 35 missions. This forced LeMay to make another important decision. He had to decide between using his crews for not more than 60 combat hours each month, the maximum they would be able to stand over an indefinite period, and pushing them to as high as 80 combat hours a month, a rate that had been reached during the March fire raids, but could not be sustained for any length of time.

LeMay made his choice and in a message to General Arnold wrote:

"In choosing between long-term and short-term operating policies, I am influenced by the conviction that the present stage of development of the air war against Japan presents the AAF for the first time with the opportunity of proving the power of the strategic air arm. I

consider that for the first-time strategic air bombardment faces a situation in which its strength is proportionate to the magnitude of its task. I feel that the destruction of Japan's ability to wage war lies within the capabilities of this Command, provided its maximum ability is exerted unstintingly during the next six months, which is considered to be the critical period. Though naturally reluctant to drive my force at an exorbitant rate, I believe that the opportunity now at hand warrants extraordinary measures on the part of all sharing it. I, therefore, suggest we adopt the short-term operating policy.... It will not produce the maximum results of which this Command would be capable were the combat crew flow adequate, but it represents an all-out effort to achieve the utmost from that with which we are provided."

Nothing could stop them now—certainly not flying extra hours or squeezing extra missions into an already crowded schedule. They were bringing the war home to the Japanese!

Morale was at an all-time high. Aircrews and the men on the ground at Saipan, Guam, and Tinian were growing more and more proficient. The good ones were becoming better; the mediocre ones becoming good. Men returning from missions bounced out of their planes, and after the interrogation sessions, gathered in their huts to talk flying, and fighting, and training. They speculated on their next mission as they studied the seared bottoms of their planes and remembered how their incendiaries had sent up whole portions of a city in smoke. And they laughed when Captain Samuel B. Hanford brought his Superfort back to the Marianas after a raid on Osaka with a piece of roofing from a Japanese house snagged on his wing.

"If we go any lower, someone will bring back a bowl of *sukiyaki*,"[31] quipped one of the gunners.

In addition to continued incendiary attacks against carefully selected urban targets, precision strikes were staged against Japanese war industries. Enemy fighters and flak still rose to meet the B-29s over Japan, and that meant that the Superforts were being shot at and sometimes shot down. And planes still ran into trouble because something went wrong with the engines or the fuel supply. And brave men were still called upon to put the safety of their crewmates ahead of their own welfare. One such

---

[31] A meat (usually beef) and vegetable broth.

airman was 23-year-old Red Erwin, who had flown ten flak-blanketed, bullet-ridden missions as the radio operator on the "City of Los Angeles." Then on the morning of April 12, 1945, came what was to be the final mission for Red.

On that morning Captain George Anthony Simeral, commander of the City of Los Angeles, piloted the big bomber down a coral runway and pointed its long, shining nose toward a target 1,500 miles away. The plane was leading a formation against a chemical plant in Koriyama. The gasoline production plant 120 miles north of Tokyo would be the longest strike ever made by Marianas-based Superforts. In addition to the regular crew, Lieutenant Colonel Eugene Strouse, their squadron commander, was aboard as an observer, for Tony Simeral's B-29 was to lead the formation for the 52nd Bombardment Squadron. The formation roared out over the Pacific and shortly passed high over Iwo Jima.

About 550 miles north of Iwo and 175 miles from the target they were nearing the assembly point, the place in the sky where all the planes met and gathered into a tighter formation before going on. It was the duty of Sergeant Red Erwin, as radio operator in the lead plane, to drop phosphorus smoke bombs to indicate where the other B-29s were to assemble for the attack. Harried by fighters and flying through flak, the City of Los Angeles finally reached the assembly point and Pilot Tony Simeral waved his right hand. Red released the colored parachute flares. Tony waved his hand again. Then Red started to release a phosphorus smoke bomb. Bare-armed and bareheaded, he picked up the smoke bomb, carefully pulled the pin of the six-second, delayed action fuse, then dropped the bomb down the release tube.

But the fuse was damaged, and the flap at the end of the tube had jammed shut when the last parachute flare went through. With a resounding blast the bomb exploded at the end of the narrow release tube. The projectile blew back, straight up, out of the tube into Red's face and then back into the interior of the plane. Red was knocked off his feet.

The inside of the B-29 was immediately illuminated by ignited phosphorus burning at a temperature of 1,300 degrees Fahrenheit. In an instant the sizzling, white-hot phosphorus had seared Red's eyeballs; his nose was gone and most of his right ear; patches of skin from his face and flesh from his right arm melted away. The bomb bounced around on the floor of the plane, then started to burn through the metal.

Below, in the great bomb bays, were 6,000 pounds of incendiaries. The fate of the eleven-man crew was in Red's hands.

The B-29 filled with thick black smoke that blotted out the instrument panel and the controls. Tony Simeral, blinded and choking, lost control of the plane and it dropped to 700 feet. The tons of high explosives aboard could not be jettisoned at that altitude because the explosion would wreck the ship; if the plane crashed into the sea, the bombs would blow up instantly. In another few seconds, the B-29 would crash unless the phosphorus bomb could be forced from the plane.

There was only one thing to do, and Red did it. Barely able to see, with the flesh burning from his body, he leaned down and clutched the spewing, white-hot bomb in his bare right hand. Then he inched forward, through the plane, toward the copilot's window. His hand was soon burned almost to the bone, but he held on to that bomb. With shocking, grinding pain stabbing his body like a million knives, Red stumbled on. He bumped blindly into the remote-control turret and squeezed around it, only to hit the navigator's table which completely blocked his passage. Placing the bomb under his arm like a runaway football, tight against his seared body, Red used his hand to unlatch the table and move it out of his way. Then he staggered into the smoke-filled pilot's compartment screaming, "Open the window!"

He half-fell across the lap of Roy Stables, who was trying to tell him that the window was open. Then he found it, hurled the bomb out, collapsed on the floor of the diving plane.

All this happened in just twelve seconds.

As the smoke began to clear, Tony was able to bring the plane out of its dive—at 300 feet. Then he leveled off and began climbing for altitude.

By now Red was completely on fire, his rubber lifejacket a mass of flames. Gene Strouse grabbed a fire extinguisher and sprayed him until the flames were out. Tony swiftly turned the City of Los Angeles back to Iwo.

For an hour and a half Red sprawled on the floor of the cabin and suffered in silence. He wasn't granted the mercy of unconsciousness. The crew tried to deaden the pain with morphine, but it didn't seem to help. Blood plasma was given. It was a grim twist that the first-aid man for the plane was Red himself. He had to direct one of his crewmates in administering the plasma.

Finally, the B-29 dived toward Iwo. But Iwo was under air attack!

The plane landed while American P-51s and enemy planes were scrapping it out in the air. Bullets whizzed around and bombs exploded as Red's crewmates rushed him to the hospital.

Then began a desperate battle by the doctors. They fought death, hour after hour. For four long days Erwin's life hung in the balance. Taking a long chance, the doctors ordered him flown to a larger hospital at Guam, where there were better medical facilities.

Five weeks later, Major General Willis Hale flew in from Hawaii with the Congressional Medal of Honor. A few hours later, young Erwin, his entire body swathed in bandages, was presented with the nation's highest award. He was the only member of the Twentieth Air Force to be so honored. Through the haze of pain, with sound muffled by the bandages that covered his head, Red could barely hear the words:

"Your gallantry and heroism, above and beyond the call of duty, saved the lives of your comrades."

The medal was pinned to the bandages on Red's chest as generals and colonels stood by in respectful silence, and doctors stood by to resume treatment when the ceremony was over.

Red was praised by everyone from the citizens of his native Alabama to General Hap Arnold, who said, "The country's highest honor will still be inadequate recognition of the inspiring heroism of this man."

But nothing changed Red. He told reporters: "They made a fuss about my being a hero. It didn't occur to me that way at the time. I knew the bomb was bunting, and I just had to get it out of there!"

The April skies were filled with Superforts on their way to Japan in aid of the Okinawa campaign, or to lay more mines, or to drop more bombs. From India came Brigadier General Roger Ramey and his 58th Wing, which had been without a strategic mission after operations began in the Marianas. Among the planes that moved to Tinian with the 58th was the "Eddie Allen," a B-29 of the 45th Bomb Squadron; employees of the Boeing

Airplane Company at Wichita, Kansas, made the plane and then paid for it with bond purchases in the Fifth War Loan drive.

The Eddie Allen was sent to the 20th Bomber Command in India, where it was assigned to the 45th Bomb Squadron; and on September 26, 1944, it flew over the Hump into China on the first leg of its first mission. Briefing was held that night at the advance China base. The target was to be the Showa Steel Works at Anshan, Manchuria, a target important to the Japanese war effort and high on the priority list of the 20th Bomber Command Early the next morning, before the sun had risen, the Eddie Allen took off to receive its baptism of fire. Mist shrouded the target, but the B-29 was able to drop its bombs and get away without being hit by flak or the fighters that rose to defend the target. When the Eddie Allen returned to its base in India, a red bomb was painted on its nose under the pilot's window. It was a good airplane and would earn more of those red bombs.

In October, there were two raids against targets in Formosa, and then the Eddie Allen went to Japan to bomb an aircraft plant at Omura. On November 3 it was among the B-29s that flew through heavy flak and fighter opposition to hit the marshaling yards at Rangoon. There were other trips to Manchuria, to Japan, to Hankow, China, to Singapore, and to Formosa. The line of bombs on "Eddie Allen's" nose kept growing.

During the last days of its stay in India the Superfort participated in raids designed to aid the Burma campaign. Then in April, the Eddie Allen was moved to Tinian in the Marianas, where it began at once to take part in the stepped-up bombardment of Japanese cities. Missions came in close succession—to Tokuyama, Hamamatsu, Tokyo—some staged at night, some during the day.

In the records of the 45th Bombardment Squadron, an entry dated 25 May 1945 stated under the heading "Aircraft lost" that Aircraft No. 42-24579, the Eddie Allen, was sent to salvage due to "damage sustained in combat." In its eight months of active service the Eddie Allen had bombed targets in seven countries—Malaya, Burma, Thailand, China, Manchuria, Formosa, and Japan. It was a fitting tribute to the man who had done so much to make the long-range bomber a reality.

After the surrender of Germany on May 7 and the end of B-29 support of the Okinawa operation on May 11, a month of holocaust started for Japan. The situation there was becoming critical, and airmen were more than ever convinced that the B-29s could bring the Pacific war to an end without a costly invasion.

By the fifteenth of June, 17 maximum effort incendiary attacks had taken 6,960 B-29s to Japan; 41,592 tons of bombs were dropped on the country's six most important industrial cities. Nagoya, Tokyo, Kobe, Yokohama, Osaka, and Kawasaki were turned into fire-blackened ruins.

The bombers mixed daylight attacks with night raids to make it more difficult for the Japanese to put up an effective defense. All the missions were major ones, with over 500 planes being dispatched on most of them, enough to fill the skies over the target cities and greatly overtax air raid protection systems.

Again and again the B-29s went to Japan, their huge bomb bays filled with M47 and M69 incendiaries, the combination that had proved to be the most successful. With pathfinder planes to locate their aiming points, they flew through flak, fighter attack, and the glare of the searchlights to wipe out one area after another.

When the planes returned to their home bases in the Marianas, the excited crewmen pounded one another on the back and described their missions in awed voices. Intense fires, smoke at times so dense that some of the bombardiers were forced to use radar, thermal updrafts so powerful that they bounced the mighty Superforts like balloons, became part of every trip. Each crew had a raid story more spectacular than the last.

The destruction continued to mount: 3.15 square miles of Nagoya burned out, and two days later, 3.82 more; 22.1 square miles of Tokyo wiped out in two raids; a third of Yokohama destroyed in one day-fight attack; 3.15 square miles of Osaka, 4.35 square miles of Kobe, then 2.21 more square miles of Osaka burned out. The parade of the Superforts seemed without end.

In the month of intensive effort, 136 B-29s were lost; an average of not quite two per mission, a rate much less than that suffered in the beginning of Superfort operations. The glare from the Japanese searchlights was so blinding it was sometimes impossible to see flak bursts. The searing heat from the burning cities created heavy thunderheads whose lightning was an additional hazard. Enemy fighters were often up in force to attack the

Superforts. But the results were there for all to see; the towering columns of oily smoke, the fiery glow on the clouds, the burning cities below. The men of the 21st Bomber Command knew that the enemy could not survive long under the strain of the Superfort attacks.

The big bombers traveled to Japan, came back, and went out again. Ground crews worked around the clock to repair battle damage and keep the planes flying. As June drew to an end and the fateful days of August came ever closer, the Superforts were embarked on a program of using good weather for daylight precision missions and radar weather for incendiary missions against industrial cities of secondary importance.

Enemy opposition was growing more and more feeble. In order to step up the pressure, General LeMay began issuing warnings of impending attacks to selected cities. The warnings, delivered in the form of leaflets by B-29s, called upon the residents of the cities to leave in order to save their lives. About a dozen cities would be notified and of these a certain portion would be raided. Even with the forewarning the Japanese were no longer able to inflict much damage on the B-29s; it was becoming increasingly apparent that they were no longer safe on their islands.

The Journey's End

SHORTLY BEFORE CHRISTMAS, 1944, at an isolated base in northwestern Utah called Wendover Army Air Field, a new bombardment unit, designated the 509th Composite Group, was organized. Thousands of miles away the 20th Bomber Command, in its last month under the leadership of General Curtis LeMay, was bombing Mukden, Bangkok, Hankow, and Omura from its bases in India and China. In the Marianas, 111 B-29s had taken off from Isley Field for the first raid on Tokyo to be staged from Saipan; this was followed by more attacks on Tokyo and on Ota[32] and on Nagoya.[33]

Like the 20th and the 21st, the 509th was equipped with B-29s. But the B-29s of the 509th had no turrets or guns except the twin .50-caliber tail guns. The 509th differed from other very heavy bomber groups in many ways. It was organized to be self-sufficient, with its own engineering, matériel, and ordnance sections, and five C-54s to act as transports. It operated under the strictest security conditions: each man knew about his own job, but no more than that; he was warned about talking to anyone about what he was doing; security agents were everywhere to see that he didn't. The bombardiers of the 509th were expected to achieve an accuracy beyond anything that the AAF had ever asked before. Radar operators and flight engineers were put through a rigid training program. Pilots practiced sharp, near 180-degree turns after dropping dummy bombs, a maneuver new to Superfort bombing procedures.

This unusual unit was under the command of Colonel Paul W. Tibbets, Jr., who, in the summer of 1944, had been called from his job of test-flying B-29s to a new assignment. The assignment was the organization and training of a special heavy

---

[32] Targeting the Nakajima aircraft plant at Ōta City; in Japan's Gunma Prefecture.
[33] Targeting a Mitsubishi military factory at Nagoya; in the Chūbu region of Japan. Nagoya military installations were also the target of the April 18, 1942 Doolittle Raid.

bombardment group to use a powerful new weapon in combat for the first time. The weapon was the atomic bomb.

In 1939, physicist Albert Einstein had written a letter to President Roosevelt[34] in which he pointed out that the creation of an extremely powerful uranium bomb was possible. Although such a bomb might prove to be very large and heavy, Dr. Einstein urged immediate American action to develop it before Germany did. Some progress in atomic research was made in the next few years; after the Japanese attack on Pearl Harbor, development was more rapid. By 1943, when the atomic laboratory at Los Alamos was established, it seemed possible that the bomb could be made in a size small enough to be delivered by air, although it would still be large compared to conventional bombs.

By 1943 the AAF had the B-29 in production. Its size and range made it the logical choice to deliver the new bomb, should one be developed. By September of that year the decision had been made: the B-29 was to carry the atomic bomb. General Arnold was told to arrange modification of 15 B-29s for this new role and the training of a combat unit to drop the bomb.

The search for men to fill the new unit was an exhaustive one. The nature and importance of the project made it imperative that only men of great skill be chosen, and they had to be men who could pass rigid security checks.

Paul W. Tibbets, Jr., had graduated from flying school in 1938, a year after he entered the Army Air Corps. In 1942 he was sent to England, where he flew 25 combat missions in the B-17. He was the pilot who flew General Mark Clark to Gibraltar in preparation for the invasion of North Africa. On the night of the invasion he flew General Eisenhower and his staff to Gibraltar and General Clark to Algiers. Then Tibbets flew bombardment

---

[34] In 1905, Einstein had shown that a large amount of energy could be released from a small amount of matter with his revolutionary equation $E = mc^2$ (energy = mass times the speed of light squared). Others later discovered that a chain-reaction could amplify the release of this force. Einstein was a pacifist, and did not advocate for nor was he involved in the development of the atomic bomb. However, after Hitler's rise and the splitting of the uranium atom in Germany in December 1938, Einstein modified his position of 'absolute pacificism,' and gave his endorsement to the project by signing the letter to Roosevelt urging that the bomb be built.

missions in North Africa for thirty days; he led the first heavy bombardment mission in support of the invasion.

By March of 1943, when he returned to the United States, he was assistant operations officer in charge of bomber operations. His next job was with the Air Matériel Command, testing the new Superforts that were just beginning to come out of the Boeing factories. After a year of work with the B-29 program, he became director of operations at a B-29 instructor transition school. Then came his assignment to the atomic bomb project.

He was selected from a list of four names—a brigadier general's, two full colonels', and his own. Tibbets was a lieutenant colonel; he was 29 years old.

At Fairmount Army Air Field in Nebraska, a B-29 squadron had already begun its training for combat including a great deal of high altitude flying, long-range navigation and radar work. This squadron, the 393rd Bombardment Squadron, was moved to Wendover in September to become the combat arm of Colonel Tibbets' 509th Composite Group. These were the men he would train to drop the atomic bomb.

Since it might be necessary to drop as many as five of the new bombs, 15 highly skilled crews had to be developed. Each combat element would require three planes, one to carry the bomb, one to carry instruments for measuring the effect of the blast, and one to carry camera equipment. For the job of instructing these crews, Tibbets chose combat-tested airmen, most of whom had been reassigned back to the United States as test pilots or instructors. To train his pilots for their all-important job he picked Major Charles Sweeney, Captain Robert Lewis, and Captain Charles Albury, all of whom were test-flying B-29s. Major Thomas Ferebee and Captain Kermit Beahan, bombardiers who had been wounded in action and reassigned as instructors, were sent to the 509th. The navigators were put in the charge of Major Theodore Van Kirk and Captain James Van Pelt. Master Sergeants Wyatt Duzenbury and John Kuharek were to train the flight engineers.

It had cost the United States Government in the neighborhood of $2B USD to develop the atomic bomb. Now that work on the first bombs was nearing completion, much was going to depend on how effectively they could be delivered. And it wasn't to be a one-way trip to the target; a Kamikaze mission. The B-29s that dropped the bombs were going to get away, although they'd have to do it very quickly or be caught in the explosion.

Colonel Tibbets and his instructors went to work. Bombardiers practiced dropping dummy bombs within a 900-foot circle from a height of 30,000 feet, high enough to give a B-29 time to get away. In order to get his planes up that high, Tibbets stripped them of armor, guns, and sighting blisters. Some of the bombs that were dropped were shaped like a falling drop of water, fat at one end and tapering to fins at the other.

This practice bomb actually was the shell of the plutonium bomb still under development. Studies were made of the way it acted in the air, of the fuse action, and of its electronic equipment. These bombs, called "pumpkins" by the men of the 509th, contained no plutonium, of course, but they did contain the conventional explosives to be used with the plutonium. The drops by Tibbets' men provided the scientists at Los Alamos with valuable information on the ballistics of the bomb they were designing; information that they could get in no other way. The plutonium bomb was to be tested only once before its use in combat, and that was a ground test.

Severe shockwaves would follow an explosion as violent as the one to be produced by the atomic bomb, so scientists worked with Tibbets to figure out how far away the planes would have to travel to be safe and what kind of maneuver would best get them out of the danger zone. A steep, diving turn of 158 degrees would place the plane the necessary eight miles away in the 43 seconds available for escape. Pilots were sent up over the Utah flats to practice these tight, diving turns.

By January, enough progress had been made for ten crews to go to Cuba for intensive training in high-altitude bombing and long over-water flights. There was no practice of formation flying, always a big part of B-29 training. The mission of the 509th would not require it. By May, the men of the 509th were ready to move overseas to North Field on Tinian, which was to be their new base. They had been equipped with B-29s that had all the latest improvements: fuel-injection engines, reversible-pitch propellers, and fast-acting, pneumatic bomb-bay doors. The 509th had been enlarged by the addition of the 1st Ordnance Squadron, the men who were to handle the atomic bomb.

The bomb itself was nearing completion. Actually, there were two bombs, each one constructed of a different fissionable material and design. One contained uranium 235 arranged at each end of a long gun barrel. When the two masses of uranium were brought together by the action of a proximity fuse, the bomb would explode. This bomb was called the "Little Boy," and it was the one that destroyed Hiroshima. Because scientists were virtually certain that it would work, it was not tested before it was used in combat. The second bomb used plutonium as its fissionable material, and it was designed to be set off through implosion, or bursting inward. In the bomb, pressure would be evenly applied to all sides of the mass until a critical stage was reached. This action had never been tested on a large scale, and when it was, it proved so successful that it made the "Little Boy" obsolete before it was used. The second bomb was called the "Fat Man" because of its shape; it was dropped on Nagasaki.

The 509th's advanced air echelon reached Tinian on May 18; the first ground echelon arrived on the 29th. By the middle of June, the combat crews, flying their new B-29s, began arriving. The men immediately became absorbed in a life of C-rations, pup tents,[35] mail call, and washing dirty socks in combat helmets. Tinian itself pleased them. It was cooled by ocean breezes, the vegetation was lush, and because the island resembled Manhattan in shape, its streets bore the names of well-known New York thoroughfares. By early July, the 509th was settled in its own section near the runways and hardstands of North Field, which it shared with the 313th Wing.

During May and June, when the 509th Composite Group was moving to the Pacific and getting settled on Tinian, the B-29s of the 21st Bomber Command completed the ruin of Nagoya, Tokyo, Yokohama, Osaka, and Kobe, and then began to appear over a series of smaller Japanese cities to drop their destructive firebombs. The 313th Wing, the 509th's neighbor at North Field, was busy bottling up Japanese shipping with its aerial mines.

And in Washington, far away from the bombing, the mine laying, and the B-29s parked wingtip to wingtip on the coral

---

[35] Small, basic tent or shelter-half.

hardstands, the hour of decision had arrived. The atomic bomb was ready. Was it to be dropped on Japan?

In the beginning, back in 1939, 1940, and 1941, the idea had been to develop a bomb as quickly as possible, and to use it. Gradually as the awesome nature of the new weapon became more apparent, some doubts were raised. The responsibility that went with the power of the bomb was great indeed, and it would trouble men forever.

President Truman assumed responsibility for the use of the atomic bomb almost as soon as he assumed the office of President of the United States. Immediately after he had taken the oath of office, Secretary of War Stimson told him of the new weapon soon to be ready for use against the enemy. A few weeks later, after the President had received a thorough technical explanation of the bomb, Stimson suggested that a committee be formed to work out just how it should be used.

Named to the Interim Committee, as it was called, were: Secretary Stimson, chairman; George L. Harrison, acting chairman in the absence of Stimson; James F. Byrnes, personal representative of the President; Undersecretary of the Navy Ralph A. Bard; Assistant Secretary of State William L. Clayton; and scientists Vannevar Bush, K. T. Compton, and J. B. Conant. These men were handpicked by the Commander in Chief to deal with the most fearsome weapon ever developed by man. It was their task to recommend what was to be done with the top-secret bomb which would be ready by August 1.

On June 1, after a series of conferences, the Interim Committee officially adopted a series of recommendations concerning this weapon and sent them along to the President. And with them went the blueprint of a new era of warfare.

The recommendations were:

1. The atom bomb should be used against Japan as soon as possible.
2. It should be used on a dual target that is, a military installation or war plant surrounded by, or adjacent to, houses and other buildings most susceptible to damage.
3. It should be used without prior warning of the nature of the weapon.

The principal considerations in reaching these decisions were later disclosed by Mr. Stimson:

"As we understood it, there was a very strong possibility that the Japanese Government might determine upon resistance to the end in all areas of the Far East under its control. In such an event, the Allies would be faced with the enormous task of destroying an armed force of 5,000,000 men and 5,000 suicide aircraft belonging to a race which had already amply demonstrated its ability to fight literally to the death.

"We estimated that if we should be forced to carry this task to its conclusion, the major fighting would not end until the latter part of 1946, at the earliest. I was informed that such operations might be expected to cost over a million casualties to American forces alone. Additional large losses might be expected among our Allies, and, of course, if our campaign were successful and if we could judge by previous experience, enemy casualties would be much larger than our own.

"My chief purpose was to end the war in victory with the least possible cost in the lives of the men in the armies which I had helped to raise. In the light of the alternatives which, on a fair estimate, were open to us, I believe that no man, in our position and subject to our responsibilities, holding in his hands a weapon of such possibilities for accomplishing this purpose and saving those lives, could have failed to use it and afterwards looked his countrymen in the face."

Unaware of the momentous decisions being made in Washington, the combat crews of the 509th went through the weeklong indoctrination course given to all new arrivals. By the end of June, they were ready to resume their flight training. First came three weeks of navigation training flights and bombing missions against Rota, Guguan, Truk, and Marcus with regular 500- or 1,000-pound bombs instead of the dummy bombs carried at Wendover. Then on July 20, training began to take the 509th to Japan. By the 29th they had made 12 strikes, each one a precision attack against a target near, but not actually in, one of the cities chosen for the atomic bomb.

A list of potential targets for the bomb had been drawn up after the Interim Committee had made its report. The Committee had pointed out the advisability of choosing a target that included a military installation plus a surrounding civilian area.

The choice was further limited by the fact that the bomb's effectiveness could be measured only if it were dropped in an area still relatively undamaged. Weeks of intensive bombing by General LeMay's 21st Bomber Command had already destroyed the largest Japanese cities. Of those left, Kyoto was the largest, followed by Hiroshima, Niigata, and Kokura. This list met with the approval of General Arnold; on July 3 the Joint Chiefs of Staff ordered that there be no bombing of the four cities. Secretary Stimson, however, questioned the presence of Kyoto on the list. It was a religious and cultural center, and Stimson felt that its destruction would never be forgiven by the Japanese. With the approval of President Truman, Kyoto was removed from the list and replaced with Nagasaki at the suggestion of General LeMay's staff, although it was far from ideal as a target.

The four target cities were studied carefully so that the practice strikes of the 509th could be planned to give the crews as much experience as possible for the important mission they might someday have to fly. The navigation and bombing procedures used and the sharp turn away from the target were all similar to what would be the case if an atomic bomb were dropped. The bombs that were dropped were 10,000-pounders with ballistics similar to the atomic bomb.

The 509th was a highly trained outfit; its marksmanship on these training missions was impressive. But all its bombing reports and strike photos went straight to General LeMay, bypassing the usual lines of communication with higher headquarters, and so the other groups based in the Marianas wondered about the 509th. It had the very best of beautiful, new equipment, yet it didn't take part in the big fire raids on Japan. Its planes bore different markings; a black circle bisected by a black arrow. Its section of the base was full of restricted areas surrounded by barbed wire and guards, and there seemed to be numerous civilians about; the scientists and technicians who were to assemble the bomb. Curiosity about the 509th, plus the resentment always felt toward a unit that seemed to be getting preferred treatment, resulted in gripes. Soon a verse was making the rounds:

Into the air the secret rose,
Where they're going nobody knows;

*Tomorrow they'll return again,
But we'll never know where they've been.
Don't ask about results or such
Unless you want to get in Dutch;
But take it from one who is sure of the score,
The 509th is winning the war.
When the other groups are ready to go
We have a program on the whole damned show;
And when Halsey's Fifth shells Nippon's shore,
Why shucks, we hear about it the day before;
And MacArthur and Doolittle give it out in advance,
But with this new bunch we haven't a chance.
We should have been home a month or more,
For the 509th is winning the war.*

If the rest of the Twentieth Air Force was in the dark about the mission of the 509th, the members of the unit didn't know much more about it. They all knew they were going to drop a special kind of bomb. Each of the men was working on his own part of the project, but security forbade discussion, even among themselves. They did not know what kind of bomb it was or how powerful it would be. They certainly hadn't seen it, because not until August 1, in one of the 509th's bomb huts where temperature and humidity could be carefully controlled, was the first bomb assembled.

Six days before, on the morning of July 26, the cruiser Indianapolis had dropped anchor in Tinian harbor long enough to discharge a cargo consisting of a lead cylinder and a long crate. In the crate was an alternate casing for the bomb; in the cylinder was the target chunk of U-235. Another shipment of U-235 was divided into three parts and shipped to Tinian by air. The 509th was almost ready to go into action.

The bomb lying in the air-conditioned hut on Tinian was the "Little Boy." It had never been tested, but the scientists were sure it would work. Since the 16th of July they had been sure that their second bomb, the "Fat Man," would work even better than the "Little Boy." At 5:30 A.M. on the 16th the plutonium bomb had been exploded in the desert near Alamogordo, New Mexico, with results that exceeded the expectations of its designers.

President Truman and Secretary Stimson received the news of the successful test explosion while they were attending the Potsdam Conference. The President had agreed with the recommendations of the Interim Committee, and now he reaffirmed his earlier decision to use the powerful new weapon in the hope of saving the millions of lives that would be lost in an invasion of Japan. Japan was warned on July 26 to surrender unconditionally to avoid "inevitable and complete" destruction. Two days later the Potsdam Declaration was rejected by Premier Suzuki.

The chain of command that extended from President Truman down to the crew of the "Enola Gay" had already started to function. On July 25, General Carl A. Spaatz, commander of the United States Army Strategic Air Forces, had been given a directive which ordered the 509th Composite Group to drop the first atomic bomb as soon after August 3 as the weather would allow visual bombing. Spaatz immediately left Washington for Guam where his United States Army Strategic Air Forces headquarters had taken over the functions of the Washington headquarters of the Twentieth Air Force; he arrived there on July 29.

By August 1, it was just a matter of waiting for the 3rd, the earliest date set for the attack, and after that, for suitable bombing weather. There were now two bombs available; the scientists and technicians needed to handle them were on Tinian; the 509th had made 12 training strikes at targets in Japan; and the crew had been selected to deliver the first bomb.

Colonel Tibbets was going to lead the mission. He chose the plane and crew of Captain Robert Lewis, one of his instructors, to carry the bomb. With them would go one B-29 to measure the effect of the blast and one to carry camera equipment. In addition, three Superforts would precede Colonel Tibbets to check the weather, and there would be another Superfort waiting at Iwo Jima to take the bomb in case Tibbets' plane developed trouble.

On August 2, President Truman made his final decision to use the bomb against Japan, and Lieutenant General Nathan Twining issued the field orders for the strike. The primary target was to be Hiroshima; the alternates were Kokura and Nagasaki. The bombing was to be visual, from 28,000 to 30,000 feet, the airspeed 200 miles per hour; the date was to be August 6.

The Superforts making the trip had their group insignia and names marked out. Tibbets later arranged to have Enola Gay, his mother's name, painted on the nose of the plane that was going to carry the bomb.

On August 4, the briefing of the crews began. At the first session they were shown pictures of the Alamogordo explosion and told that the bomb they were going to drop would have a force equal to 20,000 tons of TNT. The word "atomic" was not used to describe the bomb. Polaroid glasses were issued to all the men scheduled to go. They were given the details usual at a pre-mission briefing: take-off times, altitudes, routes, fuel loads. And they were given special instructions about avoiding clouds and keeping a critical distance from target area after the bomb had been dropped.

The next day, the Enola Gay was given a test run. Later she was taxied to a loading pit where the bomb waited. The five-ton "Little Boy" was raised by hydraulic jacks up into the forward bomb bay of the Superfort. The doors were closed, and a sign posted to indicate that the plane was "cocked" and ready to go.

At midnight there was a weather briefing; the weather looked good. The crews were told of the arrangements that had been made for air-sea rescue and given final details on the procedures to be followed during the mission. Then came breakfast, and then the three weather planes took off. Take-off time for the Enola Gay was to be 2:45 A.M.

The crew started to assemble at the Enola Gay at two o'clock. Besides Colonel Tibbets there were Captain Robert A. Lewis, who was acting as copilot; Major Thomas W. Ferebee, the bombardier; Captain Theodore J. Van Kirk, the navigator; Lieutenant Jacob Beser, a radar countermeasures officer; Master Sergeant Wyatt E. Duzenbury, the flight engineer; Staff Sergeant Joe S. Stiborik, radar operator; Sergeant George R. Caron, the tail gunner; Sergeant Robert A. Schumard, the waist gunner; and Pfc. Richard H. Nelson, radio operator. Also making the trip were Navy Captain William S. Parsons, who had worked at Los Alamos and was in charge of the bomb, and his assistant, Lieutenant Morris R. Jeppson.

After Army photographers had taken their pictures of the plane, the ground crew, and the crowd gathered to see them off, one by one, the men climbed into the Superfort. Tibbets appeared at the pilot's window; he waved and started the four powerful engines one after another. Slowly, the Enola Gay taxied to her runway. The camera plane, piloted by Captain George W. Marquardt, and Major Charles W. Sweeney's "Great Artiste," which had been transformed into a flying laboratory, were waiting for their take-off time. The Enola Gay left the ground at 2:45 to be followed at two-minute intervals by the other two planes. The "Little Boy" was on its way to Japan.

The bomb was still not armed. There had been a series of bad take-off crashes which had made everyone worry about having the Enola Gay take off with a live bomb on board. Captain Parsons had decided to put off the final assembly of the bomb until after they were safely airborne. To make sure that he would be able to do it smoothly when the time came, he had practiced putting the explosive charge in the end of the bomb over and over again. Now, as the Enola Gay leveled out over the Pacific, Parsons and Jeppson went to work in the bomb bay. The charge was inserted, and the final connections made. The bomb would now explode after it had dropped to an altitude of 1,850 feet.

At Iwo Jima, the Enola Gay began a slow climb to the altitude from which the bomb was to be dropped. The decision to strike the primary or the alternate targets rested with Colonel Tibbets and was to be made on the basis of information transmitted by the weather ships flying ahead of the Enola Gay.

At 8:15, the report on Hiroshima was received:

"2/10 lower and middle lower, and 2/10 at 15,000 feet."

Visual bombing conditions at the primary target! The decision was quickly made. Hiroshima!

The doomed city, Japan's eighth largest, was exactly what the Interim Committee had recommended as a target for the first atomic bomb: a military installation surrounded by houses and other buildings. It was an important army transport base and contained large ordnance, food, and clothing depots. It also had a shipbuilding yard, textile mills, oil-storage facilities, electrical works, and a large railroad yard. Because Hiroshima was on the list of targets reserved for the 509th, it had received so little damage that some of its residents had come to believe they were going to be spared the fate of Tokyo and Yokohama.

As the Enola Gay flew toward Hiroshima with her deadly cargo, the crew passed the time in various ways. Some of them tried to sleep, some read, some just sat and thought about the job that lay ahead. They were all a little awed by the bomb that rode in the forward bay. It was gray and long—close to ten feet— and about a yard in diameter. It was the biggest bomb they had ever seen.

Colonel Tibbets crawled back through the tunnel from the pilot's compartment to give the men in the rear a final briefing on the bomb. He asked the tail gunner, Sergeant George Caron, if he had figured it out yet.

Caron asked, "Is it some chemist's nightmare?"

Tibbets said it had nothing to do with chemistry. Then Caron recalled something he had read about a cyclotron and asked if it were a physicist's nightmare.

To this Colonel Tibbets replied, "I guess you could call it that."

As he started to return to the pilot's compartment, Caron stopped him with another question: "Are we going to split atoms?"

The colonel just smiled and went back to his flying.

As the Enola Gay neared the Japanese coast, Captain Parsons went back to take one last look at the bomb. With Jeppson he had been keeping an electronic check on it from the forward compartment. Everything seemed to be all right. The bomb run was begun 25 miles out. Each man had his goggles ready to pull over his eyes when he heard the bombing signal. When they were 12 miles from target, Ferebee, the bombardier, took over. Below he could see Hiroshima on the delta of the Ota River.

It was 8:15 in Hiroshima when the bomb was released. The continuous tone of the signal cut off, warning the crew and those in the accompanying Superforts that the bomb was away. The Enola Gay was at 31,600 feet, traveling at 328 miles per hour. It was clear and sunny. There were no enemy aircraft visible and the flak was far below them. The men sat behind their dark goggles and waited. The bomb, set to go off above the ground to increase the effect of its blast, exploded in less than a minute. By that time Tibbets had put the Enola Gay into a steep, tight turn— the same turn he had practiced so often—and was leaving the target behind.

Far below, the 245,000 people who had not been evacuated from Hiroshima were up and beginning a new day. There had been an air-raid alert when the weather planes had passed over, but the all-clear had sounded. War workers were either en route or had already arrived at their destinations while others were busy building firebreaks and removing valuables to safety in the country. Probably few heard the Enola Gay as it passed over Hiroshima. The Japanese jammed in the vast Bushido Arsenal or hurrying through the heart of town to their jobs had no warning of the holocaust that was to envelop them. Suddenly, a fight brighter than a thousand suns filled the sky. The world's first atomic bomb had exploded. At that moment, air became fire, walls crumbled to dust, and lives flickered out by the thousands.

The explosion started hundreds of fires almost simultaneously—fires whose intense heat sucked in air from all directions, creating a fire wind which helped to spread the numerous blazes. An area measuring 4.7 square miles in the heart of the city was completely destroyed. According to Japanese figures, 71,379 residents of Hiroshima were either dead or missing as a result of the bombing; almost that many more were injured. Many of the casualties were among the personnel of the Second Army and the Chucogu Regional Army units stationed in Hiroshima.

When the bomb exploded, the Enola Gay was racing away from Hiroshima. In spite of the bright sunlight, the flash of the explosion lit up the inside of the Superfort. The crews of the two escort planes, observing the explosion through their protective goggles, reported that the flash after the explosion was deep purple, then reddish. It reached to almost 8,000 feet. The cloud, shaped like a mushroom, was up to 20,000 feet in one minute. Then the top part broke from the stem and eventually reached 40,000 feet.

Sergeant Caron, riding in the tail of the Enola Gay, was in the best position to view the effects of the blast. He saw a flash followed by a tremendous buildup of light which grew and then faded out.

"After what seemed like an eternity," Caron reported, "I saw shockwaves coming up. I reported this to the Colonel and started taking pictures. He called back and told me to keep talking. I added that the shockwaves resembled a series of circles like those caused from dropping pebbles in water. Seconds later they struck the airplane and one of the pilots asked if we had been hit by flak.

"Colonel Tibbets kept asking me what was going on. Then I saw the cloud and was never so busy in my life—trying to take pictures and keep the Colonel and the rest of the crew up to date on the blast.

"By the time the cloud rose slightly into the air we were far enough away, and I could see the entire city. I commented that the whole area was covered with a thick, purplish mass that looked like fluid. It looked like it was a hundred or more feet thick and flooding out over the city from the center of the blast. Then flames started breaking up through the smoke and dust. The Colonel asked me to count them. I tried but lost track. In the meantime, I was still taking pictures.

"Then Colonel Tibbets turned the Enola Gay so all crewmen could see, and each gave his impression over the intercom and into the wire recorder. As we headed for home, the Colonel told me to keep my eye on the 'mushroom' and tell him when it disappeared from view. The crew for the most part was quiet on the return. I just sat there and watched that cloud. Finally, I called up that I was losing sight of it. We then were 363 miles from Hiroshima."

Captain Parsons later described what he was able to see: "A few fires were visible around the edges of the smoke, but we could see nothing of the city except the dock area where buildings were falling down. The boiling dust and debris continued for several minutes, as a white cloud plumed upward from the center to 40,000 feet and an angry dust cloud spread all around the city."

The crew felt a sense of relief that the bomb had been dropped successfully after their many months of training. But it was relief tinged with awe at the unearthly flash, the shock of the distant explosion, and the sight of a city disintegrating before their eyes.

The Superfort whose single bomb had destroyed Hiroshima sped back to Tinian, 1,600 miles away. So did The Great Artiste, whose instruments had measured the blast, and the B-29 camera plane. Messages had preceded them that the bomb had been dropped successfully.

The trip back was uneventful. Captain Lewis described their landing:

"I looked at 'Ole Bull' [Colonel Tibbets] and his eyes were bloodshot, and he looked awful tired. He looked like the past ten months at Wendover and Washington and New Mexico and overseas had come up and hit him all at once. I said to him, 'Bull, after such a beautiful job, you'd better make a beautiful landing.' And he did."

The Enola Gay touched down at 2:58 P.M., 12 hours and 13 minutes after she had taken off on her momentous journey into the Atomic Age. Close to 200 people were waiting as the Superfort taxied to her hardstand. Among them was General Spaatz, who pinned the Distinguished Service Cross on Tibbets' flying suit.

President Truman received news of the successful dropping of the bomb as he was returning from Potsdam on board the Augusta. His public announcement of the bombing was released in Washington 16 hours after it happened—still August 6 in the United States because of the time difference. The President again warned the Japanese people of what was in store for them.

The men in the Marianas received their first word of the powerful new bomb that had been dropped on Japan from the President's message. The 509th now became the center of attention, but the other B-29 units still had work to do. On the 7th, 131 Superforts struck at Tokokawa. The next day there was an incendiary attack on Yawata.

When no offer of surrender came from Japan, the decision was made to drop a second atomic bomb on the 9th, This time the primary target was to be Kokura in northern Kyushu, the site of a large army arsenal. Nagasaki was the secondary target. It was an industrial city covering a series of hills and valleys on the west coast of Kyushu.

"Fat Man," the plutonium bomb that had been tested at Alamogordo on July 16 and found to be more powerful than the one dropped on Hiroshima, was made ready and placed aboard the Superfort, "Bock's Car." Major Charles W. Sweeney, who had been in charge of one of the observation planes on the Hiroshima mission, was the pilot; his copilot was Lieutenant Frederick Olivi; the bombardier was Captain Kermit K. Beahan; and Captain James F. Van Pelt, Jr., was the navigator. Lieutenant Commander Frederick Ashworth was in charge of the bomb, which this time had to be armed before the plane took off.

Sweeney's regular B-29, The Great Artiste, which had been filled with instruments, accompanied Bock's Car as an observation plane and was flown by Captain Frederick Bock, who usually flew Bock's Car. This switch of planes between Sweeney and Bock led to confusion in stories about the dropping of the second atomic bomb. For years afterward, there were accounts of the mission that had The Great Artiste carrying the bomb to Nagasaki. Once more, in the early hours of an August morning, Superforts were prepared for take-off. Two observation planes went with Bock's Car; two weather planes were sent ahead to check bombing conditions at Kokura and at Nagasaki. A spare B-29 would be waiting at Iwo Jima in case Bock's Car couldn't make it all the way with the bomb.

The strike force got safely off at 3:49 A.M., much to the relief of the scientists, who feared a crash with the armed bomb would destroy half of Tinian. At 9 A.M. the report received from the Kokura weather plane indicated visual bombing conditions over the primary target. With orders that called for a visual drop, Sweeney headed for Kokura.

But by the time Bock's Car arrived over the target, the weather had closed in and visual bombing was impossible. In his report Major Sweeney described what happened:

"The navigator made landfall perfectly. We passed over the primary target, but for some reason it was obscured by smoke. There was no flak. We took another run almost from the LP. Again, smoke hid the target. 'Look harder,' I said to the bombardier, but it was no use. Then I asked Commander Ashworth to come up for a little conference.

"We took a third run with no success. I had another conference with the Commander. We had now been fifty minutes over the target and wanted to drop our bomb in the ocean. Our gas was getting low. Six hundred gallons were trapped in one of the tanks.

"We decided to head for Nagasaki, the secondary target."

The report received from the Nagasaki weather plane at 9:19 had been "ceiling and visibility unlimited," but when Bock's Car reached there the target had an 8/10 cloud cover. Because of their fuel shortage Sweeney and Ashworth had decided to make one run and drop the bomb by radar if they had to. Commander Ashworth took the responsibility for the change in procedure.

The big ship was on instruments for 90 percent of the bomb run. At the last moment, Captain Beahan, the bombardier, called out, "I can see it, I can see the target!"

He took over and made a visual release of the bomb. It was 10:58 Nagasaki time. As the thundering Superfort turned in a tight arc and sped south, the city vanished in a sky-searing flash of light.

Nagasaki had had an air-raid alert at 7:45 A.M.; the all-clear had sounded at 8:30. When Bock's Car was sighted, the raid signal was given again, but few people bothered to go to the shelters. If they had, the loss figures would have been less than the estimated 35,000 killed, 5,000 missing, and 60,000 injured.

The Nagasaki bomb's blast effect seemed greater than that at Hiroshima because of the difference in topography and the type of bomb used. The area totally destroyed was an oval 2.3 miles long and 1.9 miles wide; every building in it was destroyed, with severe damage extending in an irregular pattern beyond that. Over 68 percent of Nagasaki's industrial area was destroyed.

The men in Bock's Car had donned their polaroid glasses before the bomb was dropped, but they were nearly blinded by the flash. Sergeant Raymond C. Gallagher, the assistant flight engineer, told of a tremendous white flash such as he had never seen before; this was followed by a black cloud which billowed up like a balloon. The tail gunner, Staff Sergeant Albert T. Dehart, saw what looked like a big red ball coming up at him. On the ground was a big black cloud and out of it came a huge white cloud.

The shock of the explosion was felt by those in the strike plane.

"The turbulence of the blast," said Major Sweeney, "was greater than that at Hiroshima. Even though we were prepared for what happened, it was unbelievable. Seven or eight miles from the city shockwaves as visible as ripples on a pond overtook our plane, and concussion waves twice thumped against the plane, jolting it roughly. The underside of the great clouds over Nagasaki was amber-tinted as though reflecting the conflagration at least six miles below. Beneath the top cloud mass, white in color, there gradually climbed a turbulent pillar of black smoke and dust which emitted a second fireball less vivid than the first. It rose as solid as a stump, its base dark purple, with a reddish hue in the center that paled to brown near the top."

The last look they got at Nagasaki showed a thick cone of dust covering half the city. On its rim near the harbor, great fires were raging.

Aboard Bock's Car there was serious debate as to whether to bail out over an air sea rescue craft in the Pacific or to try to reach Okinawa's Yontan airfield on their shrinking fuel supply. The decision was to make a run for Okinawa. As Bock's Car, practically dry of gasoline, descended to land at Okinawa, Sergeant Dehart, the tail gunner, saw smoke from Nagasaki 385 miles away.

All the Superforts of the Nagasaki mission were safely back at Tinian by midnight of August 9. They were not the last B-29s to make the trip to Japan because the expected surrender did not come. On the 10th, H4 B-29s were airborne and a total of 828 on the 14th. Before the last of these planes returned to the Marianas, Japan had agreed to an unconditional surrender.

The "Tokyo Hitch Hiker," 398th Squadron of the 313th Wing, had become the last Superfort to drop bombs on Japan. The target had been Nobeoka, a small town near Bungo Strait, where the Superfort had covered a mine-laying mission. While returning to their base at Tinian, the "Hiker's" radio operator picked up a message announcing the capitulation of the Japanese Empire.

The B-29 had dropped 147,000 tons of bombs on Japan in a little more than a year, with results that convinced the Japanese their cause was hopeless and the AAF that strategic air power was of the utmost importance to the future defense of the nation. Although the B-29 attacks on Japan had been planned as a prelude to invasion, invasion had not been necessary; the million or more casualties expected from such an operation were never lost.

The 509th Composite Group's pictorial history carried this tribute to the B-29 and the men who made it:

"To the builders and designers of the B-29, the best, the biggest, the fastest bomber, for bringing our crews safely from each mission, for helping conclude the war from the skies, and making unnecessary an invasion into Japan itself."

Epilogue

ON THE MORNING OF SEPTEMBER 2, 1945, aboard the United States battleship Missouri riding at anchor in Tokyo Bay, an austere ceremony began. Surrounding the cleared space on the deck stood military leaders and representatives of the Allied Powers, watching carefully as the Japanese spoke to General MacArthur. Gray clouds swirled about in the sky as radio announcers, in hushed tones, described the signing of the surrender document.

At 9:08 A.M. the instrument of the capitulation of Japan was signed by fidgety Foreign Minister Marnoru Shigemitsu, on behalf of Emperor Hirohito and the Japanese government. For the surrender of the Japanese armies, Chief of Staff General Yoshijiro Umezu abruptly scrawled his signature.

Now it was General MacArthur's turn to sign. Slowly he eased his tall, angular figure into the chair, looked at the Japanese, then picked up a pen. This was the moment of which he had dreamed, for which he had fought, in which he had come back from defeat to glorious victory. This was the greatest day of his 65 years.

As the General started to write, the clouds overhead parted. The defeated and the victorious stood perfectly still as a shaft of sunlight illuminated the deck of the Missouri.

And as MacArthur finished signing his name and looked up, a Superfortress, high in the sky, flashed down through the thin line of sunshine, casting its shadow on the ship below. It was followed by hundreds of B-29s representing every squadron of the Twentieth Air Force, and the drone of planes slowly rose to a deafening crescendo.

The journey was over. The giant had become a symbol of peace.